Comrades in conflict

Manchester University Press

Comrades in conflict

Labour, the trade unions and 1969's *In Place of Strife*

Peter Dorey

Manchester University Press

Copyright © Peter Dorey 2019

The right of Peter Dorey to be identified as the author of this work has been asserted by him in accordance with the Copyright, Designs and Patents Act 1988.

Published by Manchester University Press
Altrincham Street, Manchester M1 7JA, UK
www.manchesteruniversitypress.co.uk

British Library Cataloguing-in-Publication Data is available

ISBN 978 1 5261 3828 6 hardback
ISBN 978 1 5261 4803 2 paperback

First published by Manchester University Press in hardback 2019

This edition published 2020

The publisher has no responsibility for the persistence or accuracy of URLs for any external or third-party internet websites referred to in this book, and does not guarantee that any content on such websites is, or will remain, accurate or appropriate.

Typeset by Toppan Best-set Premedia Limited

Contents

List of tables	*page* vi
Acknowledgements	vii
List of abbreviations	viii
Introduction	1
1 Emergence and identification of the problem	9
2 The Donovan Commission and its Report	24
3 The initial political response	46
4 Cabinet demurrals and diminishing Ministerial support	73
5 Increasing antipathy in the Parliamentary Labour Party	110
6 The trade unions' implacable hostility	133
7 A 'solemn and binding' agreement	162
Conclusion	189
Bibliography	213
Index	220

List of tables

1 Number, types and examples of written evidence, from institutions, received by the Donovan Commission. *page* 29
2 The main themes and papers discussed at the Sunningdale Conference. MS. Castle.273, Seminar on the Donovan Report, 15–17 November 1968. 58
3 Results of the 1970 general election, with corresponding figures for 1966. 191

Acknowledgements

In writing this book, I have made extensive use of archival sources, some of which have only been made available to scholars relatively recently, while others have largely been neglected or overlooked, not least because the topic examined by this book has received only limited academic attention. I am therefore extremely grateful to the following individuals and organisations who very kindly and efficiently made sundry archives from 1968–9 available to me: Colin Harris and his colleagues at the Bodleian Library, Oxford, where I examined the papers of James Callaghan, Barbara Castle and Harold Wilson; the staff at the National People's Museum in Manchester, who provided me with the minutes of meetings of the (backbench) Parliamentary Labour Party, as well as the records of Tribune Group meetings; Mike Parker, who provided me with digitalised back issues of *Tribune*, the weekly paper published by the Tribune Group; James King and his colleagues at the Modern Records Centre, Warwick University, for providing me with the minutes of meetings both of the TUC's General Council, and its Finance and General Purposes Committee; the staff at the National Archives, Kew, for retrieving or photocopying Cabinet papers, correspondence between Ministers, minutes of a crucial weekend seminar held at the (then) civil service training college in mid-November 1968, and policy advice and proposals written by senior civil servants, as well as papers detailing the drafting of the 1968 Donovan Report.

Pete Dorey
Bath
May 2018

List of abbreviations

AESD	Association of Engineering and Shipbuilding Draughtsmen
BOAC	British Overseas Airways Corporation
CBI	Confederation of British Industry
CIR	Commission on Industrial Relations
DEA	Department of Economic Affairs
DEP	Department for Employment and Productivity
EEC	European Economic Community
IRC	Industrial Relations Commission
NEC	[Labour Party] National Executive Committee
NIRC	National Industrial Relations Court
PLP	Parliamentary Labour Party
PPS	Parliamentary Private Secretary
TGWU	Transport and General Workers' Union
TUC	Trades Union Congress

Introduction

It was fifty years ago, in 1969, that a Labour Government sought to introduce legislation to reform industrial relations, and place Britain's trade unions within a clear legal framework. The proposals, enshrined in a White Paper entitled *In Place of Strife*, aimed both to imbue the unions and workers with various statutory rights and to impose particular responsibilities on them. The purported objective overall was to foster more orderly and responsible industrial relations, primarily in order to reduce the incidence of unofficial strikes, but also, ostensibly, as part of Labour's professed objective of establishing a Socialist society. A core component of this latter objective was much greater planning and regulation of the economy, coupled with the goal of establishing a fairer, more egalitarian, society. These objectives and goals were deemed to be seriously impeded by an apparently anarchic industrial relations 'system', and the readiness with which many trade unions used their 'industrial muscle', via strike action, to pursue short-term economic goals for their members, without regard for the longer-term material interests of British society overall.

The two senior Ministers most closely involved in pursuing industrial relations reform via *In Place of Strife*, Prime Minister Harold Wilson and his Secretary of State for Employment and Productivity, Barbara Castle, were convinced that their legislative proposals were fair and equitable, in that they aimed to establish a balance between the rights of workers and trade unions on one hand, and the interests of 'the community' on the other. They were adamant that their proposed legislation would not – and was not intended to – prevent or ban the trade unions from engaging in strikes in connection with disputes with employers, but that certain conditions should be met, and procedures adhered to, before strike action was embarked upon; it was about improving organisational processes, not imposing outright prohibition.

Yet while *In Place of Strife* appeared eminently reasonable to its political advocates, it aroused strong opposition from key sections of the

Parliamentary Labour Party (PLP), a prominent Cabinet Minister, the Home Secretary James Callaghan, and from the trade unions themselves. Some of this antipathy had been anticipated by Castle and Wilson, but what surprised them, and ultimately proved fatal to *In Place of Strife*, was the scale of the opposition which it aroused, and the extent to which this increased during the first half of 1969. Castle and Wilson had envisaged that initial opposition would dissipate once opponents of *In Place of Strife* were persuaded of its alleged virtues, most notably the number of provisions it proposed to strengthen the trade unions and workers' rights. In this regard, Castle had immense faith in her skills of persuasion, linked to a strong belief in the capacity of rational, reasoned argument to win over initial opponents.

Instead, the opposition aroused by *In Place of Strife* increased during the next few months, and was exacerbated both by the mid-April announcement of an 'interim' Industrial Relations Bill (as a prelude to more comprehensive legislation planned for the next parliamentary session), and the appointment of a new Chief Whip, the supposedly disciplinarian Bob Mellish, who was widely expected to ensure the compliance of rebellious Labour MPs. Instead, his appointment inadvertently fuelled further anger among sundry Labour backbenchers.

Meanwhile, Castle and Wilson encountered implacable opposition from the trade unions, whose leadership, via the Trades Union Congress (TUC), bitterly resented statutory intervention in their internal affairs, and legal regulation of activities pursued in connection with collective bargaining. Some of the proposals enshrined in the White Paper and interim Bill offended against the unions' long-standing commitment to 'voluntarism', whereby the State mostly maintained a non-interventionist stance towards industrial relations, thereby permitting unions and employers to negotiate terms and conditions of employment with a high degree of autonomy.

For the trade unions, this *free* collective bargaining was of the essence, and the 'penal clauses' proposed by *In Place of Strife* were not rendered any more acceptable by virtue of emanating from a Labour government. Nor were the unions pacified by Castle's insistence that the 'penal clauses' would be invoked only rarely and sparingly, because even if she did exercise the utmost constraint, a subsequent Conservative Secretary of State was very unlikely to practice similar reticence. Some trade union leaders even viewed *In Place of Strife* as the first step on the road to State control of trade unions, notwithstanding the many measures included in the White Paper which aimed to strengthen trade unions and workers' rights.

Castle also reminded the unions that, in spite of their professed commitment to voluntarism, they and their members already benefitted from State intervention, most notably via legislation concerning sundry conditions of employment. Indeed, some laws to provide workers with greater statutory employment rights and protection had only been enacted during the previous six years. Yet such arguments failed to reduce the unions' hostility to the Labour Government's proposed industrial relations legislation, which was also criticised by some union leaders for deriving from an out-of-touch view of industrial life. Indeed, it was sometimes suggested that Castle and Wilson were middle class, Oxbridge-educated academics who had never done a proper day's manual work or got their hands dirty in their lives, and as such, knew nothing about life on the factory floor, down a coal-mine, or on a building-site.

By June 1969, the scale and strength of the opposition from the PLP *and* the trade unions had prompted some Cabinet Ministers to concede that the Government could not win, and that Castle and Wilson should therefore accept counter-proposals which the TUC drafted, and then emphatically endorsed at a special conference in Croydon. Initially, Wilson rejected the TUC's counter-proposals as inadequate and ineffective (or likely to prove so). However, as Cabinet support for industrial relations legislation steadily ebbed away, amidst dire warnings of a serious, and possibly fatal, split between Labour and the unions, Castle and Wilson negotiated a last-minute 'solemn and binding' agreement, whereby the TUC's General Council would take responsibility for resolving inter-union disputes and unofficial or unconstitutional strikes, in return for the Government abandoning its imminent industrial relations legislation. Apart from slight presentational differences, which ostensibly saved Castle and Wilson from complete political humiliation, this agreement was largely based on the TUC's counter-proposals which Wilson especially had rejected just weeks previously.

When Labour subsequently lost the 1970 general election twelve months later, much of the Party's *de facto* post-mortem focused on the events surrounding *In Place of Strife*, the ensuing interim Industrial Relations Bill and the 'solemn and binding' agreement with the TUC. Those Labour MPs and Ministers who had continuously supported Castle and Wilson's pursuit of reform argued that it was the abandonment of industrial relations legislation which was largely responsible for the electoral defeat, and rendered the Conservative Party's own, more radical, proposals for industrial relations reform attractive to those voters – doubtless including some erstwhile Labour supporters and trade unionists – who were exasperated with the industrial and social disruption (and perhaps loss of wages) caused by strikes, of which at least 90 per cent were unofficial.

Conversely, some critics argued that it was Castle's and Wilson's six-month pursuit of industrial relations reform, following several years of pay curbs and cuts to social provision in the context of deflation, which had alienated many workers who had voted Labour in 1966, but had thereafter become disillusioned with the re-elected Government's economic, industrial and social policies. Certainly, for many on the Left, the 1966–70 Labour Government was a classic example of 'leadership betrayal'.

Yet in spite of the controversies engendered by *In Place of Strife*, and the ensuing developments and intra-Party divisions, as well as deep tensions between Labour and the trade unions, this important episode in British labour history has received scant academic attention. Indeed, the only book on this topic is Peter Jenkins' *The Battle of Downing Street*, which was published the following year, and according to the blurb on the back cover, was written in the style of a political thriller (Jenkins, 1970). Thereafter, the adoption and then abandonment of *In Place of Strife* was only addressed by academics in the guise of chapters (or sections of chapters) in more general historical accounts of industrial relations or government–trade union relations since 1945, or in biographies of the key political figures. The main examples of historical accounts are Barnes and Reid (1980: 112–26), Dorfman (1979: 8–49); Panitch (1976: 171–203), Ponting (1990: 350–71), Sandbrook (2006: Chapter 33) and Taylor (1993: 159–73), while the relevant biographies are by Morgan (1997: 330–45), Perkins (2003: chapters 13 and 14), and Pimlott (1993: chapter 23).

However, the authors of these works mostly lacked access to key archival sources, many of which have only become available to scholars in relatively recent years, due to such factors as the thirty-year rule which applied to the release of government papers, or the bequeathing and/or cataloguing of the personal papers of the three central political figures involved in promoting or opposing *In Place of Strife*, most notably Barbara Castle, James Callaghan and Harold Wilson. As the Acknowledgements to this book indicate, this author has made extensive use of archival sources now stored in Coventry, London, Manchester and Oxford, and in so doing, has been able to offer new or richer, more nuanced, insights into the origins, developments and subsequent abandonment of *In Place of Strife*.

For example, having provided a fuller and more reflective account of the role and *modus operandi* of the 1965–8 Donovan Commission in chapter 2, we then consider, in chapter 3, how Barbara Castle and her senior Departmental 'team' resolved to go further than the (to them) disappointingly cautious Donovan Report. We examine the often overlooked or underestimated importance of the mid-November 1968 'Sunningdale seminar', at which Castle, a couple of other Ministers and her senior civil servants discussed the increasingly evident inadequacies of the hitherto 'voluntarist' approach to industrial relations, under which the State mostly refrained from intervention either in collective bargaining between employers and trade unions, or in the internal affairs of the unions. With this voluntarist system of industrial relations deemed no longer 'fit for purpose', the Sunningdale seminar was instrumental in crystallising Castle's ideas for placing industrial relations and trade unionism in a clear legal framework. This was evident in the White Paper which was published two months later: *In Place of Strife*.

One other factor which chapter 3 highlights, in examining the post-Donovan adoption of a more legalistic industrial relations policy, is the changing ethos among senior civil servants, which reflected and reinforced the growing conviction that voluntarism was no longer adequate. Although mandarins in the previously pro-voluntarist Ministry of Labour had begun to doubt the continued efficacy of a 'hands-off' approach to industrial relations and trade unionism during the course of the 1960s – largely due to economic and industrial developments which are discussed in chapter 1 – what ultimately proved decisive in heralding the paradigm shift in Whitehall was the 1968 merger of the Ministry of Labour with the Department of Economic Affairs (DEA).

Many senior civil servants in the latter had already been strongly inclined to a more legalistic industrial relations policy, primarily because they witnessed more directly, on an almost daily basis, the apparent impact of strikes and restrictive practices on the British economy, especially with regard to economic modernisation, planning and productivity. Thus it was that when the DEA was formed in 1968, many of its senior civil servants were already supportive of a new, statutory, industrial relations policy.

However, it must not be assumed that Castle was unduly influenced by these civil servants, as some trade unions subsequently suggested (in so doing, perhaps they revealed their own sexist attitudes towards her). As we emphasise, to a very considerable extent, Castle had already arrived at such a conclusion about the need for a statutory industrial relations policy, and as such, it was very much a mutually reinforcing meeting of like minds between her and her Departmental officials. Indeed, it is more likely that her mandarins were themselves greatly encouraged and emboldened to have a Secretary of State who had already resolved to adopt a statutory industrial relations policy.

Meanwhile, chapter 4 offers a more in-depth and nuanced analysis of the responses to *In Place of Strife* within the Cabinet. Most studies of the events surrounding the White Paper have focused mainly on the strong opposition of James Callaghan, the Home Secretary, and while we fully acknowledge the undeniable importance of this, we also draw attention to the attitudes and responses of other Cabinet Ministers, for these have generally been overlooked. For example, Callaghan's opposition to *In Place of Strife* was wholly shared by Richard Marsh, the Transport Secretary, who was another 'working-class trade unionist' in the Cabinet. He shared the Home Secretary's view that most of those in the Cabinet who were promoting or supporting *In Place of Strife* were 'middle-class academics', who therefore lacked any real experience of life in industry or trade unionism. Consequently, their backgrounds supposedly meant that they did not really understand industrial relations, and so had a naïve faith in the ability of legislation to inject order and stability into this often complex and conflictual sphere of human interaction.

Nor were attitudes within the Cabinet merely a binary division between enthusiastic supporters and implacable opponents because, as on any political issue, there were positions in between. In this instance, a few Ministers expressed doubts about specific measures proposed by *In Place of Strife*, or demurred from them, and as such, their support was tentative or qualified: they were ambivalent or apprehensive about aspects of the White Paper, and so their cautious endorsement was in the expectation that the planned period of consultation would lead to modification of particular features.

The other aspect of intra-Cabinet debates and disagreements over *In Place of Strife* which has tended to be neglected concerns the timing of the proposed legislation. Castle envisaged spending most of 1969 undertaking consultations with the trade unions, in order to persuade them of the professed merits of *In Place of Strife*, prior to introducing an Industrial Relations Bill in November. However, a few Cabinet Ministers warned that a lengthy period of consultation would provide the trade unions, and sections of the Labour Party, with ample time in which to mobilise opposition to the White Paper; the longer Castle left it before introducing legislation, these Ministerial colleagues warned, the greater the difficulties she would face when she eventually did so. Consequently, their advice was 'the sooner, the better'.

Having initially rejected such haste (believing that this itself would mobilise widespread opposition to her proposals), Castle subsequently agreed to introduce a 'short' Bill, to be scheduled for late spring or early summer, with more comprehensive industrial relations legislation in the next Parliamentary session. Yet the April announcement of an imminent interim Bill unwittingly served to weaken support, both in the Cabinet and on the Labour backbenches, among Ministers and MPs who felt that they were being 'bounced'. To the extent that they had previously supported *In Place of Strife*, it had largely been on the basis that it was a basis for lengthy discussion, yet now they were being expected to endorse industrial relations legislation just three months after publication of the contentious White Paper.

What also led some formerly supportive Ministers to change their minds was the TUC's response to the mid-April announcement of the interim Industrial Relations Bill, for the unions were simultaneously outraged and yet galvanised into developing counter-proposals of their own for tackling various forms of industrial action (as discussed in chapter 6). Some Ministers deemed that the TUC's proposed measures were sufficiently credible and robust to warrant the Government withdrawing its own proposed Bill, or at least the 'penal clauses'. That Wilson (especially) and

Castle instantly dismissed the TUC's counter-proposals antagonised those Ministers who were suitably impressed and enamoured with what trade union leaders were offering, and strained their loyalty; they considered Wilson and Castle to be intransigent and obstinate, and engaged in a reckless game of brinkmanship which threatened to cause irreparable damage to the relationship between the Labour Party and the trade unions.

The other factor which prompted the withdrawal of most Cabinet support for *In Place of Strife* and the interim Industrial Relations Bill during the second quarter of 1969 was the growing opposition in the PLP, as examined in chapter 6. Although much of this opposition emanated from the Left, particularly the Tribune Group's 33 MPs and the 127 trade union-sponsored Labour MPs (a few MPs belonged to both, so that their combined number was slightly less than 160), other Labour MPs who were not aligned to either group also opposed *In Place of Strife* or/and the interim Industrial Relations Bill, so that opposition effectively spanned all sections and ideological tendencies or factions in the PLP.

Moreover, whereas many Labour MPs opposed industrial relations legislation, especially the penal clauses, from the moment that *In Place of Strife* was published, other backbenchers became opposed in response to subsequent developments, namely the announcement of the interim Industrial Relations Bill, Wilson's appointment of the apparently disciplinarian Robert 'Bob' Mellish as the Government's Chief Whip, and the apparent credence and efficacy of the TUC's counter-proposals for tackling strikes, which were summarily rejected by Wilson. Some Labour MPs had initially endorsed *In Place of Strife* out of a personal loyalty to Castle herself, but became disillusioned by these subsequent developments and the perceived obstinacy or bloody-mindedness of Wilson and/or Castle in refusing to accept the TUC's counter-proposals.

In some respects, the growing intra-Cabinet opposition to industrial relations legislation and the parallel growth in PLP opposition became reciprocal. Some Cabinet Ministers reasoned that because the interim Bill would fail to muster sufficient support among Labour MPs to secure its successful parliamentary passage, Wilson and Castle should abandon it, and accept the TUC's counter-proposals instead. Similarly, as it became increasingly clear that many Cabinet Ministers were withdrawing their erstwhile support for the proposed Bill, so did more Labour MPs become emboldened in opposing it, secure in the knowledge that their concerns and views were now shared among a growing number of senior Ministers. As a consequence, Wilson and Castle became effectively isolated, and their political authority seriously weakened. Not even Wilson's occasional threats of resignation could reverse the decline in support in the Cabinet and on the backbenches; on the contrary, some Labour MPs and Ministers would have welcomed a change of leader, and so called Wilson's bluff.

Thus it was that, as we examine in chapter 7 (again relying extensively on archival sources), Wilson and Castle brokered a deal with the TUC's General Council, whereby the latter would take responsibility for resolving inter-union disputes, and unconstitutional or unofficial strikes, in return for which the interim Industrial Relations Bill would be withdrawn. In many respects, this 'solemn and binding' agreement was extensively based on the TUC's counter-proposals which Wilson and Castle had previously rejected as inadequate, but which were subsequently amended slightly, albeit more in presentation than in substance, largely in order that Wilson in particular could 'save face' when announcing this deal.

When Labour subsequently lost the 1970 general election a year later, the inevitable intra-Party post-mortem included consideration of the role of *In Place of Strife* in the loss of support, as we discuss in the conclusion. There was a divergence of views between those Labour politicians who blamed Labour's defeat, in large part, on the failure to implement the reforms enshrined in *In Place of Strife*, while others claimed that it was the time and energy devoted to industrial relations legislation in the first place which had alienated many erstwhile Labour supporters.

Against these two perspectives, we argue that Labour's loss of support in the 1970 election derived from more general and longer-term disillusionment among many of the Party's former voters, this pre-dating *In Place of Strife*. Furthermore, Labour's defeat in 1970 owed less to Labour voters switching to the Conservatives, as was widely assumed at the time, than to abstentions by many people who had voted for the Party in 1966, or to former Labour voters switching to the Liberal Party in some seats which the Liberals had not contested in 1966. Moreover, the Conservatives benefitted enormously from an increase in turnout among their own supporters, this significantly exceeding the decline in Labour's support.

1

Emergence and identification of the problem

It was during the 1960s that concern about industrial relations and trade unionism moved firmly on to the political agenda, whereupon many senior politicians and civil servants increasingly became convinced of the necessity of reform which entailed legislation. Since the end of the Second World War a voluntarist approach had prevailed, under which governments studiously sought to avoid being embroiled in industrial relations, and instead repeatedly insisted that relations between employers and employees, and management and trade unions, could only be improved through the conscious and concerted efforts of those directly involved. In effect, governments promoted a form of industrial self-government, with the State refraining from intervening so far as was deemed practicably possible.

There was, of course, an irony in this, namely that since 1945 successive governments had increasingly intervened in economic and social affairs, via regulation of the economy, Keynesianism, the promotion of full employment and the welfare state. Yet while often welcoming such intervention, due to its positive impact on jobs, standards of living (most notably via higher earnings) and the 'social' wage (child allowance/benefit, old-age pensions, unemployment benefit, etc.,), the trade unions still insisted that the State should not intervene in 'collective bargaining' between the so-called two sides of industry, nor in the internal affairs and governance of the unions themselves.

However, during the 1960s, four discrete factors fuelled growing concern about industrial relations in Britain, and the conduct of trade unions, namely: emerging evidence of Britain's relative economic decline; the changing structure of British industry; new data about the incidence of unofficial and unconstitutional strikes; the recourse to incomes policies in order to secure wage restraint aiming to curb inflation and the additional problems which accrued from these pay policies. In addition, the critical attention which was increasingly being directed towards the conduct of the trade unions was reinforced by a landmark judicial decision in 1964, which fuelled demands for a formal inquiry into the law pertaining to trade unionism.

Britain's relative economic decline

Although it is widely acknowledged that Britain's economy experienced *relative* decline during the twentieth century (Alford, 1996; Dintenfass, 1992: chapter one; Elbaum and Lazonick, 1986; Gamble, 1981: chapters one and two; Kirby, 1981; Robbins, 1983: chapter 33; Smith and Polsby, 1981: chapter one; Supple, 1994: 441–58),[1] it was during the 1960s that increasing – or increasingly evident – economic problems moved on to the political agenda: the genial confidence of the 1950s was replaced by genuine concern during the 1960s. A range of economic data and statistics seemingly illustrated the scale and scope of this economic deterioration. For example, whereas Britain had enjoyed 33 per cent of the global market in manufactured exports at the very end of the nineteenth century, its share had fallen to 25.5 per cent by 1950, and then to 16.5 per cent ten years later. By the end of the 1960s it had dwindled to barely 11 per cent. Throughout this time, Britain was being challenged and outperformed by several other advanced industrial countries, such as Japan and West Germany.[2]

Another clear manifestation of Britain's ailing economy was its low rate of growth, particularly when compared to its economic competitors. By 1960, it had become apparent that, during the previous decade, Britain's rate of economic growth had been lower than that attained by France, Italy, Sweden, the United States and West Germany, and there was little improvement during the 1960s. Indeed, towards the end of the 1960s, Britain's average annual rate of economic growth was just 2 per cent, whereas Japan achieved a remarkable 16.5 per cent, and the six-member European Economic Community (EEC), officially formed in 1957, was enjoying a 6.5 per cent economic growth rate. Incidentally, the relative economic decline of the British economy, and the parallel success of the fledging EEC, were major reasons why Britain subsequently applied to join the Community: economic pragmatism and financial calculation rather than genuine political principle and firm commitment.

In turn, Britain's declining share of world trade in exports, coupled with the domestic economy's low rates of economic growth, yielded a corresponding deterioration in the country's balance of payments during the early 1960s. Britain's overall current balance was in deficit for three out of the five years from 1960 to 1964 inclusive (we were importing more than we were exporting), whereas during the 1952–9 period the balance of payments had consistently been in surplus. What further fuelled concern was that the deficit on the 'visible' earnings account increased from an average of £377 million in the second half of the 1950s, to an average of £1,277 million during the first half of the 1960s. That Britain's overall balance of payments account was ever in credit was due entirely to the strength of her 'invisible' earnings (i.e. banking, financial services, etc.).

One other economic trend which fuelled growing political concern during the 1960s was steadily rising inflation, for whereas the average annual rate had been 3.5 per cent during the first half of the decade, it had risen to 5.4 per cent by 1969. It was largely to tackle inflation that Conservative and Labour governments alike resorted to a series of incomes policies in the 1960s: attempts to restrain annual pay increases in order to reduce the price increases which employers or companies often invoked to offset them. Yet incomes policies subsequently served to highlight problems of authority within the trade unions, for rank-and-file or local-level members and officials often secured higher wage increases – sometimes by pursuing unofficial strikes – which circumvented those formally agreed by their national-level leaders in London, an issue which we return to below.

All of these statistics and trends prompted rapidly growing political concern about the economic problems facing Britain. Yet crucial though they were, other developments during the 1960s also contributed significantly to the emerging 'trade union problem'.

The changing structure of British industry

By the 1960s the British economy was increasingly dominated by large firms and industries, due to two factors. First, much of the private sector was characterised by semi-monopolies and oligopolies, as a consequence of corporate amalgamations, mergers and take-overs. These often accrued from the pursuit of 'economies of scale' which derived from a conception of economic rationality and industrial efficiency via large-scale production.

Second, alongside these private sector oligopolies were several industries and utilities which had been nationalised by the 1945–50 Labour government led by Clement Attlee, such as coal, electricity, gas, the railways and water. With the subsequent 1951–64 Conservative governments pursuing only very limited de-nationalisation (the term 'privatisation' was not deployed at that time), most of these industries remained as State-owned entities throughout the 1960s.

This trend towards private sector oligopolies and State-owned monopolies had four particular consequences which served to push industrial relations reform on to the political agenda during the 1960s. First, industrial concentration mean that there were correspondingly fewer trade unions than had hitherto been the case, but they were larger (in terms of membership). As noted by the 1965–8 Royal Commission on Trade Unions and Employers' Associations – hereafter referred to simply as the Royal Commission, and discussed fully in chapter 2 – whereas at the start of the twentieth century there had been 1,323 trade unions, with a combined membership of 2,022,000 workers, by the mid-1960s the number of unions had fallen to 574 but their total membership had risen to 10,111,000, with more than half of these members belonging to just nine trade unions. Furthermore, almost 9,000,000 of the total membership belonged to 170 trade unions (Royal Commission, 1968: 7, para. 28). The trend to fewer, but larger, trade unions had also been facilitated by the 1964 Trade Union (Amalgamations, etc.) Act, which streamlined the procedures and requirements which had to be met or adhered to before two (or more) unions joined together.

The second reason why the trends towards industrial oligopolies and monopolies pushed industrial relations and trade unionism on to the political agenda was that, because of the increased size and scope of many industrial enterprises and companies, senior management was increasingly remote from the workers at factory level or on the shop-floor. This served to weaken both the sense of corporate allegiance among employees, and comprehension of why particular decisions were being taken: the larger the firm or organisation, the more likely it is that workers will view senior management as being out-of-touch, especially in the absence of effective consultation or channels of communication.

Crucially, this trend was replicated inside many trade unions themselves, as their increased size resulted in a similar centralisation, and the concomitant upwards transfer of power,[3] so that trade union leaders similarly appeared remote to their grass-roots members; negotiations over terms and conditions of employment were increasingly conducted in London, far away from the workplace. This meant that senior or national-level trade union officials also appeared increasingly out-of-touch with their members' concerns and grievances in the workplace. A major consequence of this was an increase in the *de facto* authority and factory-floor activism of shop stewards and other local-level trade union officials. These were often able to secure the respect and trust of their rank-and-file members by virtue of their proximity and visibility, and thus their ability to respond immediately to grievances. According to Davies and Freedland (1999: 242) 'the number of shop stewards was estimated at 90,000 in 1961, and at 175,000 in 1968'.

One study attributed four closely connected characteristics to shop stewards, namely: their identification with the workplace itself and thus the workers employed there; the relative organisational and operational autonomy of shop stewards from their official trade union leadership; their parallel autonomy from senior management control systems when negotiating with local-level managers and factory foremen; the relatively strong influence of shop stewards over local-level pay bargaining (Terry, 1983: 67–8).

The third reason why the trend towards industrial concentration and economies of scale fuelled growing political concern about the character and conduct of Britain's trade unions was that larger companies and industries were more prone to inter-union or demarcation disputes. These occurred when unions competed with each other in claiming that a particular task was part of their jurisdiction, so that it could, or should, be performed exclusively by their members, rather than by any worker(s) belonging to another trade union. As we will note in subsequent chapters, these demarcation disputes were to become a key concern of politicians seeking to reform industrial relations in the late 1960s, most notably the Labour Prime Minister Harold Wilson and his Secretary of State for Employment and Productivity Barbara Castle.

However, there was a fourth reason why the growth of industrial oligopolies and monopolies fuelled political concern about industrial relations and trade unionism, namely that these trends were also rendering the British economy increasingly inter-connected and inter-dependent: a strike in one company or industry was highly likely to have a negative impact on other companies and industries with whom there were trading relationships. As such, even an ostensibly small or local industrial dispute could have much wider repercussions, and cause disruption far beyond the original source.

The incidence and impact of unofficial strikes

As their name clearly implies, *unofficial* strikes are those which are not called or endorsed by the union leadership. Indeed, such strikes might well be contrary to the advice or instructions of trade union leaders. In such instances, *unofficial* strike activity would be pursued by ordinary union members acting independently of their union leaders, quite possibly in defiance of them. Political concern over unofficial strikes increased during the 1960s, both because of the afore-mentioned size of many companies and the general inter-dependence of British industry, and because of the manner in which such stoppages often reflected the growing gulf between official trade union leaders (who might be based in London) and union members in the workplace. The vacuum which nature abhors was readily filled by local trade union officials and shop stewards, a process which further fuelled growing political concern about the erosion of authority and discipline inside trade unions. Moreover, it was only in 1961 that the Ministry of Labour began distinguishing between official and unofficial strikes when compiling statistics on industrial stoppages, whereupon it was discovered that at least 90 per cent of strikes were unofficial.

The 1960s also heralded concern about 'unconstitutional' (or 'wildcat') strikes, which were industrial stoppages that occurred before grievance procedures or other recognised methods of resolving a workplace dispute had been fully pursued. Indeed, in some instances, these procedures simply did not exist. Such strikes invariably flared up instantly, seeing a group of employees immediately cease work, often in protest against a seemingly arbitrary decision or apparent injustice perpetrated by an employer. Of course, 'unconstitutional' strikes were almost always unofficial too – because they were not endorsed by the national union leadership. However, 'unofficial' strikes were not necessarily 'unconstitutional', because they often occurred after the pursuit of established procedures had failed to elicit a decision or response satisfactory to the workers involved. In such instances, local-level union officials or shop stewards might then call a strike, albeit one still not endorsed by senior union leaders at national level.

The recourse to incomes policies

Although senior Conservatives had increasingly exhorted workers and their trade unions to practice wage restraint during the latter half of the 1950s, in order to curb inflation and prevent higher unemployment, it was not until July 1961 that Harold Macmillan's Government took direct action, via a nine-month 'pay pause' invoked by Chancellor Selwyn Lloyd. By this time, Macmillan (1972: 376) himself was ruminating on 'the next great struggle that awaits us – and the most important – the Battle of Wages'. Applying only to the public sector and nationalised industries – albeit expected to set an example to the private sector – the 'pay pause' was intended to constitute an immediate, short-term measure pending a long-term policy for securing wage restraint, albeit on a consensual basis; a voluntary or non-statutory incomes policy.

This was part of a general shift in intellectual and political opinion towards a more active and direct role for the State in pay determination, in order to control inflation and maintain full employment, both of which were heavily dependent on restraining wage increases; 'excessive' pay rises would fuel inflation – as employers passed on higher labour costs to the consumer through higher prices – and/or cause higher unemployment – as employers laid off workers to offset their company's higher wage bill. There was also concern that higher wages were themselves contributing to Britain's balance of payments problems, as the increased incomes were then spent on imported goods. Hence incomes policies often sought to link wage increases to higher productivity and *inter alia* greater industrial output.

Of course, this recourse to incomes policies was itself a manifestation of the growing political concern about the strength of workers and trade unions in an era of full employment and industrial oligopolies. Initially, though, it was envisaged that if wage increases could be curbed or regulated via incomes policies, then this would obviate the need for industrial relations legislation. Yet it soon became apparent that recourse to incomes policies exacerbated another problem, namely that of 'wage drift' (on the history of incomes policies in post-war Britain, and the problems they caused or encountered, see Dorey, 2001). This was the term used to characterise the phenomenon of *actual* pay increases exceeding the permissible level stipulated in any particular incomes policy. In other words, local-level wage increases were often higher than those agreed at national level via negotiations between trade union leaders and employers or Ministers. Or, as the Ministry of Labour (1965: 22, para. 62) observed in its submission to the Donovan Commission (see chapter 2), 'earnings are now consistently higher than wage rises ... earnings are rising faster than wage rates'. This is certainly not to suggest that wage drift had not occurred previously; however, recourse to incomes policies simultaneously compounded the problem by increasing its scope and impact, thereby imbuing it with greater visibility, and thus rendering it politically (rather than just economically) problematic. Needless to say, this further fuelled concern about 'the trade union problem' from the early 1960s onwards.

This phenomenon further reflected the growing role of local-level or factory-floor trade union officials or shop stewards, who were sometimes able to negotiate a better (higher) pay rise than that secured by the union's official leadership based in London. Indeed, the recourse to incomes policies from the early 1960s served to fuel this phenomenon, because the increased role of national trade union leaders in accepting wage restraint through negotiations with Ministers unwittingly enabled local or workplace union officials to attract more respect and allegiance from workers on the factory/shop-floor. Ironically, as national-level trade union leaders acquired an aura of power and prestige by virtue of regular meetings and discussions with Ministers (with whom they were on first-name terms), so their actual authority inside the trade union often dissipated, as their rank-and-file members suspected them of 'selling out' or being bought off by political leaders.

This was certainly a perception or suspicion which some local-level union officials were happy to encourage, for it often enabled to them to enjoy greater authority and allegiance among workers, on the basis that they could secure higher pay increases than their more senior officials and leaders; they were still 'down here' on the factory-floor fighting alongside union members to improve wages, not 'down there' in London colluding with Ministers to hold down wages. This created something of a schism inside many trade unions, and was subsequently identified by the Royal Commission on Trade Unions and Employers' Associations as a major source of unofficial strikes – as we will also note in the next chapter.

Turning attention to the trade unions

In response to these developments, criticism of Britain's trade unions steadily became more vehement and vocal, to the extent that they increasingly became, in the words of a labour historian, 'the scapegoats of national decline' (Taylor, 1993: 1–15). For example, in 1961 the recently created Organisation for European Economic Co-operation (subsequently to become the OECD) asserted that:

> [p]ost-war experience suggests the [British industrial relations] system is less well suited to the new conditions of almost continuous full employment ... The haphazard fragmentation of collective bargaining and the weakness of central organisations has facilitated competitive bidding between unions, and at the same time, political factors bearing on wage determination in the nationalised industries ha[ve] had a very strong influence on wages in the economy as a whole. (Organisation for European Economic Co-operation, 1961: 8)

Much of the early criticism of Britain's system of industrial relations in general, and of the trade unions in particular, emanated from journalists working for broadsheet newspapers. For example, in his 1961 book *The Stagnant Society*, Michael Shanks (a labour correspondent and industrial editor with the *The Financial Times*) castigated the unions for 'failing to adjust themselves to the changing pattern of industry and society'. This alleged failure rendered them 'increasingly dated ... The smell of the music hall and the pawnshop clings to them.' Moreover, he argued, Britain was experiencing an expansion of non-industrial sectors, and a corresponding increase in white-collar jobs, which left the trade unions representing a declining working class, and 'trapped among the slogans and banners of the past.' As a consequence, Shanks deemed many trade unions to be backward-looking and resistant to change or modernisation, as well as amateurish in their organisation and operation (Shanks, 1961: 44).

Another journalist who published a 1961 book critical of the trade unions was Eric Wigham, a labour correspondent for *The Times*. His book was bluntly called *What's wrong with the Unions?*, and constituted part of a 'What's wrong with...?' series of Penguin paperbacks published in the early 1960s: other books focused on the Church, Parliament, British industry, etc. Each book in this series focused on the alleged deficiencies and conservatism of the chosen institution, which was deemed in urgent need of 'modernisation' in order to retain its relevance in a rapidly changing society.

Although Wigham commenced his book by readily acknowledging many positive characteristics and qualities of Britain's trade unions, he then proceeded to delineate the sundry ways in which they had not only become increasingly powerful in an era of full employment, but had displayed a growing tendency to exercise their enhanced power in a destructive and negative manner, with damaging repercussions for the British economy and wider British society. He lamented that what had once been virtues had become vices, such as:

> when comradeship becomes conspiracy for selfish gain, when loyalty becomes sheeplikeness, when unpaid service turns to officiousness and even bullying, when respect for tradition turns to rigidity, resoluteness to obstinacy, dignity to insolence, acceptance of majority decisions to subservience, tolerance to irresponsibility, and democracy comes near to anarchy. (Wigham, 1961: 9)

Yet Wigham also highlighted something of a paradox concerning the growth of trade union power, namely the relative weakness of many national-level or official union leaders, largely due to the economic and industrial trends already noted in this chapter. In this context, 'there has in recent years been no central leadership with authority. The T.U.C General Council ... cannot control the policies of individual unions', especially as their leaders 'are themselves subject to executive committees, which in their turn are responsible to rank-and-file opinion' (Wigham, 1961: 21). This was to become a common trope in many criticisms of the trade unions, whereby they were simultaneously condemned for being too powerful, yet not powerful enough.

Indeed, during the 1960s and 1970s, political criticism of the trade unions oscillated between bemoaning the apparent inability or unwillingness of trade union leaders to exercise authority over their rank-and-file membership, and berating the same union leaders for acting like bullies or feudal barons *vis-à-vis* their union members. Of course, which of these criticisms was advanced at any juncture depended largely on who was deemed responsible for strikes. If and when rank-and-file trade unionists pursued strike action, the political demand was for the official union leadership to be imbued with greater authority or power over their members. Yet when trade union leaders themselves instigated strikes, many politicians and much of the press – invariably without any sense of irony or awareness of cognitive dissonance – demanded that their 'irresponsible' power be curbed, and the unions 'democratised' so that they were 'handed back to their members'. This was precisely the stance adopted, and the discourse deployed, by the 1979–90 Thatcher Governments (see Dorey, 2016b).

The TUC's lack of authority over its affiliated trade unions

A key problem which became apparent in the context of these economic and industrial developments, coupled with the governmental recourse to incomes policies as a means of curbing inflation, was the structure of the trade union movement, and the concomitant power relations within them. We noted earlier the trade unions' implacable commitment to voluntarism, jealously guarding their autonomy from State interference in industrial relations and the unions' internal affairs, but the unions also sought to maintain a high degree of independence from the TUC in their day-to-day activities.

The voluntarism which the trade unions overall subscribed to *vis-a-vis* the State was strongly replicated in their attitude towards the TUC itself. To individual trade unions, the TUC was an umbrella organisation which provided a collective voice on their behalf, and which could campaign and lobby more effectively at national-level than unions could separately, but many trade unions were wary of ceding authority to the TUC over their own internal affairs. As Flanders highlighted, the voluntarist ethos meant that trade unions:

> want to order their own affairs according to their own preferences with as little outside interference as possible. This applies at all levels of trade union organisation, to union affairs within a plant in their relations with district or higher union authorities, as well as to national unions ... Self-government is the essence. (Flanders, 1974: 362, emphasis added)

Consequently the federal structure of the TUC itself proved to be a significant problem for politicians who were increasingly concerned to secure greater order and stability in industrial relations, particularly with regard to curbing unofficial strikes, and reducing 'wage drift'. As two historians of the TUC observed in the year before *In Place of Strife* was published: 'The untidy structure ... of the trade unions in Britain has long been recognized as a major handicap to the development and the carrying out of an effective central policy' (Lovell and Roberts, 1968: 178).

Herein lay a paradox. The growing public perception, shared – and perhaps encouraged for partisan purposes – by many politicians, was that Britain's trade unions had become too powerful, as a consequence of full employment, the vulnerability of increasingly interconnected and interdependent industries to strikes, and extensive legal immunities, as symbolised by the 1906 Trade Disputes Act. Indeed, from the 1960s onwards, in the context of growing concern about Britain's relative economic decline, critics of the trade unions variously claimed that organised labour enjoyed almost untrammelled rights, but with very few corresponding responsibilities to wider British society. Moreover, the trade unions' legal immunities, which largely derived from the 1906 Act, were increasingly depicted by critics as 'privileges' which no other corporate bodies enjoyed, and which effectively placed the trade unions above and beyond the law (Dorey, 2016a: 194–7; Hayek, 1960: 268, 269; Hayek, 1980: 52, 58; Syrett, 1998: 391–3; Wedderburn, 1989: 11–12).

Yet in certain respects, the alleged power of the trade unions actually belied a weakness, namely the limited authority which union leaders exercised over their members, and, in turn, the limited authority of the TUC over the unions affiliated to it. It was this apparent power vacuum which underpinned many unofficial and/or unconstitutional strikes, and whilst many of these were sporadic, often localised, and short-lived, they were nonetheless capable of causing widespread industrial disruption and lay-offs of other workers, largely as a consequence of the growing size and interdependence of many companies and industries. Had senior trade union leaders been capable of exerting greater power over their rank-and-file members, or the TUC able (or willing) to exercise more authority over its affiliated unions, then many of these industrial disputes might have been averted.

Of course, it could also be argued that if the trade unions really ever had the power which their critics ascribed them, they would have been able to curb the enormous salaries which company bosses and 'captains of industry' were (and still are) routinely awarded, and the generous dividends often paid to corporate shareholders. They would also have been able to shape or prevent many of the managerial decisions which were detrimental to the interests of ordinary workers and union members. In short, criticisms of 'excessive' union power were at odds with the almost complete lack of union involvement or influence in the decisions taken by employers and managers. Or to put in another way, if the unions ever had so much power that were virtually 'running the country' (as was commonly and contemptuously claimed by their critics prior to the 1980s), they would not have needed to engage in strike activity to secure higher wages, prevent redundancies, and improve working conditions (on the limits to trade union power and their relative or structural weakness, see: Anderson, 1967; Coates, 1984: chapter five; Hyman, 1972: *passim*; Miliband, 1973: *passim*; Westergaard and Resler, 1976: *passim*).

Hence the paradox that while strikes in general were often viewed as clear evidence of the (blackmail) power of the trade unions to hold employers or governments (and *inter alia* society) to ransom – 'meet our demands, or else suffer the consequences' – the type of industrial stoppages and disruption which Castle and Wilson were so concerned about were, in large part, indicative of the structural weakness enshrined in Britain's trade unions and the TUC itself. As Lovell and Roberts noted, the TUC – and more specifically its governing body, the General Council – had long been 'extremely reluctant to seek the extension of its own authority ... and most cautious in exercising the powers' which it did formally possess (Lovell and Roberts, 1968: 177).

The *Rookes v Barnard* judicial decision

One particular episode which further pushed trade unionism on to the political agenda during the mid-1960s was the February 1964 conclusion of a lengthy and complex court case, whose verdict seemed seriously to undermine and weaken some of the legal rights which the trade unions had hitherto taken for granted. The origins of this landmark case stretched back to early 1956, when Douglas Rookes, a draughtsman employed, for the previous nine years, by the British Overseas Airways Corporation (BOAC) – subsequently subsumed by British Airways – resigned from the Association of Engineering and Shipbuilding Draughtsmen (AESD). However, the AESD operated a 'closed shop' (a compulsory membership scheme), and therefore warned BOAC that there would be a strike if it continued to employ Rookes. BOAC did terminate Rookes' employment, albeit giving him the statutory seven-day period of notice. The judicial decision was that BOAC had *not* acted in an unlawful manner, and Rookes was thus unable to sue the company.

He did, though, pursue legal action against three officials of the AESD. His case was that the union and BOAC had hitherto operated a no-strike agreement, and as a consequence, the threat by AESD to instigate a strike if BOAC did not sack him constituted a 'conspiracy' to induce other union members to break their contracts. The court found in favour of Rookes, and awarded him damages, but this decision was overturned when the AESD challenged it in the Court of Appeal. However, the original verdict was restored when the case was subject to a further appeal in the House of Lords (via the Law Lords, who at that time constituted Britain's highest judicial body).

This decision caused considerable consternation to the TUC, for as it explained in its written evidence to the subsequent Royal Commission on Trade Unions and Employers' Associations (discussed in chapter 2), 'the judgement cast doubt on the legality of the great majority of strikes'. This, the TUC claimed, derived from a peculiar interpretation of the 1906 Trade Disputes Act, which had granted trade unions legal immunity from tort (legal liability for damages or losses incurred by others) when pursuing a trade dispute. The TUC subsequently alleged that 'the way this judgement had been arrived at ... appeared deliberately to satisfy the prejudices of the judges' (Trades Union Congress, 1966: 124: para.347).

Certainly, it left the trade unions in an ambiguous and uncertain position with regard to pursuing industrial action, for as the then (Conservative) Minister of labour, Joseph Godber noted, the Law Lords' verdict seemed 'to throw into flux some of the basic assumptions on trade union law in this country'.[4] The decision therefore provided a fillip to those politicians (usually Conservatives) who had already been calling for an official inquiry or Royal Commission to consider the state of industrial relations and trade unionism in Britain. Indeed, the pledge of such an inquiry was duly included in the Conservatives' 1964 election manifesto, the assumption being that a Royal Commission would serve as a prelude to industrial relations legislation which would place the trade unions in a clear framework of law. However, the election result ensured that it would not be a Conservative government which established such an inquiry, and then attempted to enact legislative reform of industrial relations.

Conclusion

If the 1950s had been a decade of economic optimism, based on the assumption that a new era of steady and sustainable economic growth, and steadily rising living standards, had been attained in the aftermath of World War Two, then the 1960s were the decade when the performance of the British economy increasingly caused political concern. Various statistical indicators and data revealed that in economic terms, Britain was not performing as strongly as it had earlier in the twentieth century, or in current comparison to several other industrialised nations. The notion of *relative* economic decline became an issue of concern to academic commentators and politicians alike.

This, in turn, prompted concern about the need for 'modernisation' and innovation, as some of the blame was apportioned to Britain's apparently antiquated administrative and political institutions, with sundry commentators claiming that institutions such as the civil service, the education system, local government, and Parliament, were ill-equipped to address the problems facing the nation as it approached the late twentieth century. Amidst such concerns, another institution which was subject to increasingly critical scrutiny was that of trade unionism, and the conduct of industrial relations in Britain. Trade unions found themselves simultaneously accused of being too radical, in terms of militancy and propensity to engage too readily in strike action, and too conservative, in the sense of resisting technological developments and changes to working practices, on the grounds of defending their members' jobs. Either way, trade unions became what Robert Taylor characterised as 'scapegoats of economic decline'.

Some of the aspects of industrial relations and trade unionism which caused mounting political concern from the early 1960s onwards were themselves a consequence of wider changes in the character and structure of British industry, and the increasing interdependence of the British economy. The inexorable trend towards larger companies and oligopolies as a result of industrial mergers, nationalisation and rationalisation, in accordance with the imperatives of 'economies of scale', had two major consequences for industrial relations. The first was that in an economy increasingly dominated by a relatively small number of large companies and industries, a strike by any one group of workers could have major and widespread damaging repercussions, by causing extensive disruption to production and/or transportation either of raw materials or finished products.

The second was that as companies and industrial sectors became larger, so the gulf between senior management and workers on the factory-floor increased, with the former appearing increasingly remote and seemingly out-of-touch. This development was matched by a corresponding gulf between national-level trade union leaders, increasingly based full-time in London, and local-level union officials and shop stewards actually based in the workplace. While formal or *de jure* power in the trade unions was increasingly centralised in the hands of a relatively small number of national leaders, actual or *de facto* power increasingly coalesced at local level, as the visibility and proximity of workplace shop stewards and union officials often earned them the respect and loyalty of union members.

A major consequence of this gulf between national- and local-level trade union officials – mirroring the centralisation of senior management itself in large firms and industries – was the propensity for strikes to be called which were neither formally sanctioned by the national-level union leadership, nor had fully utilised established procedures for resolving workplace conflicts and grievances. Thus emerged political concern about the incidence and impact of unofficial and unconstitutional strikes during the 1960s, which resulted in the 1965–68 Royal Commission on Trade Unions and Employers' Associations, and the subsequent proposals of industrial relations legislation enshrined the 1969 White Paper *In Place of Strife*.

Notes

1 Both relative to early periods of British economic history, and in comparison to the recent/current economic performance of other advanced industrialised societies.

2 At this time, Germany was divided into two entirely separate countries. West Germany was a Capitalist liberal democracy, and part of Western Europe, whereas East Germany was part of the Communist Soviet bloc which included most of Eastern Europe. The two Germanies were not reunited until 1990, following the collapse of the Soviet Union.
3 This relationship, whereby power became more centralised and concentrated as an organisation or institution became larger – regardless of its formal democratic procedures or mechanisms – had been clearly identified by Robert Michels back in 1911. Michels had claimed that 'whoever says organisation, says oligarchy', the development of which he characterised as 'an iron rule' and, as such, he considered the notion of a democratic organisation to be an oxymoron (Michels, 1911/1962: 365).
4 NA CAB 21/21/5779, Godber to Douglas-Home, 14 February 1964. See also NA PREM 11/4871, Butler to Douglas-Home, 17 February 1964.

2

The Donovan Commission and its Report

The establishment of a Royal Commission on Trade Unions and Employers' Associations was a response by the Labour Government, narrowly elected in October 1964, to the problems and issues delineated in chapter 1. However, it was also a *quid pro quo* for passing the 1965 Trade Disputes Act to restore the unions' legal position following the judicial decision in *Rookes v Barnard*. In spite of the Royal Commission's title, it was clear that the primary focus of its investigation was the role and activities of trade unions, rather than employers' associations, for the political concern was with the incidence and impact of unofficial and unconstitutional strikes. Some senior Labour Ministers, including Prime Minister Harold Wilson himself, had hoped that the Royal Commission, chaired by Lord Donovan, would publish a report containing radical and far-reaching proposals for reforming industrial relations and trade unionism, whereupon the Government could mollify trade union outrage by offering a rather more modest and 'reasonable' package of reforms.

However, although the membership of the Royal Commission did include a few critics of the trade unions, the inclusion of some senior trade unionists, alongside academics associated with the 'Oxford School' of industrial relations – who were firmly committed to 'voluntarism' or collective *laissez-faire* – meant that its final Report, published in June 1968, strongly endorsed the extant system of industrial relations, and so rejected legal curbs on trade union activities, including strikes. Instead, while acknowledging the problem of unconstitutional and unofficial strikes, the Donovan Report strongly recommended the reform and strengthening of existing modes of collective bargaining and associated institutional machinery. In effect, the Royal Commission sought to rescue, not reject, voluntarism, and as a consequence its Report was a deep disappointment to those who were increasingly impatient for legislation to regulate industrial relations and place the trade unions within a clear statutory framework. The cautious character of the Donovan Report also meant that the Labour Government felt obliged to pursue a programme of industrial relations and trade union reform which was more far-reaching than it had originally anticipated.

Establishing the Donovan Commission

A few weeks before the 1964 general election, which saw Labour elected with a four-seat Parliamentary majority, the Party's leader Harold Wilson had informed delegates at the TUC's annual conference that Royal Commissions 'took minutes and wasted years', and that any changes in the sphere of industrial relations could be achieved through informal discussions between a Labour government and the TUC. As such, there was no pledge in Labour's 1964 election manifesto to establish such an inquiry into industrial relations or trade unionism. The nearest that the manifesto offered pertaining to any such critical reflection was the suggestion that 'we shall seek to evoke an active and searching frame of mind in which all of us, individuals, enterprises and trade unions are ready to re-examine our methods of work, to innovate and to modernise' (Labour Party, 1964: 24).

However, the newly elected Labour Government then pledged to enact legislation, in the guise of the 1965 Trade Disputes Act, which would remove the legal liability and uncertainty to which the trade unions had been exposed as a consequence of the *Rookes v Barnard* decision in the House of Lords, thus restoring the *status quo ante*. In return for such legislation, though, the trade unions were persuaded, 'after considerable discussion', that a major inquiry should be conducted into 'more important general problems of industrial relations as well as the specific question of trade union law'.[1] As had been the case in 1903, following the 1901 *Taff Vale* judgment, a Royal Commission was established to examine aspects of trade unionism following a judicial decision which placed the unions in a very precarious legal position.

At this initial stage, it was envisaged that the inquiry would be conducted by a Royal Commission consisting of people who were representatives neither of the trade unions nor of employers' organisations, although the likelihood of union opposition to such exclusion was foreseen.[2] When this opposition was duly expressed, Ray Gunter (Minister of Labour) conceded that the trade unions and the employers could each be represented by two senior figures, with the remainder of the Royal Commission's members appointed either on the basis of their industrial and occupational backgrounds, or their academic expertise in industrial relations. Thus did the final membership of the Royal Commission consist of:

- Lord Donovan, a former Labour MP prior to becoming a High Court judge

- Professor Hugh Clegg, Professor of Industrial Relations, Warwick University
- Lord Collison, General Secretary of the National Union of Agricultural Workers
- Dame Mary Green, headmistress
- Professor Otto Kahn-Freund, Professor of Comparative Law, Oxford University
- Sir George Pollock, QC, former director of the British Employers' Confederation
- Lord Robens, Chairman, National Coal Board
- Andrew Shonfield, Director of Studies, Royal Institute of International Affairs
- Lord Tangley, solicitor and chairman or director of several companies
- John Thomson, Chairman of Barclays Bank
- Eric Wigham, labour correspondent, *The Times*
- George Woodcock, General Secretary, TUC.

Yet even the appointment of the two trade unions representatives had initially been a cause of disagreement with the TUC, for the Minister of Labour himself had intended to nominate them, possibly with one representative *not* being a member of the TUC's General Council – maybe even a retired trade union official. His reasoning was that the members of the Royal Commission would be appointed 'on the basis of their personal qualities and experience, and not as representatives of particular organisations'. However, George Woodcock, then General Secretary of the TUC, protested against this method of selection, whereupon Gunter invited the TUC to nominate five or six senior members, from whom the Minister would select two. In doing so, he pointed out that employers would be entitled to similar representation on the Royal Commission, in order to ensure equity and genuine representativeness.[3]

At the time, Wilson had been sceptical about the wisdom of including trade union leaders and employers' representatives on the Commission, lest its inquiry be overly influenced by sectional pressures and partisan perspectives, but he subsequently conceded that Gunter had been right to ensure that the two sides of industry were directly represented on the Royal Commission (Wilson, 1971: 537–8).

The remit of the Royal Commission was:

> to consider relations between management and employees, and the role of trade unions and employers' associations in promoting the interests of their members, and in accelerating the social and economic advance of the nation, with particular reference to the law affecting the activities of these bodies. (Royal Commission, 1968: 1)

Originally, it had been intended that this remit would also require the Commission to consider how trade unions and employers' associations could contribute to improved productivity and efficiency, but this specific issue was excised from the final text, after opposition from the trade unions, although they acknowledged that the topic would be implicit in much of the inquiry. The other notable change between the initial and final draft of the Royal Commission's remit was that the former had referred to the objective of 'advancing the social and economic well-being of the nation', but this was replaced by 'accelerating the social and economic advance of the nation', in order to imbue the inquiry with a greater sense of urgency.[4]

Although the Royal Commission's remit implied an even-handed approach between trade unions and employers' organisations, it was evident that the real source of concern to many Ministers was the conduct of trade unions, and especially the incidence of unofficial or unconstitutional strikes. This was something which the TUC was keenly alert to, hence Woodcock's insistence that 'the Trade Union Movement should not in any way be put on the defensive in this inquiry', nor should it become an exercise in 'dragging-up … particular union practices in isolation from their background'.[5]

Meanwhile, relatively little attention was given to the role of the trade unions 'in accelerating the social and economic advance of the nation', at least not directly or explicitly. It was tacitly assumed that if industrial relations problems could be ameliorated via more orderly collective bargaining and a significant reduction in unofficial and unconstitutional strikes, then the British economy and society would advance as a consequence. Thus did Vic Feather, who became Acting General Secretary of the TUC in late February 1969 (pending formal confirmation at the TUC's annual conference in September 1969), subsequently express regret that 'the Royal Commission seems to have been primarily a Royal Commission on collective bargaining. Very little said about the remainder of its terms of reference' (Feather, 1968: 341).

The Donovan Commission's work

The Donovan Commission conducted its inquiry over a period of three years, its weekly meetings usually commencing at 10.40 on Tuesdays, adjourning for lunch at 13.00, and then resuming at 14.00 for two hours. In total, it sat on 128 days. Its invitation for written evidence was accompanied by a 330-question 'survey', which potential respondents were asked to refer to when drafting their submissions; they were not asked to answer any of the questions directly (let alone all of them), but to identify the key issues and problems highlighted by them, and draft their written evidence accordingly. Moreover, the questions were divided into five categories or themes, namely:

> The role of trade unions and employers' associations in accelerating the economic and social advance of the nation.
> Relations between managers and workers in the workplace.
> The role and relationship of the trade unions *vis-à-vis* their members.
> The role and relationship of employers' associations *vis-à-vis* their members.
> The law in relation to the activities of trade unions and employers' associations.

Under each of these headings was a series of more specific questions, also arranged thematically. For example, under the heading 'The role and relationship of the trade unions *vis-à-vis* their members', there were questions focusing on such aspects as finance and funding, communication, discipline, strikes, other forms of industrial action, organisation and operations, advisory and 'welfare' services or support, inter-union relations, the role of the TUC, etc.

In total, the Royal Commission received written evidence from 261 organisations, not including the eight government Departments which also submitted statements. The number and range of institutional or organisational sources from which written evidence was received is provided in Table 1.

The Royal Commission also received 163 written submissions from individuals (Royal Commission, 1968: Appendix 2, 330–33). Some of these were citizens writing in a private capacity on an issue they felt strongly about, while several other written submissions emanated from senior academics with particular expertise in industrial relations, such as Professors Allan Flanders, H. Phelps Brown, B. C. Roberts, and K. W. Wedderburn. Another noteworthy individual who tendered written evidence was Douglas Rookes, the plaintiff in *Rookes v Barnard*, cited in chapter 1. The Royal Commission also heard oral evidence (in public) from sixty-four individuals and organisations, while a further thirteen sessions took oral evidence in private.

The TUC's written evidence

Although the Donovan Commission was appointed in April 1965, the TUC did not submit its written evidence until the following year. Part of the reason for this delay was that the Royal Commission wanted to garner written submissions from individual trade unions before it received evidence

Table 1 Number, types and examples of written evidence, from institutions, received by the Donovan Commission

Category of institution	Total number of submissions	Examples of institutions
Government Departments	8	Department of Economic Affairs Department of Education and Science Ministry of Agriculture, Fisheries & Food Ministry of Defence Ministry of Health Ministry of Labour Ministry of Social Security The Treasury
Trade unions	106	Amalgamated Engineering Union Civil Service Clerical Association General & Municipal Workers Union National Union of Bank Employees National Union of Railwaymen Royal College of Nursing Society of Telecommunications Engineers Trades Union Congress (TUC) Transport & General Workers Union Union of Shop, Distributive & Allied Workers
Employers' associations	71	British Iron & Steel Federation Engineering Employers' Federation Federation of Master Builders National Association of Master Bakers, Confectioners and Caterers National Federation of Builders' and Plumbers' Merchants National Grocers' Federation National Union of Retail Confectioners Newspaper Proprietors' Association Shipbuilding Employers' Federation
Companies	46	British Oxygen Company Dunlop Rubber Esso Petroleum John Lewis Partnership Massey Ferguson Mobil Oil Rolls Royce Scottish & Newcastle Breweries Unilever Vauxhall Motors

Table 1 Number, types and examples of written evidence, from institutions, received by the Donovan Commission (Continued)

Category of institution	Total number of submissions	Examples of institutions
Political, professional and voluntary bodies	38	Association of Liberal Trade Unionists Bar Council British Housewives' League British Medical Association Conservative Trade Unionists' National Advisory Committee Consumer Council Law Society National Citizens' Advice Bureau Council Socialist Medical Association Workers' Educational Association (WEA)

Source: Royal Commission, 1968: Appendix 2, 320–29.

from the TUC itself.[6] The TUC's 202-page (including Appendices) submission strongly reaffirmed the voluntarist ethos of British trade unionism (discussed more extensively in chapter 5), insisting that:

> [t]he essential characteristic of free trade unions is that they are responsible to the workpeople themselves who comprise their membership, and cannot be directed by any outside agency ... In general ... Government stands aside. Its attitude is one of abstention, of formal indifference. (Trades Union Congress, 1966: 29–30, 31: paras 85, 90)

The TUC was adamant that this 'attitude of abstention ... still remains largely true', because '[n]o state, however benevolent, can perform the function of trade unions in enabling workpeople themselves to decide how their interests can best be safeguarded' (Trades Union Congress, 1966: 68–9, 69, para. 174).

However, the TUC acknowledged that 'a significant change has come about over the last five years', mainly as a consequence of a more active and interventionist labour market policy pursued by successive governments. This, though, was attributed, not so much to a new role being adopted by governments, but to 'a new interpretation by Government as to what this role should involve', namely 'to make labour market policy the key to economic growth' (Trades Union Congress, 1966: 69, 70, para. 176). While this undoubtedly yielded some measures which were beneficial to workers – such as the 1964 Industrial Training Act and the 1965 Redundancy Payments Act – the TUC confessed that when it came to various other measures associated with an active labour market policy, such as productivity agreements and increasing reliance on incomes policies (usually a euphemism for wage restraint), 'the trade union movement is naturally looking at them with some misgivings' (Trades Union Congress, 1966: 71, para. 179).

Moreover, although the TUC readily paid homage to the plethora of positive measures which governments had implemented in order to provide trade unions and workers with statutory rights and employment protection, it insisted that 'legislation favourable to unions does not logically strengthen the argument for unfavourable legislation as a sort of *quid pro quo* ... Improving terms and conditions of employment and enhancing the freedom and dignity of workpeople is essentially a one way process' (Trades Union Congress, 1966: 70, para. 178). This perspective was to prove especially pertinent in view of the so-called 'penal clauses' subsequently proposed by *In Place of Strife*, and then enshrined in the 'interim' Industrial Relations Bill, during the first half of 1969.

With regard to strikes, the TUC's evidence to the Donovan Commission insisted that many industrial stoppages were a consequence of employers' conduct or decisions concerning 'non-recognition, dismissals, management breaking agreements or introducing changes without consultation', and yet '[t]he responsibility of employers for strikes is largely ignored or played down'. Indeed, the TUC claimed that it was often the case that '[e]mployers or managements are shown as the injured party. Usually, this is not so'. While conceding that trade union officials were not always blameless, and sometimes made mistakes or errors of judgement, 'the fault [when strikes occurred] is more likely to be caused by poor management, taking hasty decisions and causing rumour through withholding information' (Trades Union Congress, 1966: 109, 110, paras 296, 297).

The TUC's written evidence to the Donovan Commission also emphasised the trade unions' lack of confidence in the judiciary, arguing that judges had a propensity to interpret laws in a manner different to that intended by governments and Ministers themselves in many cases. In referring to this 'problem of language', the TUC cited the examples of the 1901 *Taff Vale* judgment and the 1909 *Osborne* judgment, when judicial decisions seemed at variance with the trade unions' erstwhile interpretation or understanding of the law, and consequently placed the unions in a precarious legal position, until Parliament provided new legislative remedies. It was argued that the 'problem of language has bedevilled the interpretation of the law on trade disputes for over 50 years', and that this problem was 'of considerable importance, as the judges exercise considerable ingenuity in deciding how Acts [of Parliament] should be interpreted, without reference to the purpose of the Act in question'. This, the TUC claimed, was 'a perennial difficulty' facing the trade unions in relation to the judiciary, and largely explained why 'many trade unionists have always been, and continue to be, very suspicious of the law and the judges who appear to make the law in their own image' (Trades Union Congress, 1966: 124, 125, paras 349, 352).

The Ministry of Labour's submission

Throughout the 1950s, the Ministry of Labour had strongly endorsed the voluntarist perspective on industrial relations (Ministry of Labour, 1957; Ince, 1960), and much of its written evidence to the Donovan Commission constituted a restatement of the apparent virtues of this non-interventionist approach. For example, the Ministry was adamant that outlawing unofficial strikes would be 'impracticable', because 'in the last resort, it is not practicable, nor would it be conducive to good industrial relations, to try and put large numbers of people in jail' (Ministry of Labour, 1965: 7, para. 30). As to any counter-suggestion that it should be the trade unions, rather than individual members, that ought to be punished through the imposition of fines when unofficial strikes occurred, the Ministry argued that in some instances this 'might lead to the crippling of certain trade unions in circumstances where it might well be that there is little or nothing that the union itself could do'. Moreover, to avoid such fines, a trade union might feel 'compelled, in their own interests, to call official many strikes which now remain unofficial' (Ministry of Labour, 1965: 7, para. 30).

With regard to the oft-mooted suggestion that there should be statutory ballots prior to a strike, the Ministry was deeply sceptical, and as such, again adhered to its voluntarist stance. It argued that 'there is no sound reason for supposing that compulsory secret ballots would reduce the number of strikes. The very compulsion to hold a ballot might harden the opinion of the workers concerned in favour of striking.' There was also a risk that having been endorsed by a statutory secret ballot 'might make it more difficult for it [the strike] to be called off' (Ministry of Labour, 1965: 79–80, para. 24). For similar reasons, the Ministry of Labour was also reluctant to propose a statutory cooling-off period prior to a strike, noting that attitudes were at least as likely to harden during such a pause, and thus make a strike more likely at the end of it, while also militating against a swift or amicable settlement thereafter (Ministry of Labour, 1965: 79, para. 23). Ultimately, the Ministry of Labour (1965: 43, para. 54) was emphatic that 'most of the changes in the law commonly suggested to solve the strike problem are unrealistic and unacceptable'.

However, the Ministry did evince some modification of its erstwhile voluntarist stance, for it suggested that more might be expected or required of the trade unions either to address the activities of the shop stewards who often instigated unofficial strikes, or to introduce more clearly defined procedures which would need to be followed prior to embarking upon such industrial action. It was suggested that 'if it were to be provided that a union could be sued in the event of any of its members going on strike in breach of an agreement, that could have great practical effect', for it would 'have the effect of encouraging unions to reform their internal organisation, and to take disciplinary and other measures to reduce the number of, or eliminate, unofficial strikes' (Ministry of Labour, 1965: 81, para. 32; 80, para. 28). In this context, the Ministry argued that the unions might be expected to 'show to some independent tribunal that they had taken all the steps open to them to prevent the unofficial strike taking place, or to bring it to an end as soon as possible' (Ministry of Labour, 1965: 7, paras 30–31).

Nonetheless, the Ministry of Labour conceded that sometimes individual trade unionists might engage in strike action in defiance of their union, in which case legal action would be unreasonable if it could provide 'clear proof that the union had made a real effort to prevent the breach' (Ministry of Labour, 1965: 82, para. 33). The Ministry also recognised that even if collective agreements were made legally enforceable, an employer might be reluctant to instigate legal proceedings where a breach occurred, for fear of exacerbating grievances harboured by the workers involved, and thus worsening industrial relations. Given that the State, via the Government or a relevant Minister, might also be reluctant to become directly embroiled by prosecuting a trade union in such circumstances, the Ministry proposed that jurisdiction in such cases ought to reside with a new system of labour courts, the membership of which might include representatives from the two sides of industry (Ministry of Labour, 1965: 92, para. 77).

With regard to inter-union disputes, which themselves were sometimes the source of strikes, the Ministry of Labour suggested that in cases where the TUC's own 'disputes procedure' was unable to resolve a disagreement between two (or) more trade unions, perhaps because the unions or workers themselves refused to accept the TUC's decision, the Ministry might be empowered to refer the case to 'an independent statutory body', albeit very much as the last resort (Ministry of Labour, 1965: 100, para. 100).

The Donovan Report

To those who hoped that the Royal Commission would propose radical reform of Britain's industrial relations, entailing an explicit legal framework which would regulate collective bargaining and/or trade union activities, the Donovan Report was a disappointment. Published on 13 June 1968, the Report – which Andrew Shonfield had earlier hoped would provide 'a document of instruction, rather than a negotiating document'[7]

– acknowledged the extent to which voluntarism had hitherto prevailed in Britain, such that:

> ... it was a distinctive feature of a system of industrial relations that the State remained aloof from the process of collective bargaining in private industry. It left the parties free to come to their own agreements ... the parties to the collective agreement themselves rarely intend that their bargain shall be a legally enforceable contract, but rather it shall be binding in honour only ...
>
> This abstentionist attitude has reflected a belief that it is better in the long run for the law to interfere as little as possible in the settlement of questions arising between employers and workmen over pay and conditions of work. Parliament has long been committed to the view that the best means of settling such questions is voluntary collective bargaining, and has equipped Governments in various ways to support, assist and promote collective bargaining. (Royal Commission, 1968: 10, paras 39–40)

Nonetheless, the Donovan Report did acknowledge that Britain's hitherto voluntarist system of industrial relations and free collective bargaining was being placed under increasing strain, not least by governmental recourse to incomes policies. These, in turn, served to highlight the growing gulf between national trade union leaders and workplace union officials and shop stewards, whose ability to secure higher pay at local level greatly contributed to the phenomenon of 'wage drift'.

The Donovan Report also acknowledged that the first half of the 1960s had witnessed the enactment of three laws explicitly intended to benefit workers, namely the 1963 Contracts of Employment Act, the 1964 Industrial Training Act and the 1965 Redundancy Payments Act. These all signified a State that was more activist, interventionist, in the realm of industrial affairs, even though none of these laws directly sought to determine the manner in which employers and trade unions bargained with each other, nor did this tranche of legislation interfere in the internal governance of the trade unions themselves.

In one of the Report's most important passages, it was asserted that:

> Britain now has two systems of industrial relations. The one is the formal system embodied in the official institutions. The other is the informal system created by the actual behaviour of trade unions and employers' associations, of managers, shop stewards and workers. (Royal Commission, 1968: 12, para. 46)

Crucially, the Report emphasised the manner in which:

> [t]he formal and informal systems are in conflict. The informal system undermines the regulative effect of industry-wide agreements. The gap between industry-wide agreed rates and actual earnings continues to

grow. Procedure agreements fail to cope adequately with disputes arising within factories. (Royal Commission, 1968: 36, para. 149)

As a consequence:

[t]he bargaining which takes place within factories is largely outside the control of employers' associations and trade unions. It usually takes place piece-meal, and results in competitive sectional wage adjustments and chaotic pay structures. Unwritten understandings and 'custom and practice' predominate ... These developments help to explain why resort to unofficial and unconstitutional strikes, and other forms of workshop pressure, has been increasing. (Royal Commission, 1968: 261, paras 1010–11)

These key passages encapsulated three of the inter-connected problems which we identified in chapter 1. First, the manner in which local-level trade union officials and shop stewards increasingly acquired *de facto* power *vis-à-vis* their national-level leaders. Second, but following directly from this point, the incidence of unofficial strikes, themselves often at local or factory level, reflecting the power vacuum inside many trade unions, whereby local-level officials and shop stewards acquired greater allegiance and loyalty among the workforce because the national-level union leaders appeared increasingly remote, both geographically and organisationally.

Third was the phenomenon of 'wage drift', in which actual pay increases were higher than those formally agreed by the national-level union leadership and employers' representatives in London, owing to the ability of workplace shop stewards to negotiate successfully with local employers over improved pay. Of course, the phenomenon of 'wage drift' acquired much greater significance in the context of Ministerial attempts at securing pay restraint via incomes policies. Indeed, the Donovan Report noted that:

[i]ncomes policy must continue to be a lame and faltering exercise so long as it consists in the planning of industry-wide agreements, most of which exercise an inadequate control over pay. So long as workplace bargaining remains informal, autonomous and fragmented, the drift of earnings away from rates of pay cannot be brought under control. (Royal Commission, 1968: 53, para. 210)

On this particular point, when a Cabinet meeting in March 1968 considered the future of the Labour Government's prices and incomes policy, it was suggested that if the imminent Donovan Report made effective recommendations for improving trade union organisation and structure, and fostering more orderly wage bargaining, then this 'would help indirectly in promoting a sound incomes policy in the future'.[8]

However, the Donovan Report proved to be a cautious and rather conservative document, to the extent that it was reluctant to invoke legislation to tackle these problems, preferring instead to strengthen the extant system of collective bargaining rather than radically reform or replace it. Having emphasised the growing gulf between the formal and informal systems of industrial relations, the Donovan Report concluded that this would not be amenable to legislative remedies or statutory requirements. On the contrary, it was argued that:

> [a]ny attempt to deal with unofficial and unconstitutional strikes in isolation must be deprecated. This applies to the legal enforcement of procedure agreements as much to the proposal to eradicate these strikes by imposing an overall obligation to give notice before resorting to a stoppage ... None of these measures promises any success in the sense of improving our industrial relations as long as the underlying causes of the strike have not been removed. We do ... not ... think that the law could not in any circumstances assist in the reduction of unofficial strikes. It cannot do so in this country today – this is the point. To take steps in this direction would be not only useless, but harmful, and they would undo a great deal of the good we hope to see done through the reforms of the collective bargaining system which we recommend ... The British system of industrial relations is based on voluntarily agreed rules which, as a matter of principle, are not enforced by law. (Royal Commission, 1968: 128, para. 476; 137, para. 506; 203, para. 751)

This unwillingness to recommend legislation owed much to the intellectual influence of the 'Oxford School' of industrial relations, which was the label applied to a coterie of academic industrial relations experts either based at, or with strong links to, Oxford University, and who strongly endorsed the voluntarist philosophy (Bugler, 1968; Ackers, 2011). The most notable figures associated with the Oxford School were Hugh Clegg, Allan Flanders, Alan Fox, Otto Kahn-Freund and William McCarthy: 'There are seemingly an infinite number of interconnections between them; a bumps chart of them all would be filigree ... the Oxford Group is rather more than a collection of colleagues. It is also a school of thought-and-practices' (Bugler, 1968: 221).

The Oxford School's voluntarist perspective had constituted the dominant industrial relations paradigm throughout the 1950s and most of the 1960s, 'the academic orthodoxy of the time' (Morgan, 1997: 331), as evinced through their scholarly publications on industrial relations: Clegg (1970), Flanders (1964; 1974; 1975: 288–94), Fox (1974; 1985) and Kahn-Freund (1959; 1972). As noted above, Clegg and Kahn-Freund were members of the Royal Commission, while McCarthy (one of Clegg's former PhD students) served as a research director (Undy, 2015). Also, some of the evidence submitted to the Royal Commission emanated from senior academics associated with the Oxford School.

According to the author of a detailed academic study of the drafting of the Donovan Commission's Report, 'the evidence from the Oxford

School was to prove central, and its version of industrial relations would dominate proceedings'. Indeed, what really seemed to have ensured that the Final Report effectively endorsed the voluntarist approach was that much of it was actually written by Clegg himself, mostly between January and May 1968 (Ackers, 2014: 68, 70–77),[9] having worked on a 'rough draft' over Christmas 1967. As he explained to Lord Donovan, this constituted 'the kind of report that I should like to see', whereas the draft which had been written hitherto was not 'presented in a cogent and convincing manner', and focused too much on 'proposals which in the end we reject'. Furthermore, Clegg lamented that '[o]ur positive proposals, especially concerning collective bargaining, are still rather vague', and as such, he judged that the overall tone of the initial draft was 'largely negative'.[10]

Clegg's influential role was reflective of the extent to which 'Lord Donovan was content to act as chair rather than to direct the commission' (Smith, 2011: 122), although Clegg subsequently described him as a 'very weak character ... just hopeless' (quoted in Ackers, 2014: 72). Meanwhile, four months *before* the publication of the Donovan Report, one commentator was suggesting that '[i]t will be odd if the Royal Commission ... is not affected by the [Oxford] group's work' (Bugler, 1968: 221).

The Donovan Report was indeed 'affected' by the disciples of the Oxford School of industrial relations, and especially 'the inveterate voluntarism of Clegg' (Ackers, 2014: 70; see also Morgan, 1997: 331), its main proposals being as follows:

> An Industrial Relations Act should be passed, requiring that larger companies (defined as employing more than 5,000 people), along with nationalised industries and public services, ... register collective agreements with the Department of Employment and Productivity. This requirement would eventually be extended to smaller firms.
>
> An Industrial Relations Commission (IRC) should be established, to examine issues and problems arising from the registration of collective agreements, in cases referred to it by the Secretary of State for Employment and Productivity.
>
> It should be unlawful for a contract of employment to require a worker *not* to belong to a trade union.
>
> A major expansion of factory-wide collective agreements, which would facilitate greater flexibility in response to local or workplace circumstances than could be provided by industry-wide or national-level agreements.
>
> The boards of companies to ensure that they: develop comprehensive and effective collective bargaining machinery; establish joint procedures for securing the swift but fair resolution of grievances; adopt clear, coherent and consistent rules concerning disciplinary matters; provide as much information as practicably possible to workers' representatives,

thereby fostering greater understanding of the objectives and key decisions taken by management.

Workplaces to enshrine clearer and more consistent rules or machinery to protect workers from unfair dismissal. This would also expressly exclude discrimination on the grounds of gender, marital status, race, religion, or trade union membership.

Encourage more trade union mergers, with the aim of having just one or two unions in some industries or sectors, when and where practicably possible.

In making these recommendations, the Royal Commission was at pains to emphasise that 'we are not suggesting a sharp break with policies which the Government have hitherto pursued ... We suggest, rather, how that policy can be made fully effective in modern circumstances' (Royal Commission, 1968: 276, para. 1109).

At this juncture, it is worth noting the main potential measures which the Donovan Report explicitly rejected, namely rendering collective agreements legally binding or enforceable, and compulsory strike ballots. Yet these were precisely the two measures most favoured by critics of the trade unions, which thus compounded their subsequent dismay at the caution and conservatism of the Donovan Report, which they viewed as a thoroughly wasted opportunity.

The issue of making collective agreements legally binding and enforceable had been considered in some depth when the Royal Commission was drafting its Report during the first few months of 1968, but had ultimately been rejected, partly because of the pervasive intellectual influence of the Oxford School of industrial relations such as its steadfast commitment to the principle of voluntarism or collective *laissez-faire*, and partly because of various issues of practicability. Of course, the latter were sometimes cited precisely in order to justify and reinforce the principle of voluntarism.

For example, with regard to the oft-mooted proposal to render procedural agreements legally binding – explicitly requiring trade unions to pursue a specified series of procedures prior to embarking on strike action (thereby militating against 'unconstitutional' and/or 'wildcat' strikes) – the Donovan Report was adamant that the increasingly fragmented and two-tier system of collective bargaining in British industry, in which negotiations were often conducted at local or factory level, would make such legal enforceability ineffective: 'Until this defect is remedied, all attempts at making procedure agreements legally binding are bound to defeat themselves'. Moreover, imposing statutory measures in this sphere would 'divert attention from the underlying causes to the symptoms of the disease' (Royal Commission, 1968: 128, para. 475). Only if or when collective bargaining was imbued with greater order and stability might it be feasible to invoke legally enforceable collective or procedural agreements

– although if stronger order and stability were achieved, via the industrial relations reforms proposed in the Donovan Report, then there might be no need for such agreements anyway, a point which had been trenchantly expressed by Clegg during the drafting of the Report.[11]

The same concern over practicability (or lack of) was cited as justification for rejecting statutory curbs on unofficial and unconstitutional strikes, and/or imposing a legal obligation on trade unions to conduct pre-strike ballots, with Kahn-Freund proving a staunch ally of Clegg in 'fighting a long, subtle, rear-guard, action against crude, precipitate legal measures against unofficial and unconstitutional strikes' (Ackers, 2014: 75; see also Clegg, 1983). To pursue such measures would be to neglect the underlying causes of many industrial disputes, and thus result in the implementation of inappropriate, and thus ineffective, remedies.

The Royal Commission's rejection both of legally binding and enforceable collective agreements (procedural or substantive), and of statutory strike ballots, reflected another industrial relations conundrum with which it had grappled with when drafting its Report during the first few months of 1968, namely the precise relationship between trade unions and their individual members: to what extent could or should the agreements entered into by trade unions *qua* corporate institutions be deemed binding on their rank-and-file membership? Or to express it another way, when unconstitutional or unofficial strikes occurred, who should be deemed responsible from a legal perspective: a trade union for failing to control its members, or the members for failing to adhere either to agreements entered into by their union, or to their union's rulebook? According to the TUC's then General Secretary, George Woodcock, 'trade unions were simply not in a position to make binding contracts on behalf of their members', a point reiterated both by Professor Otto Kahn-Freund and Lord Donovan himself.[12]

This might have been construed as a tacit acknowledgement that unofficial, unconstitutional or 'wildcat' strikes were thus the responsibility – fault – of individual trade union members, rather than the trade unions or their leaders themselves, but this perspective was also rejected. Instead, as previously noted, the trade unions' stance was that such strikes were frequently a response to arbitrary or/and unjust decisions taken by employers or workplace managers.

Ultimately, the Donovan Report broadly endorsed the perspective that establishing a more orderly and stable system of industrial relations was the key to reducing such industrial stoppages: 'We expect the reform of the collective bargaining system to lead to a very considerable reduction in unofficial strikes'; although it was conceded that, if this expectation was not subsequently realised, 'it may then be necessary to reconsider the desirability and practicability of giving some legal support to procedure agreements' (Royal Commission, 1968: 128, para. 476).

This last point suggested that the Donovan Report was not quite the uncritical and unequivocal defence of voluntarism that has often been assumed. While it broadly reaffirmed that good industrial relations could not be secured by legislation, and that, ultimately, the two sides of industry needed to work more closely and constructively together, the Donovan Report cautiously acknowledged that the law could play a small part in fostering more order and stability in British industry. For example, as Davies and Freedland note, '[t]he registration of collective agreements is not an obviously significant step in itself, but the [Donovan] Commission had taken a decisive step towards a legal framework for industrial relations'. Indeed, the proposed registration of collective agreements, in tandem with the suggested role of the IRC, entailing the codification of its operational principles, constituted 'the starting-point for a very important extension of the role of the state in industrial relations'. Certainly, such proposals enshrined 'the idea of a legal matrix for industrial relations' (Davies and Freedland, 1999: 260–1, 261).

Furthermore, although the Donovan Report refrained from advocating statutory curbs on the activities or internal affairs of trade unions themselves, it is not difficult to see – particularly with the political historian's benefit of hindsight – how governments might devise ways of making trade union immunities (bequeathed by the 1906 Trade Disputes Act) conditional on registration with a body such as the IRC, and perhaps acceptance of, or adherence to, its recommendations if and when it had been called upon to adjudicate in an industrial dispute.

However, several other factors meant that the Donovan Report's defence of voluntarism was qualified or somewhat equivocal. First, there was an allusion to the potential for future legislation if collective bargaining was not reformed or strengthened in a manner which imbued greater order and stability in industrial relations, and thereby reduced the number of unofficial strikes. As the relevant passage explained:

> The effect of the reform of collective bargaining will be to reduce greatly the problem of unconstitutional strikes, which may not however disappear. It will then be possible to identify any circumstances in which it would be neither unjust nor futile to apply legal sanctions, because satisfactory disputes procedures are available and because legal penalties are appropriate where irresponsibility or ill-will is the root cause of their breach. If legal sanctions have to be applied – and whether this will happen cannot be predicted at present – it will have to be done *ad hoc* ... The Industrial Relations Commission should be instructed to keep the matter under review in the light of progress with the reform of industrial relations in general and disputes procedures in particular, with a view to advising the Secretary of State whether legislation for the enforcement of procedure agreements has become imperative... (Royal Commission, 1968: 268, para. 1055)

Second, Lord Donovan himself provided an 'Addendum' to the main report, in which he confessed that, while improved procedures were essential to reducing the incidence of unofficial and unconstitutional strikes, he remained 'reluctant to trust entirely to the expected effect of better procedural agreements', and had thus 'sought some interim remedy which would be both workable and just'. He had, though, found such a solution to be 'very elusive' (Royal Commission, 1968: 279, para. 5).

Lord Donovan also admitted that he had initially been attracted by the notion of treating participation in an unofficial or unconstitutional strike as breaking continuity of service, which would therefore have implications for the amount of redundancy pay that an employee might be entitled to in subsequent years. Ultimately, though, he recognised that, for reasons of practicability, this would not be a viable option, not least because such a measure would almost inevitably prompt a tranche of (often complex) appeals, with employers required to attend evidence-giving sessions in tribunals. He therefore conceded that 'the effect on production might be worse than was the strike itself' (Royal Commission, 1968: 279, para. 7).

One final reason adumbrated by Lord Donovan to explain the Royal Commission's overall refusal to recommend legal sanctions for industrial relations transgressions such as unofficial and unconstitutional strikes, or other breaches of the employment contract, was the extant 'reluctance by employers to pursue remedies already provided by the civil and the criminal law', often because recourse to such action 'might simply make industrial relations worse'. Clearly, if employers were already reticent about seeking legal redress against their employees, or the unions in their workplace, for various misdemeanours or transgressions, then it was highly unlikely that introducing new or additional laws into the realm of industrial relations would have the desired effect (Royal Commission, 1968: 280–1, para. 11).

Third, Lord Tangley also submitted a 'supplementary note' (Royal Commission, 1968: 282–7), confessing his 'regret that I cannot without some qualification join my colleagues in presenting our Report' His demurral derived from a firm belief that the proposed IRC needed to be vested with more power than the Report proposed, for whereas it was envisaged that the Commission 'will rely on persuasion and publicity', Lord Tangley lamented that 'there are ample instances in which there have been ample persuasion and publicity that have produced no results at all'. He therefore feared that if the IRC remained 'as powerless as is proposed in the Report, it will become yet another voice crying in the wilderness'. Consequently, he was convinced that in cases where national or industry-wide agreements were not registered with the IRC, the relevant company or trade union(s) should be required to state their reasons for not registering, whereupon the IRC could submit a report to the Secretary of State, who would then be entitled to make an order binding on those concerned.

Lord Tangley also wanted the IRC to have more power to ensure that the internal rules adopted by trade unions pertaining to 'admission, expulsion, suspension or other disciplinary action' were clear, consistent and equitable. This might entail the adoption of new rules, or the amendment of existing ones. Where such rules did not exist, or were not applied in a fair and reasonable manner, the IRC could urge the Secretary of State to draft the rules to be adopted by the recalcitrant trade union(s).

In extreme cases where a trade union consistently or flagrantly failed either to comply with its own rules or to adhere to registered agreements, the IRC should be empowered to 'de-register' it. Crucially, this would mean that if a de-registered trade union subsequently called a strike, or engaged in other forms of industrial action, it would cease to be protected by the legal immunities provided by Section 3 of the 1906 Trade Disputes Act. In other words, the union(s) concerned could be sued for damages by an employer or company, as was the case immediately following the 1903 *Taff Vale* decision.

Fourth, a 'supplementary note' – comprising just one paragraph – was written by three (of the twelve) members, which expressly endorsed Lord Tangley's recommendation that the IRC should have the power to 'de-register' a trade union which failed to adhere to its own rules, or acted in defiance of registered agreements, if and when these were judged to be of sufficient 'frequency' in their occurrence or 'gravity' in their consequences (Royal Commission, 1968: 287).

Fifth, Andrew Shonfield wrote a fifteen-page 'note of reservation', which conveyed his disappointment that the main report had shied away from recommending more radical reform. He believed that, sooner or later, Britain's system of industrial relations would need to be placed in an explicit legal framework and on a firm statutory basis, for he deemed it:

> inconceivable in the long run that in a society which is increasingly closely knit, where the provision of services to meet the elementary needs of a civilised daily life depends more and more on the punctual performance of interrelated work tasks of a collective character, trade unions will be treated as if they had the right to be exempt from all but the most rudimentary legal obligations. This is the traditional view, which has bitten deep into the British system of industrial relations. (Royal Commission, 1968: 289, para. 5)

Yet against the voluntarist perspective which had prevailed thus far, and which was both an article of faith for the trade unions and hitherto the in-house ideology for the Ministry of Labour, Shonfield argued that 'the deliberate abstention of the law from the activities of mighty subjects tends to diminish the liberty of the ordinary citizen and to place his [*sic*] welfare at risk' and, as such, he strongly disagreed with the Donovan Report's claim that collective bargaining should remain 'outside the law' (Royal Commission, 1968: 290, para. 7).

Notwithstanding these demurrals, most members of the Royal Commission viewed their final Report as an example of realism over radicalism, with the emphasis placed on strengthening voluntarism rather than abandoning it. This would entail the reform of collective bargaining to render it more effective, but as far as was practicably possible this was to be achieved in a consensual and piecemeal manner, with legislation playing a very limited role. That said, it was conceded that the law might play a somewhat more extensive role in industrial relations in the longer term.

To those who criticised the Donovan Report for being anodyne or even pusillanimous, one of its members, Eric Wigham (who had previously published a book critical of the attitudes and conduct of British trade unions, as we noted in chapter 1) readily conceded that, although it had clearly 'not recommended drastic laws which will solve everything in no time', he was confident that '[i]f our recommendations are adopted, the system of collective bargaining in Britain will be gradually transformed' (Wigham, 1968).

Yet as we will note in chapter 3, this envisaged gradualness was to prove unacceptable to Barbara Castle and Harold Wilson, and also to some of the senior civil servants in the newly established Department of Employment and Productivity (DEP), who were convinced that, for economic and political reasons, more substantive reform of industrial relations was needed as a matter of urgency. This conviction was underpinned by the assumption that the (institutionally conservative) trade unions were highly unlikely to take an active part in reforming collective bargaining: 'I can't see any revolutionary changes being carried through unless the government is prepared to impose them on an unwilling TUC' (Castle, 1990: 240, diary entry for 2 July 1968). Barbara Castle and Harold Wilson thus took it upon themselves to impose changes on the trade unions, although in so doing they seriously underestimated the scale and sources of opposition which would be mobilised against them.

Conclusion

Having previously claimed that Royal Commissions 'take minutes and waste years', Harold Wilson would have judged the veracity of his quip to have been sadly vindicated, for when the Donovan Report was published in June 1968, after three years and two months of evidence-gathering and deliberations, it largely endorsed the very industrial relations system which its critics deemed no longer fit for purpose. Instead of recommending comprehensive legal reform of industrial relations and trade unionism, the statutory registration of collective agreements by large (5,000 + employees) firms notwithstanding, the Donovan Report urged a strengthening of the extant system of collective bargaining, and clarification of procedures for resolving workplace disagreements and disputes. As such, statutory measures were to play no part in reducing unconstitutional and unofficial strikes, at least in the short to medium term. The key to improving industrial relations and reducing strikes was to be found in improving and rationalising the current system, which necessitated the 'two sides of industry' working more closely together. As two academic experts on labour law have noted:

> The Donovan Commission Report ... argued that the pressures for change ... could best be channelled by a process of government-led reform in which the law and the institutions of the state would support and encourage an essentially *voluntary and voluntarist* development of more efficient patterns of work, management and dispute resolution in industrial society. (Davies and Freedland, 1999: 267, emphasis added)

Although the Donovan Report was accompanied by 'addendums', 'supplementary notes' and a 'note of reservation' which indicated that it was not a wholly unanimous and uncritical endorsement of voluntarism and collective *laissez-faire*, the overall content and tone strongly reflected the influence of the 'Oxford School' of industrial relations, as personified by Professor Hugh Clegg. Indeed, Clegg wrote much of the final Report, a task which seemingly was readily relinquished by the chair, Lord Donovan. Thus it was that a Royal Commission which was widely expected to herald the death-knell of voluntarism actually provided a broad vindication of collective *laissez-faire*. The Donovan Report did not seek to bury voluntarism but to strengthen it – much to the exasperation of Barbara Castle and Harold Wilson.

Notes

1 NA CAB 128/39, CC. (64) 16th Conclusions, Meeting of the Cabinet, 18 December 1964.
2 NA CAB 128/39, CC. (64) 16th Conclusions, Meeting of the Cabinet, 18 December 1964; CAB 129/119, C. (64) 29, Memorandum by the Minister of Labour – 'Trade Disputes Bill (*Rookes v Barnard*) and an Inquiry into Trade Unions and Employers' Associations', 15 December 1964.
3 MRC, MSS. 292B/32/10, Meeting of the TUC's General Council, 24 February 1968; Gunter to Woodcock, 25 February 1965.
4 NA CAB 129/119, C (64) 29, Memorandum by the Minister of Labour – 'Trade Disputes Bill (*Rookes v Barnard*) and an Inquiry into Trade Unions and Employers' Associations', 15 December 1964; NA CAB 129/120, C (65) 2, Memorandum by the Minister of Labour – 'Inquiry into Trade Unions and

Employers' Associations', 11 January 1965; NA CAB 128/40, CC (65) 1st Conclusions, Meeting of the Cabinet, 14 January 1965.
5 MRC MSS 292B/40.2/3, Note of a Meeting of the TUC's Finance and General Purposes Committee, 18 December 1964.
6 MRC, MSS. 292B/32/10, Cassals to Woodcock, 7 January 1966.
7 NA LAB 28/609, The Royal Commission on Trade Unions and Employers' Associations, Minutes of the 108th meeting, 23 January 1968.
8 NA CAB 128/43, CC (68) 20th Conclusions, Meeting of the Cabinet, 14 March 1968.
9 NA LAB 28/607–620, 'Minutes of meetings of the Royal Commission on Trade Unions and Employers' Associations', 9 January to 30 April 1968.
10 NA LAB 28/28/229, Clegg to Donovan, 24 January 1968.
11 NA LAB 28/609, The Royal Commission on Trade Unions and Employers' Associations, Minutes of the 108th meeting, 23 January 1968.
12 NA LAB 28/610, The Royal Commission on Trade Unions and Employers' Associations, Minutes of the 109th meeting, 30 January 1968.

3

The initial political response

The conservatism of the Donovan Report was deeply disappointing to Harold Wilson and Barbara Castle. They had quietly hoped that the Royal Commission would propose a major reform of industrial relations, including statutory curbs and obligations being imposed on the trade unions, whereupon the predictable outrage by union leaders would be pacified by the Labour Government's announcement of a more modest package of policy proposals (Ponting, 1990: 352; Tyler, 2006: 467). This tactic was rather undermined by the fact that the Donovan Report was largely concerned not to bury voluntarism, but to bolster it.

Although Wilson confessed to being 'impressed by Donovan's thorough analysis of industrial relations in Britain', and many of the Report's 'detailed and constructive proposals for reforms patiently achieved throughout much of British industry', he was nonetheless adamant that 'the confessed failure of the [Donovan] Commission to find any short-term remedy for unofficial strikes … could not be accepted' (Wilson, 1971: 538, 591). In a similar vein, Castle lamented that 'I can't see any revolutionary changes being carried through unless the government is prepared to impose them on an unwilling TUC' (Castle, 1990: 240, diary entry for 2 July 1968).

Meanwhile, the Conservative Opposition was already formulating, via *Fair Deal at Work* (Conservative Political Centre, 1968), its own legislative proposals for tackling unofficial strikes and restoring the authority of the official or national-level trade union leadership over its members, with the avowed aim of imbuing industrial relations with greater order and stability. More specifically, the Conservatives were proposing mandatory strike ballots, the outlawing of the closed shop, legally enforceable collective agreements and a sixty-day 'cooling-off' period prior to some strikes.

This further convinced Castle and Wilson that the Labour Government needed to devise a clear and comprehensive industrial relations policy of its own, lest the political impetus be seized by the Conservatives, who would also doubtless argue that Labour was too financially and organisationally tied to the trade unions to reform industrial relations itself.

A further political consideration, recalled by Denis Barnes, just appointed Permanent Secretary (the most senior Departmental post for a civil servant) in the new Department of Employment and Productivity, was Wilson's commitment to modernisation of other institutions of government during the latter half of the 1960s, most notably the civil service and local government, to which we would also add the House of Lords. In this context, 'there seemed no reason to exclude trade unions from this process' (Barnes and Reid, 1980: 110).

Indeed, a few weeks before the Donovan Commission's report was published, Castle had warned Ministerial colleagues on a Cabinet committee that there was likely to be a need for some kind of industrial relations legislation in the next Parliamentary session. In so doing, she also sought to pre-empt trade union objections to such legislation by noting that the previous 100 years had been characterised by sundry laws enacted to provide the unions and workers with statutory rights and protection, hence imminent legislation could hardly be condemned as a new or unprecedented form of State intervention in industrial relations.[1]

Not whether, but when, to introduce industrial relations legislation

During the remainder of 1968, Castle's determination to reform Britain's system of industrial relations increased, so much that the question was not about *whether* to introduce legislation, but *what* the content should be, *how* it would be enacted and *when*. Yet Castle was adamant that the Government's philosophy and policy should be positive, not punitive, with the over-riding objective being to 'improve the machinery of collective bargaining' (Castle, 1990: 275, diary entry for 15 November 1968).

In fact, as early as April 1968 – two months *before* the publication of the Donovan Report – Wilson himself was urging Castle to consider, as a matter of some urgency, proposals for the reform of industrial relations and trade union legislation, albeit 'not a political study, but a serious analytical examination of the workability of the proposals'. Such a study, Wilson suggested, could either be conducted solely in Castle's new Department (of Employment and Productivity), or via a small Ministerial committee chaired by her, membership of which might include the Attorney-General.[2] The following month (May 1968), Castle acknowledged that, while there was likely to be much in the imminent Donovan Report with which the Cabinet could concur, there was likely to be a need for legislation in the next (1968–9) Parliamentary session, even if this was only in the form of a short bill.[3]

By this stage, during the spring of 1968, and thus very shortly before the publication of the Royal Commission's Report, Castle and Wilson had received indications that radical or substantial industrial relations reform was highly unlikely to be recommended. In fact, even during the previous autumn, Ray Gunter, while still serving as Minister of Labour, had written to Wilson, following a conversation 'in confidence' with Lord Donovan, warning that when the Report was finally published, 'in general it is likely to lay most stress on the need to strengthen the institutional framework of industrial relations, and to reject proposals for any general legislation regulating relations between employers and trade unions'.[4]

Castle herself subsequently recalled that the Donovan Report 'was surprisingly relaxed, and had George Woodcock's fingerprints all over it' (Castle, 1993: 413). Relaxed it might have been, but why Castle deemed this to be surprising was odd, given the already mentioned off-the-record information that she, Wilson and her predecessor, Gunter, were receiving about the likely content of the Report. Nonetheless, the conservatism of the Donovan Report reinforced Castle's conviction that industrial relations legislation would need to be introduced before the end of the following year (1969) at the latest, in order to ensure that it was on the statute book before the next general election.

Initial consultations with 'the two sides of industry'

Following publication of the Donovan Report, Castle embarked upon consultations with the TUC and the Confederation of British Industry (CBI), which then continued through the remainder of the summer and then into the autumn of 1968. These entailed both face-to-face meetings with trade union leaders (via the TUC) and senior employers' representatives (via the CBI), and a questionnaire sent to both of these bodies. Yet even at the first meeting with TUC leaders following the Donovan Report's publication, there was an early portent of their different perspectives, for when she asked the trade union leaders for their initial response to the Report, their reply was that they had attended in the expectation of hearing Castle's own views and intentions.[5] Although an innocuous misunderstanding, it subsequently proved to be the start of almost twelve months of divergent views and disagreements between Castle and the TUC leadership.

Castle envisaged that the post-Donovan consultations with the 'two sides of industry' (as employers and trade unions, or the TUC and the CBI, were often referred to) would be completed by the end of October, whereupon she and her Departmental team (of junior Ministers and senior civil servants) would draft a White Paper delineating the measures to be incorporated into industrial relations legislation the following year. However, conducting these consultations with the 'two sides of industry', prior to formulating a policy, meant that Castle had little of substance or significance to say when the Conservative Party used one of their 'Supply Days'[6] to debate the Donovan Report, within a month of its publication. As the relevant Minister, she would be the first member of the Government to reply to the opening speech by her Opposition counterpart, Robert Carr, and would be expected to provide a lengthy response, before other MPs took part in the debate. Yet she recalled that '[i]t wasn't an easy speech to make, for the simple reason that I have no policy to declare' (Castle, 1990: 244, diary entry for 16 July 1968).

Consequently, Castle's reply to Carr's opening peroration provided a judicious blend of praise for the prognosis and principles canvassed in the Donovan Report, rebuttal of Carr's criticisms of Donovan's cautious conservatism and condemnation of the Conservatives' proposed legislation enshrined in *Fair Deal at Work*. In response to Carr's questions about how and when she intended to respond to the Donovan Report, Castle merely confirmed that a White Paper would be published towards the end of the year, following consultations with the two sides of industry. She was adamant, though, that no precise date could be given for the timing of a bill, because this would largely depend on 'the outcome of the consultations … Until we know how comprehensive the legislation should be, it is clearly impossible for me to give a date for its introduction' (Hansard, 1968: Vol. 768, col. 1274).

How much industrial relations legislation: one Bill or two?

Yet almost immediately after the publication of the Donovan Report, Castle was alluding to two options for industrial relations legislation: either a 'quick, short, Bill' in the 1968–9 Parliamentary session to establish a Commission on Industrial Relations (CIR) 'and any other urgent points', followed by more comprehensive legislation in the 1969–70 Parliamentary session, or the introduction of just one, all-embracing Industrial Relations Bill in the latter session. These two options reflected the realisation that it would be impossible to put 'a comprehensive Bill on the whole range of the Royal Commission's recommendations through [in the] next session',[7] something which had been acknowledged by the Cabinet's 'future legislation' committee a month *before* the publication of the Donovan Report.[8]

More significantly, perhaps, Castle alluded to the public's increasing exasperation with unofficial strikes, such that if the Government did adhere to the Report's rejection of statutory curbs on such stoppages 'the public would want to know what were its safeguards, and the Government would have to have an answer'. As such, she suggested that some of the progressive or permissive measures, which the trade unions would welcome in any subsequent industrial relations legislation, might need to be accompanied by a few prescriptive clauses as a *quid quo pro*.[9] At this stage, though, the TUC members did not seem perturbed by this suggestion, or perhaps failed to appreciate the potential implications.

Meanwhile, senior Departmental officials, in consultation with the Cabinet Office (which is responsible for strategic oversight and co-ordination of governmental policies), were presciently keeping a space free in the planned 1968–9 legislative timetable, in case the Government decided to introduce a short Industrial Relations Bill as a prelude to a more comprehensive bill in the following [1969–70] Parliamentary session. Certainly, the Cabinet Secretary, Burke Trend, suggested – with the typically judicious phrasing articulated by senior civil servants – that 'Ministers, when they have had time to digest the Report, and public reaction to it, may themselves want to go further on some points than the report recommends'.[10] The need to keep such a space free in the next session's legislative timetable was confirmed by Fred Peart (occupying the post of Lord Privy Seal; a senior Minister without a Departmental portfolio), when he informed his Cabinet colleagues, in June 1968, that 'allowance had to be made for the possibility that it might be desired to introduce an Industrial Relations Bill of medium length in the spring [1969] to implement some of the recommendations of the Royal Commission'.[11]

The uncertainty over whether there would be a short bill followed by a longer bill, in consecutive Parliamentary sessions, or just one comprehensive bill in the 1969–70 session, was accompanied by a debate among some senior DEP officials about tensions between the economic case for such industrial relations legislation and the political case. It was suggested that, on economic grounds, such legislation should be introduced sooner rather than later, for the Donovan Report had clearly highlighted the deficiencies of Britain's extant system of collective bargaining, these being reflected and reinforced by the institutional inadequacies of trade unions and employers' associations alike.

Yet it was simultaneously acknowledged that, from a political perspective, it made good sense to defer industrial relations legislation until comprehensive consultations had been conducted with the TUC and the CBI, for whilst these would delay the introduction of a bill, it was vitally important to secure the consent and co-operation of the two sides of industry, as far as was practicably possible. The requisite trust and goodwill would be forfeited if the Government was perceived to be acting in a peremptory manner by introducing industrial relations legislation too soon and too quickly. The success of industrial relations reform in general, and reform of collective bargaining in particular, 'will need the committed support of both sides of industry', but this would not 'be forthcoming if the First Secretary went ahead without consultations with them [the TUC and the CBI]'. This, though, did not preclude explaining to the two sides of industry the need to expedite consultations, perhaps by stipulating a clear time limit, nor did it mean that some reforms could not be pursued in the meantime, either on less controversial aspects of the Donovan Report or through 'non-legislative action'.[12]

Although Castle did not have an industrial relations policy to announce in the summer of 1968, this certainly did not imply that she was bereft of ideas, or wholly uncertain of the direction in which she felt the Government should travel. Crucially, she was not willing to accept Donovan's predominantly *laissez-faire* approach in full, because she had already become convinced that at least some statutory measures were needed, albeit as part of a balanced package of industrial relations reform. If there had been an expectation that Donovan might recommend a legalistic tranche of proposals from which the Government could back-track by devising more modest reforms which were less reliant on statutory measures, then the generally non-legislative recommendations which the Donovan Report advanced effectively obliged Castle (and Wilson) to go further, by proposing a somewhat more robust package of measures; what effectively became known inside the DEP as 'Donovan-plus'. As we will note in subsequent chapters, not only did this result in serious tensions between the Labour Government and the trade unions during the first half of 1969, but it also caused strong disagreement and divisions both in the Cabinet and in the PLP.

Castle's firm belief that she needed to go rather further than the recommendations of the Donovan Report was strongly reinforced by an industrial dispute which occurred towards the end of 1968, and which she found 'impossible to justify'. The dispute took place at the Girling Brakes factory in Cheshire, when twenty-two machine-setters refused to carry out instructions issued by a supervisor belonging to a different trade union. Due to the important role of these machine-setters, there were serious repercussions as a consequence of their industrial action, to the extent that 5,000 other workers were temporarily laid-off.

This dispute seemed to epitomise much that critics deemed wrong with Britain's industrial relations in the 1960s: it both entailed unofficial industrial action and constituted an inter-union dispute, while also starkly illustrating the extent to which a small number of strikers – in this case, fewer than two dozen – could cause widespread industrial disruption, resulting in thousands of other workers being obliged to stop work and lose pay, even though they were not directly involved in the dispute. Such cases reinforced Castle's conviction that 'I would have to strengthen the Donovan Report' (Castle, 1993: 415).

Drafting an industrial relations White Paper

In order to progress beyond the Donovan Report and thereby provide the Labour Government with a robust industrial relations policy, the autumn of 1968 entailed the drafting of a White Paper heralding legislation, albeit while still conducting consultations with trade union leaders and employers' representatives. This was itself a somewhat unorthodox approach politically, because consultations in advance of a major new policy have traditionally been accompanied by, and indeed conducted in response to, a Green Paper, in which 'interested parties' and individuals are publicly invited to submit evidence and responses. These are then supposedly considered by the relevant Minister(s) when they draft a firmer or final policy, in the hope that this will secure wider support and legitimacy, and consequently prove more effective in practice. It is usually to announce imminent legislation that a White Paper is published, several months after the consultations initiated by the preceding Green Paper and consideration of the responses.

In dispensing with the Green Paper stage of policy development and legislative change, Castle's approach, while not unconstitutional, was certainly somewhat unusual. It might be argued that her approach was wholly justified on the grounds that the Royal Commission itself had provided ample opportunities for interested parties and individuals to submit their own evidence and proposals for reforming industrial relations. As such, a subsequent Green Paper would merely have prompted a repeat of the same proposals and objections, thus wasting everyone's time, while delaying the enactment of reform. Castle already knew the views and policy preferences of those involved by the time the White Paper was being drafted, yet still undertook consultations with senior representatives of the two sides of industry.

In fact, this process was the source of some bemusement to the small group of senior civil servants most closely and directly involved, namely Dennis Barnes, D. Bayliss, John Burgh (who had been assigned particular responsibility for developing the DEP's response to the Donovan Report (Tyler, 2006: 464)), I. Dewar and Conrad Heron, the Deputy Permanent Secretary. As one of them tartly observed in early October 1968, when circulating an initial set of proposals to his senior Departmental colleagues 'as a basis for further discussion', it was 'ambitiously styled a "draft White Paper", but in fact it is inevitably a half-baked document because most of the issues have not yet been fully considered', neither by the Department itself, nor by cognate Departments, and not by the two sides of industry.[13]

Yet whereas this particular official envisaged continued comprehensive consultations over the key issues and tentative proposals, one of the recipients of this draft White Paper hoped that subsequent discussions with interested parties 'won't be "more wide-ranging"' but rather more focused and detailed, with particular attention paid to the reform of collective bargaining.[14]

A changing Departmental culture?

We noted in chapter 2 how, throughout the 1950s, the Ministry of Labour had been characterised by an in-house ideology of 'voluntarism', rather like the trade unions themselves. During the 1960s, though, there were some indications that the hegemony of this Departmental philosophy was slowly being eroded, not only in response to growing concern about industrial relations problems which this stance seemed incapable of solving (and whose adoption might actually have been a contributory factor), but also as a consequence both of personnel changes and institutional reform.

With regard to the former, the Ministry of Labour's Permanent Secretary from 1959 to 1962 was Sir Laurence Helsby, who had previously been at the Treasury. Having thus previously worked in the Department most directly concerned with rising inflation and other economic problems, he arrived at the Ministry of Labour with a rather less sanguine attitude towards industrial relations problems. Indeed, it has been claimed that 'under his reign, the Ministry decided as a conscious act of policy that it could no longer automatically step in to conciliate irrespective of the economic damage it produced in the process' (Brittan, 1969: 164).

Initially, the most obvious indication of a shift in the Ministry of Labour's ethos was its conversion to supporting an incomes policy as a permanent tool of economic management, in the context of inflationary pressures accruing from the trade unions' increased bargaining power in an era of full employment, as noted by the recently retired Director of the Economic Section in the Cabinet Office, Robert Hall (1961: 1042). This clearly had implications for voluntarism, because incomes policies entailed a significant incursion into *free* collective bargaining: pay negotiations were no longer solely a matter for employers/management and trade unions, but a process in which the State increasingly took an active interest, sometimes to the extent of imposing limits on wage increases. This, in turn, served to politicise pay determination.

Furthermore, incomes policies served to highlight the extent to which nationally agreed or politically imposed pay deals were often undermined by local-level wage agreements negotiated between shop stewards and factory-level managers, sometimes against the back-drop of unofficial strikes, thus yielding 'wage drift'. In this context, some senior officials in the Ministry of Labour became more receptive to the idea of placing some aspects of industrial relations in a legal framework, most notably procedural agreements. As noted in chapter 2, this shift in perspective had been discernible in its evidence to the Royal Commission, when the Ministry cautiously suggested that the law might be extended to a couple of aspects of industrial relations and trade unionism.

The other factor which served to weaken the hitherto dominance of voluntarism in the Ministry of Labour was its merger, in April 1968, with the DEA, to establish a new Department of Employment and Productivity, whose Secretary of State was Barbara Castle. It has been suggested that some senior officials from the DEA had been rather less supportive of voluntarism for, like many of their Treasury counterparts, they were deeply concerned at what they perceived to be the increasingly damaging economic consequences of free collective bargaining and strikes. As such, the creation of this new Department meant that senior officials who had been working in the Ministry of Labour were now joined – and in some cases, perhaps influenced or persuaded by – high-ranking civil servants from the former DEA.

Consequently, those officials who still believed in voluntarism were now countered by several senior colleagues who favoured imposing a statutory framework on industrial relations. In the context of the economic and industrial problems which increasingly confronted Ministers and mandarins in the 1960s, the advocates of legislative reform within the new Department seized the initiative, and did much to shape a new agenda, albeit headed by a Secretary of State who concurred with much of their perspective (Tyler, 2006: 463–4).

For example, almost immediately upon publication of the Donovan Report, a senior official in the DEP noted its refusal to recommend that collective agreements should be made legally binding. This, the official argued, was in stark contrast to the recent Prices and Incomes Acts, which had 'intruded by statute into the field of collective bargaining', and included 'penalties … for non-observance'. While acknowledging that the labour movement was generally opposed to statutory incomes policies, the official suggested that a key argument in defence of such legislation was that 'it is necessary to have residual statutory powers to catch the "mavericks"', and as such, he suggested that '[t]he same argument could be used in relation to the Royal Commission's Report'.[15]

Incidentally, this point further illustrates the ambiguity over the relationship between industrial relations reform and incomes policies during the late 1960s: was the reform of collective bargaining, with the aim of imbuing industrial relations with greater order and stability, intended to render incomes policies more effective, or to obviate the need for them in the first place? On this particular question, proponents of industrial relations legislation, both in Whitehall, and in the Cabinet, were either undecided or divided.

Meanwhile, further evidence of a hardening of attitudes among some officials in the new Department was provided in August 1968, when in spite of – or perhaps precisely because of – the recently published Donovan Report's rejection of statutory curbs on strikes and/or pre-strike ballots, a small team of DEP officials were contemplating a 'task force' to examine potential ways in which strikes and other forms of industrial action (such as go-slows, working to rule, etc.) could be tackled. This might entail giving further consideration to measures which had been rejected in the Donovan Report, such as compulsory strike ballots and 'cooling-off' periods, for these were 'certain to be live issues in the future debates on the Royal Commission's recommendations'.[16] Indeed, it was suggested that some of the proposals emanating from such a 'task force' could be considered in the ongoing consultations with the TUC and the CBI, and then included in the subsequent White Paper – 'together with the paper on legislative sanctions which my Division [in the DEP] is preparing'.[17]

On another occasion, Denis Barnes told the recently appointed Bernard Ingham (who many years later became Margaret Thatcher's renowned Press Secretary) that unemployment in Britain would continue to double every decade until 'we got on top of the trade union problem' (Perkins, 2003: 278). This was an allusion to the increasingly prevalent view that the bargaining power of the trade unions had been greatly strengthened by full employment and the legal immunities which they enjoyed when pursuing strikes, so that they were often able to secure wage increases which were either inflationary, or eroded the profitability of the companies which employed their members. Either way, the consequences would be a continued decline in the competitiveness of the British economy and a steady loss of jobs. It was increasingly accepted that the only ways in which these problems could be tackled was by adopting incomes policies to secure wage restraint, or/and imposing statutory restrictions on the trade unions to curb their bargaining power in the first place.

The extent to which Barbara Castle herself was directly persuaded by those DEP officials who were increasingly advocating legislative curbs on some trade union activities and practices has been an ongoing question among political historians and biographers. The assumption that she was strongly influenced by them implies that this was a classic case of a Minister being 'captured' by senior Departmental officials, and thus persuaded to adopt their perspective; a political 'amateur' or non-expert seemingly persuaded by the judiciously expressed arguments advanced by senior officials, based on years of experience, and articulated with great charm and eloquence. Certainly, the biographer of Frank Cousins, leader of the Transport and General Workers' Union (TGWU) and a member of the TUC's General Council, claims that a draft version of a more legalistic industrial relations policy had been lying semi-dormant in the Ministry of Labour for many years, awaiting adoption by a suitably persuadable Minister (Goodman, 1984: 572). In similar vein, the trade union historian and former labour [industrial relations/trade unionism] correspondent of the *Financial Times*, Robert Taylor, suggests that the Ministry of Labour had become increasingly convinced of the need for a tougher industrial relations policy during the 1960s, and a more 'robust' stance *vis-à-vis* the trade unions themselves (Taylor, 1993: 157–9).

This interpretation is redolent of the 'garbage can model' of the policy process explicated by Cohen, March and Olsen (1972), which emphasises the often haphazard manner in which policies are sometimes developed or adopted. One aspect of this model is that policies are not necessarily formulated sequentially, after, and in response to, the identification of a particular problem, but can have been drafted already, and be waiting for an appropriate problem to which they can be offered as the solution. The pre-drafted policy might have been prepared in response to a similar problem in the past, but then abandoned, perhaps because the problem apparently disappeared or was solved by other means, or maybe because a change of government or Ministerial reshuffle resulted in the policy falling out of favour. The policy was thus discarded into the 'policy dustbin', but later retrieved and dusted down in response to the emergence of a similar problem, or maybe the re-emergence of the original problem.

Alternatively, a putative policy might be devised by a senior official, or team of officials, who then wait for propitious circumstances – a crisis, changes in public opinion, ideological paradigm shifts, appointment of a like-minded or amenable Minister – in which to present their preferred policy as the ready solution. Whatever the precise scenario, the central point here is the manner in which a policy can pre-date the emergence of the problem to which it is then presented as the solution.

A subsequent variant of this model of policy-making is John Kingdon's (1984) 'policy streams' approach, in which there needs to be a confluence of three 'streams' in order to establish the optimum condition or circumstances for policy change: the problem stream; the policy stream; the political stream. The 'problem stream' is when, how and why the problem is identified or defined (the scale or seriousness of the problem, statistical evidence, ideological perspective or stance, changing societal values, etc.). The 'policy stream' entails the adoption or formulation of a policy to tackle the problem (again, the policy might already exist, and have been awaiting an appropriate problem to which it can be applied). The 'political stream' refers to the circumstances required for the policy to be enacted or implemented – shifts in public or elite-level opinion, change of government or Minister, emphatic electoral victory providing the new government with a 'mandate', the dominance of an ideological faction in a governing party, available resources (funding, staffing, expertise), etc. Problems emerge (or are defined as such) almost continuously, and policies promoted to solve them, but it is only in propitious political circumstances that the policies will be applied to the problems; otherwise the 'window of opportunity' for policy change will be shut, and the three policy streams flow apart again.

Applying this model to the 1968–9 advocacy of a legal framework for industrial relations and trade unions, the 'problem stream' would be the incidence of (and economic damage caused by) unofficial and unconstitutional strikes, which, it was discovered, accounted for at least 90 per cent of all strikes in Britain. The 'policy stream' would be an industrial relations policy which placed legal curbs or statutory requirements both on aspects of collective bargaining, and the circumstances in which a strike could (or could not) lawfully be pursued. The crucial 'political stream' in this case would be sufficiently widespread concern about unofficial strikes and cognizance of the economic damage, social disruption or severe inconvenience they caused; a consensus among a sufficient number of senior Departmental civil servants that a statutory policy was now essential; and, crucially, a newly appointed Minister, fully backed by the Prime Minister, who was favourably disposed towards the proposed new policy.

However, this last point suggests a somewhat different account of Castle's role in supporting (a few) legislative curbs on the trade unions, as subsequently promoted in the *In Place of Strife* White Paper. Rather than assuming that she was 'captured' by more hard-line or hawkish senior Departmental officials who persuaded her to adopt 'their' preferred industrial relations policy, the alternative explanation is that Castle had already made up her own mind about the need for a more 'robust' industrial relations policy; she did not need to be persuaded or pressured by her senior civil servants in the new Department of Employment and Productivity. On the contrary, it is at least as likely that those high-ranking Departmental officials who hankered for a tougher policy were themselves encouraged and emboldened by the appointment of a new Secretary of State who seemingly already shared their perspective and policy preference; it was a mutual meeting of administrative and political minds, rather than the former shaping the latter. That Castle was already envisaging a more legalistic industrial relations policy became apparent at a weekend seminar which she arranged, at the civil service training college in Sunningdale (Berkshire), to crystallise the Labour Government's response to the politically unacceptable caution and conservatism of the Donovan Report.

The Sunningdale weekend

Held in mid-November 1968, this event was attended by Castle and her two junior Ministers Roy Hattersley and Harold Walker, her Parliamentary Private Secretary (PPS) John Fraser, fifteen senior officials from the DEP, two senior representatives of the National Board for Prices and Incomes, two representatives from nationalised industries, two academics (one of them Professor Hugh Clegg, who had been a key member of the Donovan Commission), Peter Shore the Secretary of State for Economic Affairs and one of his Departmental officials.

The seminar comprised a series of presentations and workshops on aspects of the Donovan Report and issues concerning industrial relations more generally. These discussions were organised around eight themes or headings (albeit some considered together in the same session), with each of these entailing one or two papers providing analysis and/or suggested remedies, as illustrated in Table 2.

Table 2 The main themes and papers discussed at the Sunningdale Conference

Theme or heading	Papers discussed (author)	Schedule for discussion
A doctrine of systematic and positive State intervention	Labour Law in Britain An Alternative Approach, section 1	Friday 21.15–22.45
The validity of the Donovan analysis Compulsory or voluntary registration of agreements?	The Application of Plant Bargaining to Different Industries An Alternative Approach, section 8	Saturday 9.45–10.45
Various trade union recognition problems Trade union reorganisation	An Alternative Approach, sections 2 and 3. Thoughts on the Donovan Report.	Saturday 11.00–12.15
Action to deal with strikes	An Alternative Approach, section 6.	Saturday 12.15–13.00
The enforcement of collective agreements	An Alternative Approach, section 5. Thoughts on the Donovan Report.	Saturday 14.00–15.30
The functions of the Commission on Industrial Relations	An Alternative Approach, section 9.	Saturday, from 15.30 onwards

Source: MS. Castle.273, Seminar on the Donovan Report, 15–17 November 1968.

Evidently, the most important paper was 'An Alternative Approach',[18] sections of which were discussed at each of these six sessions: it ran like a connecting thread through the whole of the Sunningdale Conference, and permeated all the discussions. What was most significant about 'An Alternative Approach', though, was that it had mostly been written by John Burgh, one of Castle's most senior Departmental civil servants, and clearly exemplified the extent to which some officials in the DEP were keen to move beyond voluntarism, and thus beyond Donovan. Burgh used 'An Alternative Approach' to argue that:

> [t]he doctrine of non-intervention in industrial relations never entirely corresponded with reality, and is now completely out of date. Industrial relations do not, and should not, exist in a legal vacuum. The real question is not whether there should be legislation on industrial relations, but what sort of legislation there should be.

To reiterate the point, 'An Alternative Approach' insisted that not only did non-intervention in industrial relations no longer correspond to the facts, there were now 'cogent reasons for regarding it as wrong in principle'. Whereas voluntarism had assumed that the two sides of industry were best placed to tackle workplace issues and freely pursue collective bargaining, 'An Alternative Approach' insisted that, on the contrary, 'the country's elected Government is better placed than either side of industry ... to assess the common good'. Indeed, when an elected government 'judges the common good to be threatened by either side, or both sides, of industry, the Government should have the power to take the necessary remedial action'. On this basis, it was strongly suggested that the Government would be wholly justified in going rather further than merely enacting the recommendations in the Donovan Report.

For example, with regard to inter-union disputes which resulted in strike action, 'An Alternative Approach' suggested that the Secretary of State could be granted 'reserve powers, exercisable on the CIR's advice, to make a legally binding order', although it was emphasised that such powers would need to be invoked sparingly, according to circumstances and the nature or seriousness of a particular dispute. Nonetheless, the mere existence of these reserve powers might have a salutary effect on those concerned, and perhaps encourage them to resolve their dispute without resorting to industrial action. It was also noted that if there were more amalgamations or mergers of trade unions, this would further reduce the scope for inter-union or demarcation disputes.

Another issue on which 'An Alternative Approach' suggested that statutory intervention might be warranted concerned unconstitutional strikes, especially in cases 'where there appeared to be a *prima facie* case for assuming an unreasonable breach of a procedure agreement'. This, it was readily acknowledged, was inextricably linked to the wider issue of making procedural agreements legally binding in the first place, something which the Donovan Report had shied away from, notwithstanding Shonfield's 'note of reservation'.

It was also recognised that if the Secretary of State was empowered to order a trade union or a group of workers to desist from pursuing an unconstitutional strike, the issue of penalties for non-compliance would need to be addressed, along with determining culpability; a trade union might defy an order to call off such a strike, or it might order a return to work but then be defied by some of its members. In the case of a recalcitrant trade union, it was suggested that the most obvious and feasible penalty would be a fine, with a specified sum (£500 was mooted)[19] to be paid for each day that the strike continued after the order had been issued to return to work.

In the case of individual trade union members who defied an instruction to return to work, 'An Alternative Approach' argued that, in the first instance, the trade union would need to prove that it had used its 'best endeavours' to get its members back to work. Assuming that it had done so, the question would then be what penalties to apply to the defiant union members. Imprisonment was deemed politically unacceptable (and might well result in more extensive strikes in solidarity with the trade union 'martyrs' in prison), while expulsion by and from the union would be problematic 'given the nature, purpose and functions of trade unions' – quite apart from the professed objective of strengthening collective bargaining through maximising trade union membership. As such, fines were again deemed to be the only viable penalty, with a daily sum of £10 suggested.[20]

However, as will become apparent in subsequent chapters, the whole issue of imposing fines on individual trade union members became a significant source of controversy, and provided a focal point for opponents of industrial relations legislation, whether in the Cabinet, on the Labour backbenches, or among the trade unions themselves. This was because of serious concern that in cases of non-payment the ultimate sanction might be imprisonment, even though Castle was adamant that no trade union member would be sent to prison for not paying a fine. Many Parliamentary and trade union opponents of *In Place of Strife*, however, simply did not believe her and feared that, in any court case, a potentially hostile judiciary might interpret the law differently to how Castle intended it to be enforced.

Castle's own hand-written notes from the seminar reveal her pondering whether 'collective laissez faire [should] still hold good today?', then listing four contemporary developments which showed that the State was already intervening in collective bargaining and industrial relations through its pursuit of prices and incomes policy: Industrial Training Boards, a redundancy payments scheme, the pursuit of equal pay and the continuation of Wages Councils (originally established in 1909) to ensure a minimum wage in particular industries. By this time she was already convinced that the question was no longer *whether* the State should intervene in collective bargaining and industrial relations, but *how*?

It was during the Friday evening discussions, on 'An Alternative Approach' (Section One), and 'Labour Law in Britain', that it became apparent just how far a consensus was already emerging among the participants regarding willingness to 'reject the doctrine of "collective laissez-faire" and accept State intervention in industrial relations'. As such, it was acknowledged that the key questions were now about the objectives of State intervention, and how to ensure that this more interventionist role could be pursued effectively. The objectives identified, and the methods of pursuing them, included:

> The reform of procedural agreements to reduce the scale of unconstitutional strikes.
> Extending worker participation.
> Tackling discrimination in employment.
> An active labour market policy.
> A legal right both to trade union membership, and union recognition for bargaining purposes.
> A new institution to be established, a Commission for Industrial Relations (CIR), to promote more effective collective bargaining.
> The prevention and resolution of industrial disputes.
> A fair and effective prices and incomes policy.[21]

This last point once again reflected the extent to which industrial relations reform and incomes policies were widely viewed as being inextricably linked, albeit with divergent conclusions being drawn. On one hand, some proponents of industrial relations reform envisaged that this would render incomes policies more viable and effective, because more orderly collective bargaining would reduce the phenomenon of local-level 'wage drift', which so often undermined incomes policies formally determined at national level.

Other supporters of industrial relations reform, however, envisaged that by strengthening collective bargaining machinery and procedures, and *inter alia* instilling greater order and stability into pay negotiations and wage settlements, the need for incomes policies (to curb inflation and maintain full employment) would be greatly reduced. Hence the suggestion that the proposed CIR should *not* directly concern itself with 'the actual level of wage rates ... The CIR should not be an instrument of incomes policy', although even here, it was acknowledged that 'it would be very difficult for the CIR to avoid all consideration of substantive agreements'. Nonetheless, it was argued that '[i]t should be quite feasible for the CIR to confine itself to industrial relations matters, and to avoid trespassing onto incomes policy questions'.[22]

Having identified the rationale and key objectives of a more interventionist role for the State *vis-à-vis* industrial relations, the Friday evening workshop then focused primarily on the penultimate of the above points, namely preventing and resolving strikes. It was deemed 'essential to find a means of reconciling the interests of the producer [worker] and the consumer, and at the same time to maintain full employment', while also seeking 'to prevent workers themselves acting against the longer-term interests of the economy'. The attainment of these goals meant that 'the reform of negotiating and disputes procedures was the prime requirement'.

With specific regard to industrial disputes, the Sunningdale seminar identified four main types:

- recognition disputes, where responsibility resided with management, for refusing to recognise a trade union (or even unions in general) for the purposes of collective bargaining
- inter-union disputes, for which responsibility resided with the trade unions themselves
- disputes between workers/trade unions and an employer
- disputes where the combined interests of employers and trade unions conflicted with the interests of citizens or the wider community.

In the first of these types of dispute any sanctions would be applied to employers, while in the second type workers/unions would be the subject of sanctions. In the third and fourth categories of dispute it was deemed imperative to devise methods that reduced their likelihood and frequency, which would necessitate making collective bargaining procedures and machinery more effective, and facilitating more constructive means of resolving conflicts. This would require the development and expansion of more explicit procedural agreements, coupled with more robust mechanisms for resolving industrial disputes. The latter, it was envisaged, might entail arbitration under the auspices of the proposed CIR.

However, it was readily recognised that the relationship between the DEP and the CIR would need careful consideration and presentation. This was because if cases and disputes were referred to the CIR by the DEP, then the independence of the Commission in the eyes of the trade unions, and thus its authority and legitimacy, was likely to be undermined; it would be viewed as a tool or servant of the Government, whereupon its decisions or recommendations were less likely to be accepted. Those participants in the Sunningdale seminar who harboured this concern therefore emphasised the need to ensure that the CIR was – and was seen to be – independent of the Government, whereupon it would be entitled to decide for itself which cases and disputes to investigate.[23]

Linked to the discussions about how to tackle industrial disputes was the issue of whether collective agreement should become legally enforceable, and if so, which types of agreement: procedural or substantive? The prevalent view was that in the first instance the priority should be strengthening or extending procedural agreements, for it was breaches of these, or even their absence, which often resulted in unconstitutional or 'wildcat' strikes, the intrinsic unpredictability of which frequently rendered them so disruptive. However, it was acknowledged that if reducing such strikes was a key objective of industrial relations reform, then strengthening procedural agreements ought to be part of a package of measures which included statutory trade union recognition and bargaining rights, greater disclosure (by management) of information and workers' participation via membership of company boards.

This reflected an assumption that some unconstitutional strikes were partly attributable to workers' feelings of alienation, frustration or distrust *vis-à-vis* management and corporate decisions, and in these circumstances relatively minor grievances, insecurities or suspicions could flare up into industrial disputes and walk-outs, particularly if such sentiments were exploited by shop stewards or 'militants' pursuing their own political agenda.

However, it was recognised that introducing procedural agreements would take time, and even when they were established there would still be some instances when they were breached. Consequently, the Sunningdale seminar felt obliged to consider what the political response could or should be when unconstitutional or wildcat strikes did occur, either in the absence of, or in defiance of, procedural agreements. It was from consideration of this question that the notion of a cooling-off period was embraced, with Peter Shore credited (by Castle) as the proposer of this particular policy (Castle, 1993: 415). Subsequently termed a 'conciliation pause', this would entail cessation of a strike, for a specified period of time, while an inquiry was conducted into its causes or origins, and solutions sought.

Furthermore, cognizant of the fact that some such strikes flared up in response to precipitate or provocative action by management, it was also agreed that during a cooling-off period (or conciliation pause) there should be a return to the *status quo ante*. If, for example, a group of workers had been summarily dismissed, and this then prompted an immediate walk-out by their workmates, the employer could be required to reinstate the sacked workers for the duration of the conciliation pause, pending an inquiry and, hopefully, a recommended resolution.

With regard to other types of strikes, there was general agreement that if the national interest was seriously jeopardised by such a stoppage, then the Secretary of State should have the discretionary power to order the relevant union(s) to conduct a ballot of their members, to gauge their support for industrial action (Castle, 1990: 275: diary entry for 15 November 1968).

As Castle acknowledged in the context of the Sunningdale weekend, 'a consensus emerged that we rejected the concept of "collective laissez-faire" and were in favour of state intervention in industrial relations'. She was therefore insistent that the Government could not simply endorse Donovan's overall defence of voluntarism, because of the degree of 'industrial anarchy which was doing so much harm to the economy'. Hence the essential need to seek a balance between the legitimate right of workers to defend their material interests on one hand, and the need to protect the wider community from serious disruption, and industry itself from significant damage, on the other. By the end of the Sunningdale weekend Castle noted 'a surprising amount of agreement, though some would have preferred to go further' (Castle, 1990: 275, diary entry for 15 November 1968).

Peter Shore certainly proved to be one of the Sunningdale weekend's key advocates of a tougher stance, arguing that the whole character and consequences of strikes had changed, for they now often affected the community rather than an employer. For example, he depicted a strike by dock-workers as a blockade of the nation. In this changing context, Shore was adamant that the State had the right to intervene when and where the national interest is threatened, regardless of the merits of a particular industrial dispute. He therefore favoured discretionary ballots (at the behest of the Secretary of State) prior to major official strikes, and injunctions against damaging unofficial strikes, with fines imposed if these were defied.[24] Shore was widely viewed as being on the Left of the Labour Party and, as such, his perspective might indirectly have persuaded Castle that a more hard-line stance towards industrial relations and trade unions would enjoy wider support in the PLP than it subsequently did. Certainly, as we note in chapter 5, the left-wing Tribune Group was a significant source of intra-Party opposition to the ensuing White Paper *In Place of Strife*.

Also in favour of moving beyond voluntarism was one of Castle's junior Ministers, Roy Hattersley, who confessed that he had 'no philosophical objection to more rigorous laws to control the conduct of trade unions and their members. Indeed, I am in favour of it.' He thus urged an extension of legal powers and associated sanctions, albeit on condition that these were applied to individual trade unionists who 'are both clearly identifiable and small in number', and that any such application did not occur *during* an industrial dispute, lest it exacerbate ill-feeling and foster intransigence among the participants. However, Hattersley was also cognizant that, if the Government did acquire legal powers to intervene in industrial disputes but then refused to invoke them, it was likely to 'appear ridiculous' in the eyes of the public.[25]

Meanwhile, John Fraser averred that:

> [w]e had to do something. The trade unions behaved like the Vatican State, as if they were an independent power. Yet they had been given everything. We had public ownership, but the miners and the railmen had no compunction about going on strike. They had inherited the earth and still they wanted more. (Quoted in Perkins, 2003: 281)

Castle deemed the Sunningdale conference to have been a 'fabulously successful weekend', so much so that '[w]e can all see our way on Donovan quite clearly now' (Castle, 1990: 276, diary entry for 16 November 1968). It certainly seems to have been decisive in firmly convincing her that the Labour Government's planned industrial relations legislation needed to go rather further than the Donovan Report's cautions recommendations; mere reinforcement of voluntarism would not suffice. What was needed was 'Donovan Plus'.

Indeed, even during the Sunningdale weekend itself, Castle's ideas crystallised to such an extent that by the Sunday morning she had drafted several principles and policy proposals which 'amounted to the skeleton of her industrial relations strategy'. These included a cooling-off period (or conciliation pause) in the case of unconstitutional strikes, and a secret ballot if and when a strike was deemed likely to damage the national interest. When she conveyed her tentative ideas to those colleagues still present – many had already left Sunningdale by this time, the last seminar having finished early on Saturday evening – they were greatly impressed, not just with her hand-written list of actual proposals, but with Castle's apparent confidence and conviction in presenting them. Bill McCarthy, for example, recalled that 'it was marvellous', while John Burgh averred that '[i]t was a very impressive performance. She had obviously done a great deal of work, and she was completely in command.' Further praise emanated from Peter Shore, who 'was delighted with what I thought were Barbara's very strong proposals' (Perkins, 2003: 283). Such admiration and adulation were as good as it got for Castle over the issue of industrial relations reform, though, for (as we explain in the following chapters) she and her policy were subjected to increasing criticism and opposition during the next seven months, sometimes from senior colleagues who had initially been highly supportive.

The draft White Paper on industrial relations reform

Within a fortnight of the Sunningdale weekend, the first full draft of the White Paper on industrial relations reform had been written,[26] although it was then slightly revised by senior DEP officials prior to being presented to Castle, along with those Ministers serving on the Cabinet committee on industrial relations, in December. The latter version was subsequently presented to the Cabinet at the very beginning of 1969, its main proposals being:[27]

1. To establish a Commission on Industrial Relations.
2. To require employers to register procedure agreements with the Department of Employment and Productivity.
3. Collective agreements to be legally enforceable only if the 'two sides' explicitly declare this intention in writing.
4. Provide trade unions with the right to receive certain types of information from employers, except in cases where commercial confidentiality would be compromised.
5. To provide for trade union representatives to be appointed to company boards.
6. To guarantee workers the right to belong to a trade union.
7. To prevent Friendly Societies from barring trade unionists from being members.
8. To empower the Commission on Industrial Relations to investigate trade union recognition disputes, and to arrange for a secret ballot if it considers this to be desirable.
9. When the Commission on Industrial Relations recommends that an employer shall recognise a union but there is continuing difficulty, the Secretary of State should be empowered to order the employer to recognise, and negotiate with, the union.
10. To enable the Secretary of State by order to make unilateral legally binding arbitration before the Industrial Court available in some situations.
11. Reconsider the law relating to Wages Councils.
12. To provide for the Commission on Industrial Relations to make grants and loans for trade union development.
13. To empower the Secretary of State, where an official strike is threatened, to require a ballot.
14. To enable the Secretary of State to require those involved to desist for up to 28 days (and for a further period of up to 28 days if necessary) from a strike or lockout, without the prior use of established procedures [this became the 'conciliation pause'].
15. To protect inducement of breach of a contract (other than a contract of employment) in the circumstances of a trade dispute.
16. To introduce safeguards against unfair dismissal.
17. To require trade unions to register, and to have rules concerning admission, discipline, disputes between union and member, elections and strike ballots, and shop stewards.
18. To create a new Registrar of Trade Unions and Employers Associations, the post to be combined for the present with that of Registrar of Friendly Societies.

19. To require all but the smallest unions to have professional auditors, and to make new provisions regarding superannuation funds for members.
20. To enable a union to be sued in tort, except in the circumstances of a trade dispute.
21. To make any necessary amendment to the definition of a trade dispute.
22. To establish an independent review body to hear complaints by individuals of unfair or arbitrary action by trade unions.

One 'very tricky problem' which the senior officials most closely involved in preparing the draft White Paper still felt unable to resolve, though, was the relationship between these proposed reforms and the Government's incomes policies. Some officials envisaged that the restoration of orderly collective bargaining would boost the viability of incomes policies, by rendering them a more effective and enduring tool of economic management, whereas others anticipated that the draft White Paper's proposals 'will provide an opportunity for withdrawing gracefully from the present statutory incomes policy'.[28]

There was also some uncertainty among Departmental officials about who should be responsible for invoking action against trade unions when a strike ballot was ordered, or the conciliation pause was invoked. There was concern that if Castle was the prime instigator of the 'penal clauses' she might be placed 'in an embarrassing position', due to simultaneously invoking legal powers against a trade union, while also securing their trust in facilitating a fair and equitable solution. To avoid such a dilemma, there was a suggestion that the Attorney-General might more appropriately fulfil this role, thereby leaving the Secretary of State to play a much more conciliatory or peace-broker role, either in tandem with, or via, the CIR.[29] However, this suggestion was rejected by the Lord Chancellor, George Gardiner, after he had discussed it with the Attorney-General and the Solicitor-General, both of whom were adamant that responsibility for invoking the conciliation pause should reside with the Employment Secretary, although they did not explain the reason for this decision.[30]

In the meantime, there were difficulties in agreeing on a title for the imminent White Paper. Originally, the intended title had been *People at Work: A Policy for Industrial Relations*, until it was noted that not only had the Ministry of Labour used *People at Work* as the title of a 1963 publication on communication in industry, but that *People at Work* was also the title of a series of Ladybird books about different occupations and careers.[31] Other titles mooted included *Industrial Relations: A Policy for Progress*, *Industrial Relations: Framework for the Future*, *Industrial Relations; The Way Ahead* and *A Policy for Industrial Relations*, although it was readily conceded that 'none [were] very striking',[32] albeit evincing 'varying degrees of prosiness'.³³ Even when the Cabinet discussed Castle's proposals on 14 January 1969, the policy document still lacked an official title, so continued to be referred to either as the 'Draft White Paper', or as 'A Policy for Industrial Relations'.

The White Paper's eventual title – *In Place of Strife* – was actually suggested to Castle by her husband (Castle, 1993: 417), although of course, the appellation proved deeply ironic in view of the bitter controversy it provoked during the first half of 1969. Castle had envisaged that the White Paper's nomenclature would reflect the expectation that it would herald a major diminution of strife between management and unions in British industry, and thereby pave the way for a new era of more constructive and harmonious industrial relations.

However, the title of Castle's White Paper was also a genuflection to Aneurin 'Nye' Bevan's 1952 *In Place of Fear*, which outlined his vision of democratic socialism for Britain. In invoking the legacy of Bevan Castle was evidently seeking to burnish her left-wing credentials, particularly as she would have anticipated that antipathy to aspects of the White Paper was most likely to emanate from sections of the Labour left – notwithstanding Peter Shore's enthusiastic support – as well as the trade unions themselves. Indeed, Castle recalled that not only did much of the left prove implacably opposed to specific proposals enshrined in the White Paper, they were 'outraged that I should call Bevan in aid of my proposed reforms'. Yet Castle was adamant that 'having read *In Place of Fear*, I was convinced that I understood what Bevan was about better than they did' (Castle, 1993: 206).

Giving the TUC advance notification of the draft White Paper

Having originally intended to publish the White Paper in December, its actual publication was delayed until mid-January, in order that Castle could discuss its contents and proposals with the TUC, prior to presenting it to the Cabinet. Ostensibly, such discussions were sensible pragmatic politics and tactics, because it would be difficult for the unions subsequently to claim that the Labour Government was acting unilaterally or 'bouncing' a controversial policy decision on them. However, these meetings with senior trade union leaders engendered two problems for Castle.

The first problem concerned a misunderstanding between her and George Woodcock (the TUC General Secretary) when they met on 19 December 1968. She had arranged this bilateral meeting to discuss an industrial dispute in the steel industry, but then decided, 'on an impulse', to give Woodcock advance notification of the imminent White Paper, partly to ensure that its formal announcement would not be a major surprise, and partly to ascertain the TUC's likely response to her proposed reform of industrial relations. She later confessed that 'if George Woodcock damned my proposals, I would have to give them up' (Castle, 1993: 418).

Castle believed that Woodcock's response when informed of the imminent White Paper was that he 'didn't think there was anything there that need alarm the trade union movement' (Castle, 1990: 288, diary entry for 19 December), which would have emboldened Castle to proceed with confidence: 'I was taken aback by the warmth of his response' (Castle, 1993: 418), she later recalled. Yet Woodcock's recollection was that he actually said '[t]here's nothing here that surprises me', which would not in itself have constituted endorsement of Castle's proposals, merely acknowledgement that, in view of the Government's disappointment with the timidity of the Donovan Report, 'world-weary George was hardly astonished that it was going to introduce penal sanctions against unofficial strikers' (Silver, 1973: 134).

The second problem arose when Castle met, at Feather's suggestion, with the TUC's Finance and General Purposes Committee. He had advised her that the TUC would be much less amenable if it felt that she 'was conspiring behind their backs' (Castle, 1993: 418), and presenting them with an industrial relations policy which had already been endorsed by the Cabinet, for this would imply limited scope for subsequent consultation (Dorfman, 1979: 23). Castle thus met with the Committee on 30 December 1968, albeit to outline her policy proposals and take questions for clarification, rather than engage in a detailed discussion. After all, the latter would only be possible once the TUC leaders had been given sufficient time to digest Castle's proposals. The TUC leadership's response at this initial meeting was broadly non-committal: 'The atmosphere ... was quiet and serious. Even the questions were muted, and there were certainly no attacks' (Castle, 1990: 288, diary entry for 30 December 1968).

This rather relaxed initial response by the TUC leaders is likely to have further convinced Castle of the wisdom of her proposals for industrial relations reform, and thus led her to underestimate the degree of opposition which they would encounter when subjected to wider and more detailed consideration. As soon became evident, the relative equanimity of the TUC's Finance and General Purposes Committee on the penultimate day of 1968 did not constitute agreement; silence did not mean consent. It was merely the calm before the political storm.

Conclusion

It was during the latter half of 1968 that what became *In Place of Strife* took shape. It emerged in response to the dissatisfaction which Castle and Wilson felt with the caution which characterised the Donovan Report, and their conviction that a more robust industrial relations policy was needed; what became known as Donovan Plus. However, this stance was shared by many of the officials in the new Department of Employment and Productivity, to the extent that, unlike the erstwhile Ministry of Labour, 'voluntarism' was no longer an in-house ideology. Consequently, Castle's and Wilson's support for industrial relations legislation, which would include the statutory regulation of strikes and associated financial penalties for defiance, was buttressed by several of the senior officials in a new Department. Two of the Government's most senior Ministers, and a coterie of key mandarins, were arriving at the same conclusions about both the nature of the problem and the required policy solution.

This meeting of minds was confirmed when Castle organised a weekend retreat at the civil service training college in Sunningdale, Berkshire, to discuss more fully the Department's post-Donovan approach to industrial relations. It was at this weekend gathering that the departure from voluntarism or collective *laissez-faire* was confirmed, and clarification of various principles and objectives concerning the governance of industrial relations attained. This crucial weekend in mid-November 1968 provided both Castle and her senior Departmental officials with a major spur to draft a White Paper enshrining a comprehensive package of reforms. Indeed, Castle began drafting some of them on the Sunday morning of the Sunningdale weekend, while other proposals were devised by her officials during the next couple of weeks, with a draft White Paper published in December, but not yet presented to the full Cabinet.

The crucial interplay of individual and institutional factors – agency and structure – which facilitated the development of the draft White Paper heralding a new, non-voluntarist industrial relations policy was further underpinned by a high-profile strike in autumn 1968, in the guise of the industrial dispute at the Girling Brakes company. This seemed to epitomise so much which was wrong with Britain's industrial relations in the 1960s, with an instant walk-out by just twenty-two workers, in connection with a 'demarcation dispute', resulting in thousands of other workers being temporarily laid off. Indeed, Castle and her supporters variously cited this dispute as evidence of why industrial relations legislation was so urgently needed, and why such legislation needed to include measures to tackle inter-union disputes, and unconstitutional and unofficial strikes.

Context and circumstances therefore seemed to be highly conducive to the industrial relations reform which Castle was now convinced was essential, a conviction which was also wholly shared by the Prime Minister, and by many of her Departmental officials. Ostensibly, therefore, the situation in late 1968 appeared to be highly propitious for Castle, and the timing entirely appropriate. However, what she (and Wilson) had not envisaged was just how controversial three of the specific measures in the draft White Paper would prove to be, and thus the breadth and strength of opposition which they would provoke.

Notes

1 NA CAB 134/2936, 'Memorandum by the First Secretary of State', 27 May 1968.
2 MS Wilson c.1594, Wilson to Castle, 8 April 1968.
3 NA CAB 134/2936, 'Memorandum by the First Secretary of State', 27 May 1968.
4 NA PREM 13/2165, Gunter to Wilson, 20 October 1967.
5 NA LAB 16/618, 'First Secretary's Meeting with the TUC to discuss the Report of the Commission on Trade Unions and Employers' Associations', 2 July 1968.
6 One of about twenty allotted days when an Opposition party is permitted to choose the topic of debate in the House of Commons.
7 NA LAB 16/618, 'First Secretary's Meeting with the TUC to discuss the Report of the Commission on Trade Unions and Employers' Associations', 2 July 1968.
8 NA LAB 16/618, Hattersley to Castle, 'Report of the Royal Commission', 15 May 1968.
9 NA LAB 16/618, 'First Secretary's Meeting with the TUC to discuss the Report of the Commission on Trade Unions and Employers' Associations', 2 July 1968.
10 NA PREM 13/2165, 'The Report of the Royal Commission on Trade Unions and Employers' Associations', Trend [Burke, Cabinet Secretary] to Wilson, undated, but states that the Donovan Report will be published 'on Thursday', so *circa* 10 June 1968.
11 NA CAB 128/43, CC (68) 31st Conclusions, Meeting of the Cabinet, 20 June 1968: CAB 129/138, C (68) 81, Memorandum by the Lord Privy Seal – 'Legislative Programme 1968–69', 17 June 1968.
12 NA LAB 16/618, Burgh to Smith, 'Report of the Royal Commission', 24 May 1968.
13 NA LAB 10/3478, Dewar to Burgh, 'The Donovan Report', 2 October 1968.
14 NA LAB 10/3478, Bayliss to Burgh, 'Mr Dewar's draft White Paper', 4 October 1968.
15 NA LAB 16/618, Charles to Dewar, 'Prices and Incomes Bill 1968, and the Report of the Royal Commission on Trades Unions and Employers' Associations', 17 June 1968.
16 NA LAB 16/618, Marre to Burgh, 'A Task Force on Strikes', 15 August 1968.
17 NA LAB 16/618, Burgh to Lawton, 'A Task Force on Strikes', 13 August 1968.
18 NA LAB 43/514, Department of Employment and Productivity, 'An Alternative Approach', undated but *circa* early November 1968.
19 About £8,000 today.
20 About £160 today.
21 MS. Castle.273, Seminar on the Donovan Report, 15–17 November 1968.
22 MS. Castle.273, Seminar on the Donovan Report, 15–17 November 1968.
23 MS. Castle.273, Seminar on the Donovan Report, 15–17 November 1968.
24 MS. Castle.273, Seminar on the Donovan Report, 15–17 November 1968.

25 MS. Castle.273, Hattersley to Castle, 18 November 1968.
26 NA LAB 10/3478, Burgh to Brown, 'Draft White Paper on Industrial Relations', 27 November 1968.
27 NA CAB 129/139, C (69) 131, 'Memorandum by the First Secretary of State and Secretary of State for Employment and Productivity – A Policy for Industrial Relations: Draft White Paper', 30 December 1968.
28 NA LAB 10/3478, Dewar to Burgh, 'The Donovan Report', 2 October 1968.
29 NA LAB 10/3478, Lawton, 'White Paper – Who institutes proceedings before the Industrial Board?', 2 January 1969.
30 NA LAB 10/3478, Gardiner to Castle, 'Draft White Paper on Industrial Relations', 1 January 1969.
31 NA LAB 10/3478, Bayliss to Dewar, 'Title of White Paper', 31 December 1968.
32 NA LAB 10/3478, Burgh to Bayliss, 'Title of the White Paper', 23 December 1968.
33 NA LAB 10/3478, Dewar to Bayliss, 'Title of the White Paper', 23 December 1968.

4

Cabinet demurrals and diminishing Ministerial support

The publication of the draft White Paper, soon to be titled *In Place of Strife*, which proposed comprehensive industrial relations legislation, immediately prompted disagreements and divisions in the Cabinet. However, these did not simply or solely reflect Labour's traditional ideological divisions between the Party's left and right. Instead, there were other factors which resulted in the White Paper receiving a mixed welcome, with some Ministers strongly opposed to what became known as the 'penal clauses', either as a matter of principle, or because they doubted their likely efficacy and enforceability. There were also divergent views about the proposed timescale between publishing *In Place of Strife* and enacting the legislation: how much time should be allocated to consultations with the trade unions before introducing the planned bill to Parliament?

Underpinning some of the more implacable opposition to *In Place of Strife* from within the Cabinet was a close affinity with the trade unions, this sometimes deriving from the Minister's own background prior to entering the House of Commons. In some such instances, their loyalty to the Labour Government (and the constitutional convention of collective Ministerial responsibility) was, in effect, subordinated to their loyalty to the wider labour movement, namely the Labour Party in general, both in the House of Commons and the extra-parliamentary party, and the trade unions.

However, what ultimately proved fatal for *In Place of Strife*, and the legislation which it was intended to presage, was that during the spring of 1969, Cabinet support ebbed away, as some Ministers who had initially been in favour of industrial relations legislation changed their minds. In most cases, this loss of support derived from growing Ministerial recognition of just how wide and deep the opposition was to *In Place of Strife* – and, again, particularly the penal clauses – both in the PLP and among the trade unions (these two sources of opposition are examined in chapters 5 and 6 respectively). The scale of the opposition to the proposed industrial relations legislation was such that it was highly unlikely to secure sufficient support among Labour MPs in the House of Commons. By mid-June, Harold Wilson and Barbara Castle, the two main drivers of the policy, were effectively isolated in the Cabinet, to the extent that they were faced with three unpalatable choices: persevere and face defeat in the House of Commons owing to the opposition of most of the PLP; concede defeat and resign; accept the offer of counter-proposals by the TUC, in spite of having previously rejected them as inadequate.

Presenting *In Place of Strife* to the Cabinet

The still untitled White Paper was first presented to the Cabinet on 3 January 1969, when Castle emphasised that, although the Donovan Report had provided a 'most valuable basis for changes in industrial relations', it would be 'mistaken to proceed simply on the basis that each of the Commission's individual recommendations had either to be accepted or rejected', not least because of the sundry weaknesses in the Donovan Report. She then proceeded to delineate the main features and objectives of the draft White Paper, emphasising her vision of a carefully crafted set of legislative proposals which sought to strike a balance between the legitimate rights of trade unions, their members and other employees, and the responsibilities they ought to accept towards the wider community and society, which also had rights. She simultaneously wanted to strengthen aspects of trade unionism while also tackling the apparently reckless or irresponsible behaviour which unions, or some of their members, variously indulged in.[1]

Yet even before her Ministerial colleagues responded to the actual contents of the draft White Paper, Castle had to contend with the annoyance harboured by some Ministers because she had discussed the proposals with the TUC before officially presenting them to the Cabinet. When she had met the TUC leaders at the end of December, she had naturally sworn them to secrecy, yet the press almost inevitably became aware of the meeting and therefore of what Castle was planning. Castle blamed Frank Cousins for this flagrant breach of confidentiality (Castle, 1993: 418), and while his alleged action, especially as a former Cabinet colleague, was naturally deeply disappointing to her, the real political damage was that most Ministers learned about the imminent White Paper and its controversial legislative proposals in newspaper reports on New Year's Eve, rather than first hearing about the White Paper directly from Castle herself.

This naturally irked many Cabinet Ministers who 'bitterly resented having read in the press what the proposals were before any papers were put to us' (Benn, 1988: 140–1, diary entry for 3 January 1969; see also

Wilson, 1971: 592). In fact, Harold Wilson subsequently conceded that he had been 'disturbed to learn' about Castle's intention to outline the draft White Paper to TUC leaders before it had been considered by the full Cabinet, precisely because of the likelihood of 'immediate leaks, possibly selective and tendentious', which 'would be certain to prejudice that consideration'. However, cognizant of the 'extremely tight timetable' to which the Government was working due to other major Bills, he declined to insist that Castle present her draft White Paper to the Cabinet before unveiling it to the TUC. With hindsight, though, he candidly confessed that his failure to intervene had been a mistake, and that unveiling the White Paper to the TUC before presenting it to the Cabinet 'was an error' (Wilson, 1971: 591, 592).

Castle herself was fully cognizant that she was engaging in 'a rather unusual form of consultation'[2] in discussing her legislative proposals with the TUC leadership both before formally presenting them to the Cabinet, and prior to publishing the official White Paper. However, she consoled herself with the view that the ensuing breach of trust 'merely endorsed the validity of my criticisms of their [trade union leaders'] high-handed attitude', especially as Woodcock had assured that she 'could talk to the [Finance and General Purposes] Committee in complete confidence' (Castle, 1993: 419, 418).

The 'unusual form of consultation' which Castle referred to was actually 'unusual' in another way, because she was treating the draft White Paper not only as a statement of legislative intent (which is precisely what a White Paper constitutionally is), but also as the basis of ongoing consultations with the trade unions, right up until such time as industrial relations legislation was enacted. Yet such consultation is usually associated with a Green Paper, which normally precedes a White Paper heralding a government's new policy and associated legislation. In effect, therefore, what soon became *In Place of Strife* was something of a hybrid; a White Paper with considerably green edges.

At the 3 January 1969 unveiling of the still untitled White Paper, the ensuing Cabinet discussion was so heated and protracted that it had to be resumed after lunch. This was also highly unusual, because whereas Cabinet meetings normally started at 10.00 and finished by 13.00, on this occasion the Cabinet reconvened after lunch and sat until nearly 18.00, owing to the disagreements occasioned among Ministers. During these two sessions, it became evident that were three broad perspectives among Ministers concerning the proposals in the draft White Paper.

The first was wholly supportive of the envisaged industrial relations legislation, including the 'penal clauses'. Apart from Wilson, the most unequivocal supporter of Castle's proposals was the Chancellor, Roy Jenkins, partly because he was convinced that industrial relations legislation was necessary to deal with unofficial and unconstitutional strikes *per se*, but also because he was keen to signal to 'the City' and international financiers that the Labour Government was willing to tackle a major cause of disruption to economic performance and industrial output. The Chancellor's support, in tandem with Wilson's, was key to Castle's confidence, at this early stage, that she could successfully enact the policy: 'With Prime Minister and Chancellor behind her, Barbara Castle couldn't imagine that *In Place of Strife* might not reach fruition' (Crosland, 1982: 203).

Also strongly supportive was Fred Peart (Lord Privy Seal, Minister without Portfolio), who readily accepted the urgency of imbuing industrial relations with greater order and stability. He therefore fully endorsed the proposals on pre-strike ballots in certain circumstances, and the conciliation pause when an unofficial strike was likely to prove deeply damaging to the national economic interest or/and to other workers. Peart even conceded that he would have been happy to see collective agreements made legally enforceable, a measure which had not been included in the draft White Paper.[3]

Further strong support for the proposals in the draft White Paper was provided both by Peter Shore, who had been an active participant in the previous November's Sunningdale seminar, and Tony Benn. The latter argued that the growing complexity of modern industrial life was so great that 'you simply cannot have a disturbance in the system anywhere without all of us suffering', a perspective doubtless underpinned by Benn's own political portfolio as Minister of Technology. However, he also suggested that pre-strike ballots were wholly commensurate with the left's goal of democratising British society and its component institutions (Benn, 1988: 141, diary entry for 3 January 1969).

A second strand of opinion within the Cabinet, and undoubtedly the largest one, comprised those Ministers who were either ambivalent or apprehensive about specific aspects of the draft White Paper, although these Ministers did not constitute a homogeneous 'group'. Some of them were described by Crossman as the 'doubtful ... the middle ready to be swung into support' (Crossman, 1977: 305, diary entry for 3 January 1969), with Tony Crosland, the former Education Secretary and now President of the Board of Trade among them. Crosland would have preferred the Shonfield proposal (outlined in an Appendix to the Donovan Report), under which the CIR would be strengthened and granted authority to deal with various kinds of strike, thereby avoiding the problems which were highly likely to occur if the Government itself, via Castle, imposed sanctions on trade unions or their members. As it was, Crosland was concerned that the proposed 'cooling-off period for unofficial strikes [is] likely to be ineffective, and to raise expectations which will be disappointed.'[4] This was an option which Crossman was also inclined towards (Crossman, 1977: 305, 306, diary entry for 3 January 1969).

The main concern of several of these ambivalent Ministers was the proposed 'conciliation pause', and as such, it was probably the main source of disagreement between them and Castle at this stage. Castle's defence of the 'conciliation pause' was that too much economic damage and industrial disruption was being caused by unconstitutional or unofficial strikes, even though in many instances (as in the recent Girling dispute) only a handful of workers were directly involved in the original stoppage or walk-out. Still, their negative impact, and the number of other workers temporarily laid off, often vastly exceeded the small number of employees at the heart of the dispute.

To pacify some of the opponents to this particular proposal, it was suggested that if in due course the proposed CIR succeeded in improving procedures for resolving industrial disputes, then the need to invoke the conciliation pause would greatly diminish over time. At the very least, the mere potential for a conciliation pause to be invoked might well have a salutary effect in some cases, by deterring some workers who might otherwise have embarked upon an unconstitutional strike. Such a deterrent would yield a welcome reduction in such industrial stoppages, and thus the widespread damage and disruption they often caused, without the need for the conciliation pause and penal clauses to be invoked.

Yet these arguments failed to assuage those Ministers who harboured serious reservations about the conciliation pause, either as a matter of principle, or because of concerns that it would prove impracticable. Regarding the former of these objections, Ministerial critics lamented that, as a major extension of State intervention in industrial relations *vis-à-vis* the right to strike, the conciliation pause constituted a sharp break with the voluntarist tradition, and placed considerable power in the hands of the Secretary of State to intervene in strikes. These critics and sceptics were not assuaged by the claim that the power to invoke a conciliation pause would only be used sparingly, on a discretionary basis. They were concerned that, having acquired this power, the Secretary of State would almost inevitably be under constant pressure to exercise it almost every time an unconstitutional strike occurred: 'Was it worth risking the difficulty and loss of goodwill within the unions and the Labour Party which the proposal would entail?'[5]

With regard to the objections on the grounds of practicability, some Ministers expressed concern about the perceived likelihood of workers being imprisoned if they defied an order to return to work under the auspices of the conciliation pause, and were then unable – or unwilling – to pay a fine imposed as punishment. This objection was not ameliorated by Castle's repeated insistence that the legislation would be drafted in a manner which expressly ruled out a custodial sentence for non-payment of any fines. After all, judges had historically displayed a remarkable talent for creative interpretation when presiding over cases involving trade unions and/or industrial disputes. As such, Castle's insistence that no trade unionist would end up in prison as a result of her proposed industrial relations legislation was viewed, by some critics of the conciliation pause, as naïve, if not actually disingenuous.

The third perspective within the Cabinet was outright opposition and, although this was a minority position in January, its adherents increased in number during the next few months, more especially during May and the first half of June, as it subsequently became evident just how strongly sections of the PLP, and the TUC, opposed the 'penal clauses'. At the 3 January Cabinet meeting the 'penal clauses' were the main focus of outright opponents of the Bill, who bitterly resented the attack on voluntarism which the proposals seemingly represented, and also disputed the need for industrial relations legislation in the first place, on the grounds that Britain's alleged strike problem was greatly exaggerated, often by Labour's, and the unions', political opponents and media critics.

Indeed, it was suggested (with regard to one of the draft White Paper's Appendices) that the incidence of strikes in Britain was somewhat lower than in other industrial countries, a statistic which seemed to obviate the case for the type of statutory measures and penalties that Castle was proposing: Britain's strike record was not nearly as bad as critics claimed. At the very least, it was argued, the Cabinet 'should consider very carefully the political and other consequences of introducing legal sanctions to deal with strikes in disregard of the Donovan Commission's recommendations'.[6]

In response to this particular argument, Castle argued that Britain's strike problem was not simply about the raw number of strikes, but also the nature of those strikes; there was a qualitative aspect to be considered as well as the quantitative dimension. A comparatively small number of strikes still could – and often did – cause widespread economic damage, industrial disruption, lost production and temporary lay-offs of other workers (with loss of wages).

The main opponent of the draft White Paper, and the subsequent industrial relations legislation, was the Home Secretary, James Callaghan. Indeed, his prominent role in opposing *In Place of Strife* and subsequent industrial relations legislation was so significant that it warrants separate discussion, which is provided later in this chapter. Suffice it to say at this point that Callaghan was adamant that the trade unions could, and should, be trusted to put their own house in order, and permitted to devise their own procedures for tackling unconstitutional and unofficial strikes, as well as inter-union disputes. In this regard, Callaghan strongly urged continued adherence to a voluntarist stance.

His opposition to *In Place of Strife* was fully shared by Richard Marsh, the Secretary of State for Transport, who, from the outset, 'was convinced that it wouldn't work, and the failure would be disastrous'. As soon as he read it, 'the warning bells rang loudly in my mind – I was in no doubt that I was violently opposed to this policy' (Marsh, 1978: 139). Like Callaghan, Marsh believed that the Ministers who were most enthusiastic about *In Place of Strife* tended to be 'the intellectuals with no practical experience of industry', and 'no real understanding of the unions', while the opponents were often the Party's 'proletarians' (Marsh, 1978: 133). After all, as noted above, the most prominent proponents of industrial relations legislation were Castle herself, obviously, Wilson, Jenkins, Benn and Shore – all Oxbridge-educated (at a time when many Labour MPs and Ministers had entered full-time employment, usually in industry, immediately after leaving school).

In this respect, Marsh emphasised how the issue transcended the more orthodox ideological divisions between left and right, because *In Place of Strife* attracted supporters and opponents from both 'wings' of the Labour Party. For example, Castle and Shore were on the left, while Jenkins was definitely on the social democratic wing of the Labour Party. As such, the different stances adopted towards *In Place of Strife* divided some Ministers (and MPs) who normally shared the same ideological position, while also yielding some unusual ad hoc alliances between Ministers (and MPs) who were traditionally on ideologically opposing 'sides' (Marsh, 1978: 134).

Given these differing perspectives, and the divisiveness of some of the draft White Paper's proposals, a final decision was deferred pending further discussion in the relevant Cabinet committee.[7] Yet when Castle reported back to the Cabinet just five days later, she explained that the Cabinet committee remained fully agreed on the contentious proposals to enable the Secretary of State to order a ballot prior to a major strike, and to intervene in the case of serious or protracted inter-union disputes. The only continued source of disagreement, she conceded, was that pertaining to the fifty-six-day conciliation pause which she would be empowered to invoke in the case of serious unconstitutional strikes.

A minority of the Cabinet committee remained strongly opposed to the conciliation pause, and reiterated their arguments that it would not be practicable, not least because, even if an order to return to work was obeyed, the workers involved might find other ways of *not* working as normal, for example by working-to-rule, or going-slow. Moreover, its opponents on the Cabinet committee maintained that it would be 'a major irritation for the trade unions', as initial soundings of the TUC had already made clear. As such, critics insisted that the only 'practical remedy lay in a speedy reform of procedural agreements',[8] the absence of which often underpinned unconstitutional strikes, with their damaging impact often greatly exacerbated precisely by their unpredictability.

Other Ministers on the Cabinet committee – including Castle herself, naturally – remained adamant that a conciliation pause was essential as part of a holistic approach to modernising industrial relations, one which enshrined a blend of short-term and long-term measures, some of which bestowed statutory rights on the trade unions, and a few of which imposed corresponding responsibilities. Castle reiterated that the conciliation pause was essential because of the extent to which '[t]he [industrial relations] problem in this country is the unheralded wildcat strike, in which no attempt has been made to use procedures', and as such, it was vital for the Government 'to deal with comparatively small groups of strategically placed workers whose hasty actions are likely to throw many others out of work'.[9]

Ministerial supporters of the conciliation pause also suggested that if the trade unions strongly objected to it, then they might finally be galvanised into actively seeking reform of procedural agreements, and thereby minimise the type of strikes for which the conciliation pause would be invoked. Besides, given that the clear majority of the proposals in the White Paper would benefit and strengthen the trade unions, and also the rights of their members, it was 'not unreasonable to expect the unions, in return, to accept the conciliation pause' in order to tackle unconstitutional strikes.[10] Indeed, this point was subsequently made by another (unnamed) Minister when Castle reported back to the Cabinet (on 8 and 9 January), where it was suggested that '[t]he psychological effect of its existence and the threat of its use' were themselves of the utmost importance.[11] The Cabinet also heard the argument that, despite the trade unions' professed hostility to the proposed conciliation pause, '[i]f the proposal became law, the TUC could be expected to co-operate'.

Such arguments failed to assuage the apprehension of a few Ministers, however, with Judith Hart's position being that, whilst 'a conciliation pause procedure is potentially a valuable method of encouraging a return to work in unconstitutional strikes', she remained 'deeply concerned' that what was being proposed in the draft White Paper 'will often prove either ineffective or unworkable'. She was especially concerned about the provision for imposing fines on workers who refused to return to work when a conciliation pause was invoked, for this would raise serious issues about recouping such penalties if workers did not pay them, for whatever reason, or left their current employment.

Specifically, there was some considerable concern among a few Ministers that, in the last instance, some workers might be sent to prison for non-payment, irrespective of Castle's insistence that her proposed legislation would be carefully drafted to preclude this. Yet however honourable or sincere her intentions might have been, Ministerial sceptics and critics of the 'penal clauses' were aware that if non-payment of a fine resulted in a court case, the judge(s) might interpret the law differently, and ultimately impose a custodial sentence – a major concern which was widely shared by the trade unions themselves, as we will see in chapter

6. In fact, during the final stages of drafting the White Paper, the Lord Chancellor wrote to Castle reiterating that 'it is important to keep the enforcement provisions away from the courts' and, as such, suggesting that an independent body might be given the responsibility for determining 'financial penalties'. Moreover, for presentational purposes, he suggested that the latter phrase should be deployed throughout the White Paper instead of 'fines', due to the emotiveness of the latter from the perspective both of Ministerial critics, and of the trade unions.[12]

Furthermore, Hart argued, this component of the draft White Paper risked placing the Labour Government in a no-win situation. Either the conciliation pause would only be invoked sparingly – as Castle herself claimed – in which case public opinion would be disappointed that its expectations were not being met and the Government would be viewed as weak, whereupon the Conservatives' proposals would garner greater electoral support; or the conciliation pause would be deployed regularly, in which case sections of the Labour Party and the trade unions 'will become embittered'.[13]

Such was the depth of concern over the 'penal clauses' that it required another Cabinet meeting, on 14 January, before final approval was granted to proceed with publication of the draft White Paper. At this meeting, Crossman conceded that the proposals for the conciliation pause remained the one substantive issue on which the Cabinet committee had failed to reach unanimous agreement, owing to the 'grave doubts whether the proposed power to enforce a pause can either be presented credibly or prove workable in practice'. As such, a determination to persevere with this proposal 'in the teeth of widespread trade union opposition may well be counter-productive'. He, along with Hart, therefore urged that the current conciliation pause should only be included in the planned legislation if the trade unions failed to offer a viable counter-proposal for tackling unconstitutional strikes, and therefore that Castle's proposal should be portrayed as the basis for discussion with the trade unions, rather than a firm legislative commitment.[14]

Castle's dismissive response was that this 'would indicate weakness and indecision' by the Government, which, in turn, would render it much less likely that the TUC would develop meaningful counter-proposals of its own. She was adamant that '[t]he mere existence of the powers [to impose a conciliation pause] … would be a real incentive to the trade union movement to produce a workable alternative; in so far as they did so, the reserve powers would not have to be invoked'.[15]

With Wilson's full support, which was reinforced by Tony Benn, Roy Jenkins, Fred Peart, Edward (Ted) Short, Michael Stewart and George Thomas, Castle's stance prevailed, and the draft White Paper was formally endorsed, regardless of the continued opposition of a minority of Ministers, and the reservations which some others still harboured towards the conciliation pause and associated financial penalties for non-compliance (Castle, 1990: 298: diary entry for 14 January).¹⁶

The minority of Cabinet Ministers who remained implacably opposed to the draft White Paper were, at this stage, outweighed by the combined number of senior Ministers who either fully supported it, or who supported much of it albeit with reservations about specific proposals, and those who were willing to endorse it in the expectation that the planned consultations with the TUC and the PLP would lead to the more contentious proposals being abandoned or amended, particularly if the trade unions were galvanised into devising alternative measures of their own. In this respect, some of the initial Ministerial support for Castle's proposals was tactical, so that when opposition from the rest of the labour movement subsequently increased, and the TUC did put forward counter-proposals for itself tackling unconstitutional strikes that were rejected as inadequate by Castle and Wilson, this tactical support was withdrawn.

The timing of industrial relations legislation

In addition to these doubts and disagreements within the Cabinet, there were also two distinct views about the timing of the proposed industrial relations legislation. One view was that an industrial relations bill should not be introduced until the following [1969–70] Parliamentary session, with two reasons being advanced for this approach. The first was that this would allow a lengthy process of consultation with the trade unions, via the TUC, either in the hope of securing a broad consensus over both the necessity and the content of such legislation, or to persuade the trade unions to devise alternative proposals of their own, so that the 'penal clauses' might not be necessary. Among the many Cabinet Ministers endorsing this lengthy period of consultation was Peart, who argued that '[t]ime spent in getting the White Paper right, and in negotiation with the TUC, could save much trouble later ... we should avoid rushing either', although he conceded that even this careful and consultative approach was unlikely to prevent 'continued opposition – some of it noisy – from sections of the Party and some trade union leaders'. Against such likely opposition, Peart was confident that most Labour Party supporters, as well as much of the British public generally, would endorse the Government's approach to reforming industrial relations, once it was more widely understood.¹⁷

The second reason given for delaying industrial relations legislation until the next Parliamentary session was the time needed to draft such a bill, given how comprehensive and detailed it would be. As Peart explained in the first week of 1969, the proposals would almost inevitably yield 'a long and complex Bill', one whose committee stage would almost certainly entail numerous amendments being tabled:[18] hostile Labour MPs would doubtless seek to dilute some aspects of the proposed industrial relations legislation, most notably the 'penal clauses', while Conservative MPs would almost inevitably aim to strengthen them, on the grounds that they did not go far enough. It would, therefore, be virtually impossible for a bill of such comprehensiveness and complexity to proceed through all the necessary Parliamentary stages in the current session. Consequently, such legislation would have to be deferred until the 1969–70 session. The need for such deferral was reinforced by the fact that Government's legislative timetable for the 1968–89 Parliamentary session was already congested, with several other important bills wending their way through Parliament. It would therefore be very difficult to find sufficient time to introduce a bill with content so wide-ranging, and which would almost certainly prove controversial, especially as its progress would inevitably be slowed down by its political opponents and critics.[19]

Initially, Castle was indeed content to defer industrial relations legislation until the next Parliamentary session, not just because of these two arguments, compelling though they were, but because of her confidence that a lengthy period of consultation with the TUC would assuage trade union and PLP concerns, and thus overcome initial opposition. She would use the spring and summer of 1969 to persuade them of the merits of *In Place of Strife*, so that a bill introduced in the autumn would have much more chance of proving acceptable, and thus successful. As such, Castle was adamant that she was 'not prepared to put forward a shorter [immediate] Bill in which all the emphasis will be on the penal bits. I could not imagine anything more detrimental to my whole philosophy' (Castle, 1990: 295, diary entry for 3 January), even though immediately after the publication of the Donovan Report the previous summer, she – and some of her senior DEP officials – had initially considered whether to introduce legislation in the 1968–69 Parliamentary session, albeit in lieu of a more extensive Bill the following year. This, though, was before they had fully considered their response to the Donovan Report, and drafted their own comprehensive set of proposals.

However, the second perspective concerning the timing of the proposed industrial relations legislation warned that deferring the Bill until the autumn would provide the trade unions and Labour MPs with at least eight months in which to mobilise opposition to the contentious 'penal clauses', whereupon the bill was highly likely to be rejected at the TUC's annual conference in September. This, in turn, might galvanise Labour's own opponents of the proposed legislation – or, at least, its penal clauses – to reject it at the Party's conference at the end of September. According to Crossman, deferring legislation until November 'sounds to me tactically disastrous, because it leaves almost a whole year for gnawing at the bone'

(Crossman, 1977: 307, diary entry for 3 January 1969), a view shared by Chancellor Roy Jenkins (Castle, 1990: 295, diary entry for 3 January 1969).[20] Certainly, Richard Crossman was apprehensive from the outset at just how sanguine Castle and Wilson appeared to be, observing that '[s]he and Harold have got themselves into the mood of saying that if they can get this through on Friday [3 January], there will be no difficulty in handling it, but I have the gravest doubts' (Crossman, 1977: 304, diary entry for 1 January 1969). Crossman's 'gravest doubts' were to prove highly prescient and wholly justified.

The role of James Callaghan in opposing *In Place of Strife*

As alluded to above, the most trenchant Ministerial critic of *In Place of Strife* was Home Secretary, James Callaghan. Indeed, even before Castle published this White Paper, he 'made it clear that he was going to oppose her proposals, and argue the straight Donovan line.'[21] She was probably not surprised, having already decided that 'Callaghan is the most disloyal and damaging member of the whole Government' (Castle, 1990: 283, diary entry for 4 December 1968), and five months later depicting him as 'the snake ... lurking in the grass' (Castle, 1990: 328, diary entry for 8 May 1969).

Interviewed in 1999, an unrepentant Callaghan explained that:

> I was brought up with the strong belief of voluntarism and keep away from the law as far as you can. This was probably the mistake I made but the *Osborne* judgement, *Taff Vale* judgement, were the things that made all of us suspicious of any intervention by the law. It was that which prompted in me to oppose what was going on. I believed Donovan was right and the trade unions ought to reform themselves and the law shouldn't play any part in it ... I don't regret it in the sense that it would not have succeeded in doing what it was intended to attack, namely to get rid of unofficial strikes. The legislation she proposed would have had no impact at all, in my judgement, on unofficial strikes. So I don't regret it in that sense. The other reason I don't regret it is that I believe that at that time and in that political background that it would have wrecked that Labour movement. I believe that the atmosphere was such that it would have had a devastating effect on the Labour Party ... The penal clauses were the focal point of her policy frankly. I have no regrets about opposing those at that time – within the general context of what I say about voluntarism and the legal system. (quoted in Trades Union Congress, 1999)

Not surprisingly, therefore, Callaghan raised three specific objections to *In Place of Strife*, namely that the proposed legal sanctions would fail to stop unofficial strikes; that the proposals would prove unacceptable to much of the PLP, to the extent that a bill would fail to secure sufficient Parliamentary support; and that the proposed measures would seriously damage relations between the Labour Party and its trade union allies, particularly as this relationship had already been strained by the Cabinet's pursuit of wage restraint through a series of increasingly stringent incomes policies. Callaghan (1987: 274) later recalled that '[f]rom the moment I set eyes on it [*In Place of Strife*], I knew such a proposal, which ran counter to the whole history of the trade union movement ... could not succeed. Barbara galloped ahead with all the reckless gallantry of the Light Brigade at Balaclava.' Callaghan therefore proved to be an implacable critic of *In Place of Strife*, and especially the ensuing Industrial Relations Bill's 'penal clauses'.

Another reason for Callaghan's bitter opposition was his conviction that Castle and Wilson simply did not understand the reality of day-to-day industrial relations, not least because – unlike Callaghan himself – they had no real background in the trade unions. True, Callaghan's experience was gleaned largely from his time as Assistant Secretary in the Inland Revenue Staff Federation during the second half of the 1930s, so he could hardly be considered a factory-floor proletarian (although he had been raised in a working-class family), but his union background was still one which Castle and Wilson lacked. Callaghan therefore deemed their approach to be rather academic, a criticism which also emanated from some trade union leaders, as we note in chapter 6. Indeed, Callaghan noted that other initial supporters of *In Place of Strife*, such as Tony Benn and Peter Shore, 'whatever their other qualities, know next to nothing about the Trade Union Movement'. Consequently, Callaghan was contemptuous of 'the shabby and squalid intellectual dishonesty which pretends that these [penal] clauses are going to solve unofficial strikes'.[22]

According to an 'authorised' biography of Castle, she and Callaghan had never liked or respected each other, and this meant that their political relationship was characterised by mutual antipathy and mistrust:

> Barbara was an Oxford-educated ex-journalist with a middle-class background, Callaghan was a working-class ex-trade union official who had never had the opportunity to go to university. To some extent, their mutual dislike was a reflection of the relationship between the intellectual and the working-class arms of the [labour] movement. (Perkins, 2003: 286)

However, this 'mutual dislike' apparently went further, with Callaghan having a low opinion of Castle's political skills and Ministerial status, while Castle considered Callaghan to be untrustworthy, not least because he was widely suspected of still coveting Wilson's job, having stood against Wilson (and George Brown) in Labour's 1963 leadership contest. Such suspicion meant that when Callaghan opposed industrial relations legislation, it could readily be interpreted, by his critics (and mischief-making journalists), as a ruse to undermine Wilson.

From this perspective, the Home Secretary had both a personal and a political motive for wanting the Industrial Relations Bill to fail, or be abandoned, because this would destroy Wilson's authority and credibility, thereby significantly enhancing Callaghan's chances of replacing him, buoyed by the support of Labour MPs, particularly those sponsored by trade unions, which had also opposed *In Place of Strife*. According to Defence Secretary Denis Healey, 'Callaghan campaigned tirelessly against them [the White Paper's proposals] in the hope of winning enough trade union support to force Wilson out and take his place' (Healey, 1990: 341).

Not surprisingly, Callaghan emphatically denied harbouring such motives in opposing the White Paper and ensuing legislation. He was adamant that 'it is simply not true ... that I am taking this line on legislation because I want to challenge Wilson for the leadership'. Right from the outset, he insisted, 'I have taken this line because I believe it to be right, and in the interests of the Party.'[23] If Castle suspected that he was motivated by personal career ambitions, this merely confirmed Callaghan's view that she was 'a neurotic conspiracy theorist' (Perkins, 2003: 287).

So vehement and vocal were Callaghan's objections to the penal clauses enshrined both in the White Paper and the subsequent legislation, that his continued membership of the Cabinet, with its concomitant acceptance of collective responsibility, was sporadically called into question. One instance in particular cast serious doubts on Callaghan's Ministerial future, namely a meeting of Labour's National Executive Committee (NEC) on 26 March,[24] which was subsequently described by his biographer as 'one of the most remarkable meetings of Labour's National Executive Committee ever' (Morgan, 1997: 334). At this particular meeting a motion was tabled by Joe Gormley, who later became President of the National Union of Mineworkers, calling on the NEC to reject 'any legislation designed to give effect to all the proposals contained in the White Paper'. This was amended by Callaghan to remove the word 'any', whereupon it was endorsed by sixteen votes to five. Crucially, Callaghan was one of the sixteen to vote for the motion, meaning that he was actually opposing the policy of the Cabinet of which he was a senior member.

When Wilson was duly informed, he was naturally furious with Callaghan, but was unable to act immediately because he only heard about the Home Secretary's conduct shortly before flying out to Nigeria for a summit of Commonwealth leaders in Lagos. Naturally, there was much salacious speculation about what Wilson would do to Callaghan upon his return from Nigeria. Ever the pragmatist, though, Wilson declined to sack Callaghan from the Cabinet, largely for fear that the latter would have ample opportunity to 'cause trouble from the Back Benches, and elevate the policy issue involved into an issue of principle'.[25]

Instead, at the first Cabinet meeting after his return from Lagos, Wilson strongly reminded senior Ministers – 'a constitutional homily' he later described it (Wilson, 1971: 640) – of the vital importance of collective responsibility by which all of them were bound. Although he did not mention Callaghan directly, by name, there was absolutely no doubt to whom he was alluding when he complained about:

> a growing tendency for some Ministers to act in ways which called into question the collective responsibility of the Cabinet, in so far as they had apparently felt free to, in their personal dealings both with members of the PLP and with the Press, to dissociate themselves from certain of the Government's policies and to allow this to be known to outside bodies, particularly the Trade Unions, with whom their colleagues were often conducting difficult and delicate negotiations in the name of the Government as a whole.

Wilson reiterated that, while all Ministers were free to express their views 'strongly' inside the Cabinet during discussions, once a decision was formally taken or a policy firmly adopted, then the convention of collective Ministerial responsibility required all Ministers 'to endorse it and defend it to any outside body on any occasion, whether private or public'. Lest anyone was still uncertain about who he was alluding to, he added that 'this proviso was especially important in the case of Ministers who were members of the National Executive Committee of the Labour Party, where any clash of loyalties was liable to be particularly embarrassing'.[26]

Given that he was obviously the prime target of Wilson's stricture, Callaghan felt compelled to defend himself, which he did by audaciously claiming that, as *In Place of Strife* was subject to ongoing discussions both in the Cabinet and with the trade unions, no final policy decision had yet been taken, so he could not be breaching collective responsibility. Not surprisingly, this defence failed to convince his Ministerial colleagues, and Callaghan was curtly reminded that *In Place of Strife* was a White Paper, which delineates a government's legislative intent or proposals, as opposed to a Green Paper which is wholly intended to be consultative. On this basis, Callaghan had clearly breached the principle of collective responsibility, but in order to justify *not* sacking Callaghan, Wilson concluded the meeting by declaring that he was now more interested in the future than the recent past, and that all Ministers were now expected to give their full and unequivocal public support to *In Place of Strife*.[27]

This did not prevent Callaghan, at another NEC meeting a few weeks later, from seeking to dissociate himself from the Government's industrial relations policy. At the next Cabinet meeting, a furious Crossman railed against Callaghan and shouted: 'Why don't you go? Get out' (Crossman, 1977: 480, diary entry for 8 May 1969; Castle, 1990: 329, diary entry for 8 May 1969).[28] Following this acrimonious Cabinet meeting, three (un-named) 'junior' Cabinet Ministers demanded that Wilson sack Callaghan, it being implied that if the Home Secretary was not dismissed then they might resign themselves.[29]

However, Wilson, like Castle, remained deeply concerned that Callaghan might prove even more troublesome on the backbenches, and instead dismissed the Home Secretary from the Cabinet's 'management committee' or Inner Cabinet (as it was variously known), a dismissal which had been urged by other members on this small body of senior Ministers, most notably Barbara Castle, Richard Crossman, Denis Healey and Roy Jenkins. This, it was agreed, was doubly advantageous, for while it avoided having an aggrieved Callaghan on the Labour backbenches, orchestrating PLP opposition to industrial relations legislation and *inter alia* boosting his own popularity among Labour MPs in advance of a possible leadership bid against Wilson, he would 'certainly be humiliated' by removal from the Inner Cabinet.[30]

Yet some of Wilson's critics believed that it was the Prime Minister himself whose credibility and authority were weakened by his repeated refusal to sack Callaghan from the Cabinet, particularly as Wilson variously led other Ministers, along with the press, to believe that he was going to impose his authority forcefully and unequivocally over the Industrial Relations Bill, and thereby challenge head-on his (and the bill's) political opponents. In refusing to sack Callaghan from the Cabinet, 'it was obvious that the smack of firm government had been at most a fairly mild slap' (Morgan, 1997: 337).

Having been informed of his dismissal from the Inner Cabinet during a bilateral meeting with Wilson, Callaghan returned to the Home Office and pondered whether he should resign as a Minister altogether, for this was certainly his initial inclination. However, this indecision only lasted fifteen minutes, for within the next fifteen minutes Callaghan had decided against resigning, 'because that would be playing into the hands of those members of the Cabinet who wanted me to go'. Even his senior Departmental officials were divided over his political position, with Brian Cubbon, his Private Secretary, 'very mournful' owing to a belief that Callaghan would have to resign, while the Permanent Secretary at the Home Office, Philip Allen, insisted that he 'should do nothing of the sort'.[31]

It has variously been suggested that much of the vehemence of Callaghan's opposition to *In Place of Strife* derived from his background as a senior trade union official, and especially his former role (noted above) as Assistant Secretary of the Inland Revenue Staff Association. This imbued him with an empathy for the trade unions which was not always shared by some of his more middle-class Ministerial colleagues. Although he disliked strikes – such industrial action jarring with his strong belief in dialogue and negotiation to achieve compromise or consensus; jaw-jaw always being preferable to war-war – he was adamant that the solution was not to impose statutory restrictions or penalties on the trade unions, but to leave the 'two sides of industry' to work together to improve industrial relations, which would, in turn, reduce the number of strikes. In this regard, his biographer notes, Callaghan 'took a comparatively buoyant view of the capacity of labour representatives to reach agreement, and to do so within established bargaining procedures rather than via the pressures of the law'. As such, '[h]e took the standard Labour view that the state should plan production, distribution and consumption, but remain essentially aloof from collective bargaining' (Morgan, 1997: 38).

Consequently, Callaghan was exasperated by the assumption of Ministers like Castle and Wilson that industrial relations could be improved by enacting legislation, a naïve faith which Callaghan attributed to a lack of understanding or experience of internal trade union politics. Indeed, following the abandonment of the Industrial Relations Bill, the General Secretary of the Inland Revenue Staff Federation wrote to Callaghan to thank him for his 'firm stand' in opposing the legislation, which clearly reflected both 'your Trade Union background, and your instinct and feeling for the situation'.[32]

Even the following year (1970), controversy over Callaghan's role lingered, to the extent that a book about *In Place of Strife* and its aftermath had to be slightly amended shortly prior to publication, following representations to the publisher by his lawyers. At Callaghan's behest, four specific objections were lodged against the draft of Peter Jenkins' (1970) *The Battle of Downing Street*. First, that on page 115 of the draft version, it was stated that '[d]ouble-dealing is not appreciated and Callaghan was suspected of it', an assertion which Callaghan viewed as 'innuendo'. Second, but directly following on from this, on page 116 of the draft, it was alleged that Callaghan 'seemed to be back-stabbing again', which his lawyers deemed libellous. Third, on page 82 of the draft of *The Battle of Downing Street*, the word 'malice' was used when describing Callaghan's personal qualities and characteristics – which the publisher (Charles Knight) was warned was 'offensive, and may even be libellous'. The fourth and final objection to the draft pertained to an assertion that no-one predicted the hostility which the ill-fated (1969) Industrial Relations Bill would provoke when it was first unveiled, a claim which Callaghan strongly disputed, having warned of the likely consequences of the proposed legislation from the outset.[33]

Although the publisher denied that the terms used to describe Callaghan and his role were actually libellous, it was agreed that the words 'malice', 'double-dealing' and 'back-stabbing' would be excised from the manuscript. Thus, the original sentence alleging that he was 'back-stabbing again' was changed to the rather more anodyne '[h]is conduct again seemed to be ambivalent'. Furthermore, the sentence which claimed that the publication of *In Place of Strife* had aroused 'few passionate feelings ... nobody predicted the extent of the trouble it would cause' was amended to include the qualification 'with few exceptions'.[34]

A short Industrial Relations Bill

Having emphatically rejected the call for an immediate and/or short industrial relations bill in January 1969, Castle completely changed her mind just three months later, partly because the trade unions, at this stage, were making vague pledges about being more pro-active in tackling unconstitutional strikes and inter-union disputes through existing TUC machinery, and urging the government to 'leave it to us' to sort out, but Castle and Wilson considered this to be wholly unsatisfactory, strongly suspecting that it would be a ruse for constant procrastination by union leaders.. The trade union leaders strongly opposed the Government's proposed strike ballots, conciliation pause and fines for trade unions or their members who refused to comply with an order to return to work, but were seemingly unwilling to suggest other credible or effective ways in which the underlying problems might be tackled.

Yet Castle's (and Wilson's) conversion to an immediate Bill was not solely attributable to the TUC's failure to develop adequate counter-measures, crucial though this was. By the spring of 1969, several other developments and factors were steering Castle and Wilson towards an interim Industrial Relations Bill. First, there was the relentless pressure from the 'the City' and the business community, concerned about the damaging impact of strikes on industrial output and investment. For many industrialists and financiers, the apparent irresponsibility of the trade unions and their members (or at least some of them) was deeply damaging to the British economy, and thus seriously weakened the confidence of the business community, on which investment, growth, jobs and tax revenues so heavily depended.

Second, public opinion was also favourably disposed towards industrial relations reform, as evinced by various polls conducted during this period. For example, a survey undertaken by the National Opinion Poll organisation in June 1969 found that 67 per cent of the public deemed that trade unions were in need of reform, with 61 per cent of Labour supporters and 72 per cent of Conservatives sharing this view. The same poll revealed that 57 per cent of respondents believed that the Government should reform the trade unions, while 38 per cent thought that the unions should reform themselves.[35]

These two factors were themselves influenced by a third, namely the prominence given by the press to various industrial disputes during the latter half of 1968 and early 1969, which created something of a moral panic about irresponsible trade unions and left-wing shop stewards deliberately fomenting industrial unrest to destabilise, and ultimately destroy, capitalism. Thus did Castle claim that 'I have become increasingly aware of the need for early action to improve industrial relations, and I am sure the public expects the Government to act now'.[36]

Fourth, but following directly on from these three factors, there were the Conservative Party's own proposals for radical reform of industrial relations, as enshrined in the policy document *Fair Deal at Work*. Not only were these likely to prove popular to sections of the public who were sometimes seriously inconvenienced by strikes, they were also likely to prove attractive to some workers themselves, especially those whose employment and earnings were disrupted by industrial stoppages with which they were neither directly concerned nor involved, and which they neither supported nor approved of. This scenario added to the pressure which was mounting on the Labour Government to take immediate action to tackle unofficial and unconstitutional strikes, and thereby restore greater order and stability to industrial relations.

The fifth and final factor which prompted the decision to introduce an interim Industrial Relations Bill was the recognition that many Labour MPs were opposed to legislation which would include 'penal clauses', as discussed in chapter 5. While such antipathy was expected from some quarters of the Party, it seemed that Castle and Wilson had underestimated the scale and strength of the hostility. Furthermore, they also became concerned that continued delay in enacting legislation would enable this intra-Party opposition to grow and become more organised – just as Crossman and Jenkins had warned back in January.

For all these reasons, Castle and Wilson resolved to adopt a two-stage approach, with a short interim bill to be introduced before the summer and more comprehensive industrial relations legislation to follow in the 1969–70 Parliamentary session. It was envisaged that the latter would provide Castle and Wilson with more time in which to persuade the trade unions to accept the Government's reforms, and assuage their concerns both about punitive measures in particular, and State intervention in collective *laissez-faire* in general. Furthermore, it was hoped that if comprehensive industrial legislation could be enacted during the next Parliamentary session, Labour could neutralise the issue of strikes and 'irresponsible' trade union behaviour in the run-up to the next (1970) general election, and in so doing win plaudits from voters for successfully tackling industrial disruption. If so, then Labour's chances of being re-elected might be greatly enhanced, especially if successful industrial relations legislation weakened the Conservatives' case for the package of reforms canvassed in *Fair Deal at Work*. Indeed, Labour could claim (as it was subsequently to do in 1974) that it was the only Party which could work constructively with the trade unions and foster industrial partnership, whereas the return of a Conservative government would almost inevitably result in a resurgence of industrial conflict, as the latter embarked upon class-war against trade unions and workers.

Thus did mid-April 1969 herald the announcement of an interim Industrial Relations Bill, although this declaration was actually made by Jenkins during his (15 April) Budget speech, not by Castle. This draft of this Bill contained just six measures, namely:[37]

1. Workers to have a statutory right to belong to trade unions.
2. Workers temporarily laid off, as a consequence of a trade dispute in which they were not directly involved, to be entitled to claim unemployment benefit.
3. The Secretary of State to be vested with the discretionary power to order, on the recommendation of the CIR, an employer to recognise a trade union for the purposes of collective bargaining.
4. The Secretary of State to be vested with the discretionary power to impose a conciliation pause, for a maximum of twenty-eight days, on serious unconstitutional strikes.
5. The Secretary of State to be vested with the discretionary power to order a trade union to hold a secret ballot prior to a strike which was likely to pose a serious threat to the economy or public interest.
6. An Industrial Board to be established which would be empowered to impose fines against those (employers or employees) adjudged to have defied an order to invoke a conciliation pause or conduct a strike ballot.

However, following discussions in the Cabinet's industrial relations committee, Castle readily agreed to a proposal from Crosland that the clause on strike ballots should be replaced by one on tackling inter-union disputes. She subsequently confessed that she would have preferred to have omitted the proposal on strike ballots months before, but had retained it at Wilson's behest (Castle, 1990: 321, diary entry for 14 April 1969). Now, though, the overall view in the Cabinet was that its omission might make the interim Industrial Relations Bill slightly more palatable to moderate trade unionists.

There was a suggestion from some of the Cabinet's opponents of the Bill – support for it was certainly not unanimous – that if any clause was to be dropped in order to render it less objectionable to the trade unions (and the PLP itself), it should be that pertaining to the conciliation pause, because this was the real focus of TUC hostility, particularly the provision for fines and attachment-of-earnings orders. However, the prevailing view in the Cabinet was that, as unconstitutional strikes were such a major problem, retaining this clause was absolutely vital.[38]

Although the bill received formal Cabinet approval, the degree of support is disputed by some of the key participants. Wilson, for example, recalled that this decision 'went through quietly' (Wilson, 1971: 642), but Crossman claimed that the interim bill actually prompted 'a good deal of complaint, particularly (and predictably) from James Callaghan and Richard Marsh, while the previously ambivalent Tony Crosland was unhappy at the sudden shift from the planned period of consultation with the trade unions, in lieu of an industrial relations Bill in the autumn, to imminent legislation' (Crossman, 1977: 438, diary entry for 14 April 1969). Meanwhile, Castle recalled that Callaghan had remained uncharacteristically quiet when the interim bill was announced, a silence which she attributed to his 'obviously looking for excuses not to make a resignation issue out of it' (Castle, 1990: 321, diary entry for 14 April 1969).

It had been intended that this interim bill would be introduced (given its First Reading in the House of Commons) on 22 May, but a fortnight before this date Castle proposed – and Wilson readily agreed – that this should be postponed until after the TUC's special conference in Croydon on 5 June, at which the trade union leaders' counter-proposals would be voted upon by union delegates.[39]

Those Ministers supportive of the interim Industrial Relations Bill had also agreed that it should be announced by the Chancellor in his April Budget speech, with Castle to provide the details in the House of Commons the following day. This was because it was considered 'clearly desirable that the Government's intentions about future prices and incomes policy and industrial relations should be announced together', although Jenkins had insisted that 'it was not intended that they should form a package.'[40] Yet in spite of this insistence, it was difficult *not* to interpret them as inextricably linked; an Industrial Relations Bill *instead of* continuation of a statutory incomes policy. The latter had also been bitterly opposed by the trade unions, many of which resented this interference in free collective bargaining, and what amounted to State determination of wages. By making these two policy announcements together, the message seemed to be that imminent discontinuation of the statutory prices and incomes legislation was a *quid pro quo* for the enactment of a short Industrial Relations Bill; 'a sweetener' is how Jenkins' biographer describes it (Campbell, 2014: 345). Indeed, in spite of insisting that the two policies were not part of a package, Jenkins considered this to be 'a good bargain' – industrial relations legislation instead of a statutory incomes policy – although he subsequently judged this trade-off to have been a mistake (Jenkins, 1991: 287).

This perspective was lent further credence by Denis Healey's recollection that, in January 1969, 'Harold told me, when we were lunching alone in his ultimate sanctuary, the little flat at the top of No. 10 [Downing

Street], that he had decided on union reform because he had given up hope of making his incomes policy work' (Healey, 1990: 341). Similarly, Callaghan recalled that 'Barbara and the P.M. saw the strike legislation clearly as an alternative to Incomes legislation', as well as a source of electoral popularity.[41]

A further insight into Wilson's stance was provided by Marcia Williams, his Personal/Political Secretary, who recalled that the Prime Minister was concerned that the political initiative would be seized by the Conservative Opposition. The Conservatives were opposed to governmental incomes policies (believing that 'the market' should determine wages), but were becoming increasingly vocal in canvassing industrial relations legislation (Williams, 1972: 206–7). Wilson was concerned that while the Labour Government was unlikely to gain much political popularity and electoral support by continuously holding down wages – indeed, some trade unionists might be lured by the Conservatives' promise of a return to free collective bargaining (as subsequently proved to be the case in the 1979 general election) – it certainly risked ceding kudos and credibility to the Conservatives if it failed to tackle the industrial disruption and public inconvenience caused by strikes, especially unofficial and/or unconstitutional stoppages. As such, incomes policies were tacitly traded for industrial relations legislation, even though some Ministers and mandarins continued to believe that the two would, or should, be pursued in tandem.

This was certainly the conviction of one of Wilson's economic advisers, who warned that 'while a policy to improve industrial relations may be complementary to an incomes policy, it *cannot* be a *substitute* for it'. Yet he conceded that pursuing both policies simultaneously was 'asking the unions to give up a lot', and as such, it might be necessary to pursue 'equal restraint on non-wage earners via an excess dividend tax and improved price surveillance'.[42] Such additional measures would doubtless have appealed to the left, which often resented the premise underpinning incomes policies, namely that it was the 'excessive' wage increases secured by workers which were inflationary and economically ruinous, never the very much higher salaries paid to industrialists and financiers, or the dividends paid to investors and shareholders.

Meanwhile, cognizant that the interim Bill was likely to exacerbate tensions in the PLP, Wilson opted to appoint a new Chief Whip. Since July 1966, Labour's Chief Whip had been the affable John Silkin, but some Labour MPs resented his somewhat liberal regime, which they deemed at least partly responsible for an increase in backbench rebellions and cross-voting (in which some Labour MPs voted against their Government in Parliamentary divisions); Silkin was viewed by some as too tolerant of such disloyalty, which was, in turn, deemed damaging both to the morale of more loyal backbenchers, and to the Party's public image; voters are much less inclined to vote for clearly divided parties. Wilson himself subsequently recalled the 'difficulties within the party, different in origin from, but not entirely unconnected with, the battles over the [Industrial Relations] Bill. Discipline was getting more lax in the PLP' (Wilson, 1971: 644).

He therefore replaced Silkin with the more pugnacious Bob Mellish, who 'could not abide ... those "bleedin' bastards" who voted against the party either without warning him or for some kind of perceived self-advantage within the party' (Dalyell, 1998). Thus, when he addressed the weekly meeting of the PLP for the first time as Chief Whip, Mellish warned that 'if we were defeated on the Industrial Relations Bill, we should have no alternative but to go to the country [call a general election]'.[43]

Castle, though, was adamant that the problems of backbench dissent and disunity in the PLP could not be blamed on Silkin's role as Chief Whip; the problem went much deeper. As such, she argued that '[a]s long as they [Labour MPs] feel the Government has failed, they are in no mood to accept our authority, and I can't blame them'. She thus suggested that the Cabinet's first priority should be 'an inner strategy for success – then we can talk about loyalty', although what such a 'strategy' would consist of was not explained (Castle, 1990: 324, diary entry for 29 April 1969). As such, Wilson's appointment of Mellish, and the manner in which he made the appointment, infuriated Castle, as we will note shortly.

The Wilson–Castle axis

Clearly, Harold Wilson and Barbara Castle were the two main drivers of the proposed industrial relations legislation, and displayed a determination to persevere right until the bitter end, to the extent that they acknowledged the grievous damage that might be caused to their political careers. Indeed, once they had embarked on the pursuit of industrial relations legislation based on *In Place of Strife*, they felt compelled to continue, regardless of the mounting opposition they encountered, particularly in the latter stages. For example, in the later part of May 1969, Castle was 'astonished' to be told by Wilson 'that he didn't see how we could get a settlement with the TUC, but he and I were now too committed to back down' (Castle, 1990: 334, diary entry for 21 May 1969).

Yet in some respects Wilson and Castle also found themselves in a no-win situation, because if they had abandoned *In Place of Strife* they would have been derided by their critics for cowardice and pusillanimity, and for allowing the trade unions to veto Government policies: Labour would have been depicted as totally subservient to their trade union paymasters. However, in resolving to persevere in the face of widespread and growing opposition, Wilson and Castle were equally vulnerable to allegations of arrogance and obstinacy, and perhaps defective political judgement too, the latter constituting a charge which Crossman subsequently levelled against Wilson, as we will note towards the end of chapter 7.

While Wilson and Castle presented a public image of equal determination to pursue industrial relations legislation, there were assumptions among some Ministerial colleagues and trade union leaders that one of them was more 'hawkish' than the other; but while some thought that Wilson was the more hard-line of the two, others viewed Castle as the one least willing to compromise. For example, when Wilson arranged a Chequers' weekend at the very beginning of June (discussed in chapter 7), to conduct discussions over dinner with the three most important TUC leaders, Vic Feather, Jack Jones and Hugh Scanlon, their assumption had been that Castle would not be present. They were thus deeply disappointed when she appeared, having flown back from a holiday in Italy especially to attend, for they had assumed that if they could talk to Wilson alone, he would be more amenable to the trade unions' perspective, and perhaps more willing to compromise. As Jones recalled, at the time 'we all thought ... that Barbara had made the issue her personal property, and Wilson was the less hard of the two' (Jones, 1986: 204).

Yet Castle (1993: 418) sometimes suggested that Wilson was 'far more hawkish than I was'. For example, as noted earlier in this chapter, it was the Prime Minister who had insisted on pre-strike ballots being included in the White Paper, whereas Castle would willingly have omitted this proposal. Also, as we note in chapter 7, when, at a special conference in early June 1969, the TUC endorsed counter-proposals for tackling unconstitutional strikes, it was Wilson who instantly dismissed them as inadequate, much to Castle's chagrin; she thought they ought to have been given more careful consideration, and that Wilson had been too hasty in his rejection of them. Indeed, she thought that the TUC's counter-proposals 'gave us an opportunity, if we had wanted it, to suspend the legislation in order to see what the TUC could do', but this opportunity had been spurned by Wilson: 'Harold seems very firm' (Castle, 1990: 339, diary entry for 6 June 1969).

Wilson was acutely aware of these contrasting perceptions, but emphatically rejected the assumption that one of the Bill's champions was more hard-line than the other. Consequently, when Vic Feather claimed, following a meeting between Wilson, Castle and the TUC's General Council (one of many during May and June 1969 – see chapter 7), that the Prime Minister was widely viewed to have been 'more flexible than Barbara' – the latter having 'appeared a little rigid in the form of her questions' – Wilson rejected this interpretation, and its implication that she was the obstacle to a compromise agreement. He suggested that, while 'my manner might have been more conciliatory', or perhaps 'more urbane', there should be no doubt in anyone's minds that 'Barbara and I are in total agreement about what was necessary'.[44] Still, Feather continued to view Castle as the more intransigent of the two, an interpretation he conveyed to James Callaghan towards the middle of June, when the TUC's Acting General Secretary and the Home Secretary sat together at a dinner for Lancashire miners. Callaghan recalled that 'for two hours, [Feather] gave me a continuing denunciation of B. C. He was much less sulphurous about H. W. His language was frankly unprintable.'[45] However, Feather's jaundiced view of Castle might partly have been attributable to the sexism with which many trade unionists were afflicted; a macho, male-dominated, trade union leadership resenting a woman telling them how they should conduct their industrial affairs.

Wilson and Castle's own relationship during this episode was itself intriguing. At times, they seemed close to the point of flirtation, as indicated by the April 14 Cabinet meeting which agreed to introduce the 'short' Industrial Relations Bill. At one point in proceedings, Wilson discreetly passed a note to Castle which enquired 'What are you doing tonight, baby?' to which she replied 'Meeting with my officials to start drafting a speech, daddy!' Wilson then returned the note with the words: 'Don't be a spoilsport. I was wondering whether you'd like to come and see my etchings – with Vic Feather?' signed 'D' [for Daddy].[46]

Yet their political relationship and personal friendship was strained at times during the ill-fated pursuit of the interim Industrial Relations Bill, and on at least two occasions Castle was aggrieved at Wilson's unilateral actions. The first followed the appointment of Mellish as Chief Whip, for although Silkin's more liberal management of the Party would almost certainly have made it more difficult to secure the Parliamentary passage of industrial relations legislation, Castle was adamant that she did not want the bill forced through the House of Commons in a heavy-handed manner; she wanted to secure the support of Labour MPs through exhortation and persuasion. Consequently, when Castle heard that, in spite of her robust defence of Silkin, Wilson had replaced him with the pugnacious Mellish, she was furious: 'anger ... rose in me slowly, coldly and massively'. Indeed, so great was her fury that she acknowledged 'how near I had come to resignation' (Castle, 1990: 324, 325, diary entry for 29 April 1969).

She was furious for two reasons. First, she had met Wilson during the morning of the day on which Mellish's appointment was announced, but he had not mentioned this imminent change to her. Second, she feared that Mellish would be too heavy-handed in his approach to managing recalcitrant Labour backbenchers, and thus alienate them even more. This would exacerbate the problem of securing sufficient support among Labour MPs to pass the Industrial Relations Bill.

Upon hearing of Mellish's appointment, Castle penned an angry letter to Wilson, berating him for calling upon a colleague 'to pilot the most controversial Bill of our whole Parliament through the House, and then switch Parliamentary pilots in the middle of it' without informing the Minister responsible for that legislation. She claimed that this was 'the "manner of government" of which others have complained'. Castle was so incandescent that she warned that 'faith can never be the same again', adding that 'if the strategy is to railroad my Bill through Parliament on a ... regime of reactionary discipline, I will have no part of it.'[47] She reiterated this stance in a speech in Newcastle on 4 May, insisting that 'I would reject any attempt to railroad this Bill through [Parliament] by threats of expulsion, or the clobbering of the Left'. Castle was adamant that 'I don't want to silence the critics, I want to win the argument' (quoted in Heffer, 1973: 123).

The second occasion on which Castle was angry with Wilson, as just noted (and discussed further in chapter 7), was when he summarily rejected the TUC's early June counter-proposals for tackling unconstitutional strikes, a decision he took while she was on holiday off the Italian coast. Castle subsequently recalled that, if she had been consulted, 'I would certainly have advised him against this' outright rejection of the TUC's stance (Castle, 1993: 423).

Yet Castle was also occasionally perturbed by Wilson's seemingly over-relaxed, almost complacent, stance when meeting with Vic Feather, who was deemed more pragmatic than Jones and Scanlon, and so assumed to be more probably amenable to compromise. Thus, for example, when Wilson and Castle met Feather following the Cabinet's decision to introduce an interim Industrial Relations Bill, Castle recalled that '[o]nce again, I felt uneasy at Harold's cosy way of smoothing over all the issues ... sipping brandy as if the mateyness would solve everything' (Castle, 1990: 321, diary entry for 14 April 1969).

Cabinet support ebbs away

From mid-April to mid-June, when Castle and Wilson were involved in increasingly fraught and seemingly interminable talks with the TUC leadership in an attempt at resolving the issue (see chapter 7), some Cabinet Ministers who had hitherto supported *In Place of Strife* and/or the interim Industrial Relations Bill began to harbour doubts about whether it was worth persevering. During this two-month period, a combination of exasperation and *ennui* over the whole issue developed in the Cabinet, to the extent that even some senior Ministers who had previously been keen proponents of industrial relations legislation now judged it to have dragged on for far too long, allowing erstwhile enthusiasm and momentum to dissipate, and intra-Party opposition to become too widely mobilised and too deeply entrenched – just as some of them had originally warned.

The most notable of these was Roy Jenkins, who previously, when *In Place of Strife* had been unveiled to the Cabinet back in January, had urged immediate legislation, and had subsequently announced the 'interim' Bill in his mid-April Budget speech. Yet by the middle of May 1969, even he became despondent – in the wonderful words of Peter Jenkins (no relation), the Chancellor 'slid elegantly onto the fence' (Jenkins, 1970: 154) – lamenting that 'the moment when we could have won the *In Place of Strife* Battle was past'. As he had warned, 'dilatory tactics had predictably produced a build-up of opposition which meant that there was more chance of the Government breaking-up on the issue than of getting the legislation through'. Given the extent to which '[d]elay had allowed too great a wave of desertions to build up … I had lost my faith in the ability of the Government to put the legislation through' (Jenkins, 1991: 290, 289), so much so that by mid-June, he confessed to Crossman that 'I really believe in the policy less and less' (Crossman, 1977: 526, diary entry for 18 June 1969).

Jenkins' growing disillusionment on this issue was, by early June, shared both by Denis Healey and Anthony Crosland. Healey now confessed that if he had foreseen the damaging impact which the interim Industrial Relations Bill would have on morale in the PLP, he 'would not, on balance' have supported it.[48] Crosland, meanwhile, wrote to Wilson urging that the conciliation pause should be withdrawn from the imminent Bill, and only be re-introduced in subsequent industrial relations legislation if the TUC's own proposals for tackling unconstitutional strikes proved ineffective. In view of how far the TUC had moved in recent weeks, Crosland confessed that he could not 'conceive that any marginal theoretical advantages which our proposals may have over the TUC's proposals can outweigh the likely effect on PLP morale, on public opinion of a deeply disunited Party'.[49]

In effect, Castle and Wilson were now losing the support of the Chancellor of the Exchequer and the Defence Secretary – two of the most senior and prestigious posts and personnel in the Cabinet – as well as the erstwhile support of the former Education Secretary. Jenkins, Healey and Crosland were most definitely not allies of Callaghan, but their shifting stance did mean that the Bill increasingly lacked support among Cabinet 'heavyweights', and thereby left Castle and Wilson ever more isolated among their senior Ministerial colleagues.

Furthermore, it is inconceivable that this scenario would have remained a secret, given that the Cabinet was, in Wilson's words, 'in a leaky mood'.[50] This leakiness – with Callaghan suspected of being the main source of leaks – would have meant that the other opponents of *In Place of Strife* and the interim Industrial Relations Bill, namely Labour's trade union-sponsored MPs, Tribune Group MPs and, of course, the TUC itself, would be aware of the Cabinet's changing mood. Indeed, the TUC 'decided they had the interior lines of communication, dug in and waited for the investing forces to disintegrate' (Jenkins, 1991: 289), which they duly did.

It should also be noted that, alongside the dwindling support in the Cabinet and the ever-increasing opposition within the PLP, some junior Ministers were also becoming deeply concerned at Wilson's and Castle's apparent intransigence in the face of the TUC's counter-proposals. As junior Ministers do not normally attend meetings of the Cabinet (although they do serve on Cabinet committees), they lacked a formal channel through which to convey their views. Senior Ministers had the Cabinet, left-wing MPs had the Tribune Group, trade-union sponsored MPs had the Party's backbench Trade Union Group and Labour backbenchers generally had the weekly meetings of the PLP, but there was no designated forum within which junior Ministers could routinely discuss matters and convey their views.

Thus it was that one junior Minister, David Ennals, who served under first James Callaghan and then Richard Crossman during 1967–9, wrote to Harold Wilson, congratulating him and Castle 'for forcing the TUC to accept its responsibilities ... a remarkable achievement', but then argued that 'the TUC should now be given the chance to show whether their plans will work'. If the Cabinet opted to proceed with the penal clauses now, then it would almost certainly 'undo all that has been achieved in recent months'. Moreover, he feared that if the Cabinet decided to proceed regardless, then the effect on the Labour Party might well prove 'catastrophic', as it became embroiled in 'a bitter conflict with the trade union movement'. Not only would this be deeply damaging in itself, it would also make it 'very difficult to mount an effective election campaign, let alone win it. I fear we would be decimated.'[51]

Meanwhile, another junior Minister, David Owen, who supported the proposed industrial relations legislation in principle, was conceding that by this time the mood in the PLP was 'sulphurous', and acknowledging that many Labour MPs in marginal seats were becoming increasingly anxious (Owen, 1992: 156).

Further concern from the ranks of the Government's junior Ministers was expressed by Joan Lestor. She readily acknowledged that there was much in Castle's legislative proposals which would rightly strengthen the trade unions and workers' rights, but Lestor expressed deep concern that the focus on the penal clauses was being interpreted, by many in the labour movement, as 'another bash at the workers'. Even though this was clearly not the intention, she urged Castle to exclude 'the offensive parts' from the interim bill, adding that 'I cannot understand ... why the row this has caused was not anticipated'. Lestor insisted that although the growing opposition to the interim Industrial Bill, fuelled by the ostensible attractiveness of the TUC's counter-proposals in *Programme for Action*, was not personally directed towards Castle, 'the sheer misery and dismay within the rank-and-file, here and in the country, cannot be overestimated.'[52]

During this fateful period, even Castle's PPS, Harold Walker, lamented the situation in which the Government had found itself, apparently confiding to Callaghan that Castle 'had stopped listening to him', and adding that 'the TUC document carried us on a great deal further, and that she should have accepted it.'[53]

Against this background of dwindling support and dire warnings of splits, Castle deemed 17 June 1969 to have been the 'most traumatic day of my political life'. It commenced with another Cabinet committee on this unrelentingly vexatious issue. At this meeting, it became evident that '[a]ny hope that the TUC's intransigence would have hardened the attitude of the inner Cabinet soon disappeared'. On the contrary, this meeting heard both Richard Crossman and the Chief Whip add their voices to those of other Ministers urging Wilson and Castle to compromise with the TUC, rather than pushing the labour movement to breaking-point. Crossman argued that Wilson and Castle had, by means of which he had not always approved, succeeded 'in dragging the T.U.C. forward to an astonishing degree on the disciplining of their member unions', but having achieved this much, he had been 'desperately disappointed' at their instant rejection of the TUC's counter-proposals, as endorsed at the Croydon conference. Crossman believed that these should have been welcomed, and warned of the damage to Party morale and support which would ensue if Wilson and Castle were determined to 'pick a quarrel with the T.U.C.', rather than building on the progress already achieved by doing everything practicably possible 'to reach agreement with the T.U.C.', which was certainly what the Labour Party was expecting them to do. The allusion to 'the damage to Party ... support' reflected a growing concern among some Ministers that if it appeared, publicly, that the Government was being obstinate and intransigent in its stance towards the TUC's Croydon counter-proposals, then sympathy or support might actually shift towards the trade unions, particularly among Labour's own supporters. When Wilson suggested that the Cabinet's tough stance was proving popular in the country, Crossman demurred, adding that in his Coventry constituency the mood against the Government's stance was such that he believed that he would lose his seat at the next election 'if the Government pressed ahead with its proposals without the consent of the TUC.'[54] A stance which might previously have been electorally popular risked becoming an electoral liability if persevered with.

Although its significance was not recognised at the time, Crossman suggested a way out of the *impasse* that had been reached, in which Wilson and Castle were insisting on re-writing one of the TUC's Rules *vis-à-vis* unconstitutional strikes and the TUC was raising practical and procedural objections to a rule-change and instead offering to issue a statement of clarification to affiliated unions on how they should deal with such strikes (see chapter 7). In this context, Crossman proposed that a circular be issued by the TUC which included a statement written by Wilson and Castle themselves: the words insisted upon by the two Labour Ministers could be issued in the manner insisted upon by the TUC. However, Castle immediately rejected this suggestion, arguing that the TUC would view this as evidence 'that they had got the Government on the run' and, as such, she deemed it essential to maintain a 'firm line' with the TUC.[55]

With regard to the unyielding opposition of the trade unions, Castle alleged that the TUC was being 'immensely influenced by the attitude of the PLP, and by Mr. Houghton's one-man campaign which had greatly weakened the Government's negotiating position', to which Wilson added that 'Houghton seemed to be working hand-and-glove [sic] with a member of the Cabinet', clearly alluding to Callaghan. In response, Crossman interjected to suggest that the opposition to the proposed industrial relations legislation was much more than a one-man campaign. Nonetheless, Wilson seemed determined to persevere, arguing that the logic of the 'soft centre approach' which his critics were promoting 'was that Government should always give in against pressures from the Party and unions. This was in effect saying that the TUC should govern', to which he insisted that 'it was not right that a Labour Government should be dictated to by those Labour Members who take their orders from the Trade Union movement'.[56]

The two meetings of the full Cabinet which followed the industrial relations committee reaffirmed the rapidly diminishing support for Wilson's and Castle's stance, even among some Ministers who had previously been highly supportive. The most notable addition to this growing list of recanting Cabinet Ministers was Peter Shore, who had been a keen proponent of industrial relations legislation at the Sunningdale weekend seven months earlier. Now, though, Shore argued – with 'an intensity of passion I have never seen from him before' (Castle, 1990: 342–3, diary entry for 17 June 1969) – against persevering with the Industrial Relations Bill and the penal clauses. He was adamant that, as the TUC had moved so far towards the Government in the last fortnight, it would be reckless to spurn their pledge of issuing a circular to affiliated unions (instead of amending Rule 11, as Wilson and Castle were demanding) stipulating how union leaders should respond to unconstitutional strikes.

The TUC was, in effect, offering the Government what it wanted, namely guidelines to be adopted by the unions to curb unconstitutional strikes, but in a different format. Shore was convinced that the difference between their positions was not worth continuing to fight over, and that Wilson and Castle should accept the TUC's reasonable offer. To reiterate his point, Shore asked Castle what she and Wilson really wanted to achieve:

a reduction in the incidence of unconstitutional strikes, or 'a victory over the TUC?'[57] Shore's 'most powerful speech' was deemed, by Callaghan, to have been especially significant, partly because he had previously been actively involved in developing the case for industrial relations legislation at Sunningdale, and partly because he was viewed as a 'protégé' of Wilson: 'coming at this stage, the effect was much greater than coming from known opponents'.[58]

These changes of mind among senior Ministers, 'who seemed to be gathering confidence from each other in opposition',[59] meant that by the end of these two 17 June Cabinet meetings, it was 'pretty clear that there was an overwhelming majority against the penal clauses', and as a consequence, 'Harold and Barbara were up against it' (Benn, 1988: 186, diary entry for 17 June 1969). It was not simply the number of Cabinet Ministers who now opposed proceeding with the interim Industrial Relations Bill which was politically damaging, nor the fact that some of those now opposing it had hitherto been its most enthusiastic supporters (an understandable source of deep dismay, and doubtless a sense of betrayal, for Wilson and Castle), but their seniority in the Ministerial hierarchy.

In other words, Cabinet 'opinion' can have a qualitative, as well as a quantitative, dimension to it; not only *how many* Ministers support or oppose a policy, but *who* those Ministers are in terms of seniority and/or the prestige and status of their Ministerial post. By mid-June, Wilson and Castle had effectively lost the support of the Chancellor (the second most senior post in a government), the Education Secretary, the Secretary of State for Economic Affairs, and the Secretary of State for Defence, while the Home Secretary, of course, had opposed the proposed industrial relations legislation from the outset.

In fact, at these 17 June Cabinet meetings, Callaghan proved remarkably restrained and relatively emollient, for in observing other senior Ministers withdrawing their support for the interim Industrial Relations Bill, and thereby leaving Wilson and Castle isolated, the Home Secretary recalled that 'without modifying my previous stand on substance, I began to be much less sharp in the way in which I phrased it; more in tones of appeal than demand'.[60]

Wilson's (and occasionally Castle's) allusions to resignation

Wilson and Castle were naturally bitterly disappointed that much of the Cabinet now seemed to have accepted that the TUC's General Council had conceded as far could realistically be expected, and were thus urging that the interim Industrial Relations Bill be abandoned. Their refusal to do this led many Cabinet Ministers to view Wilson and Castle as the intransigents who were being unduly obstinate, rather than the TUC, with the Prime Minister suspected of engaging in brinkmanship *vis-à-vis* his Cabinet and Parliamentary colleagues. This suspicion was fuelled by Wilson's various hints, and occasional direct threats, that he would resign if he could not secure support from his colleagues for his stance, namely that the 'penal clauses' would only be abandoned if the TUC introduced equally robust measures for tackling unconstitutional strikes, and that such measures should be enshrined in a re-writing of Rule 11 of the TUC's Congress.

For example, two days after Jenkins had announced the interim Industrial Relations Bill in his Budget speech, Wilson had warned a weekly meeting of the PLP that it was:

> [a]n essential Bill. Essential to our economic recovery. Essential to the balance of payments. Essential to full employment. It is an essential component of ensuring the economic success of the Government … That is why I have to tell you that the passage of this Bill is essential to its continuance in Office. There can be no going back on that.[61]

The phrase 'essential to its continuance in Office' strongly implied that Wilson was making this an issue of confidence in the Government, the constitutional convention being that defeat in a Parliamentary vote on such an issue would precipitate a general election.

A month later, Wilson informed Castle that he intended to make the enactment of the Industrial Relations Bill 'an issue of confidence in *him* and, if we were defeated, he would stand down from the leadership', although Castle was nonetheless 'delighted that he was no longer talking about threatening to force a General Election' in the event of such a defeat (Castle, 1990: 334, diary entry for 21 May 1969, emphasis in original).

Wilson's threats to resign continued right up to until the moment he secured a face-saving agreement with the TUC, which was deemed sufficient to enable him and Castle to abandon the Industrial Relations Bill. For example, on the day before an agreement was finally reached, Castle observed that Wilson 'is clearly determined to resign on this if necessary, but will go down fighting' (Castle, 1990: 343, diary entry for 17 June 1969). Indeed, Benn claims that in the 17 June Cabinet meetings, when it became clear that Cabinet support for proceeding with the Bill had dissipated, 'Harold threatened to resign several times, and said … they would have to look for a new Leader'. Yet few Cabinet Ministers took Wilson's threats seriously: 'His bluff was called, and he just looked weak and petty … a small man … without leadership qualities' (Benn, 1988: 187, diary entry for 17 June 1969).

Castle herself occasionally threatened to resign alongside Wilson if they were defeated over *In Place of Strife* and the concomitant industrial relations legislation. Alluding to opposition from within the Cabinet, Castle subsequently recalled that '[f]aced with such open war, Harold and I were now deep in a conspiracy. Whatever others did, we were not prepared to budge ... we would resign' (Castle, 1993: 420). On another occasion, when addressing a hostile meeting of the PLP following the announcement of the interim Industrial Relations Bill, Castle warned that '[y]ou have a right to say you will not sustain the Government. OK, but then you must find yourself a new Government' (Castle, 1990: 328, diary entry for 7 May 1969).

Castle also informed Crossman that 'she and Harold and Roy [Jenkins] ... must be prepared to resign if the [Interim Industrial Relations] Bill was so emasculated that their position was undermined', although Crossman warned that adopting such a stance might actually be exploited by those who wanted Callaghan to replace Wilson; her and Wilson's opponents in the Cabinet and PLP would have a direct interest in siding with the TUC to defeat the proposed bill, in order to engineer this threatened resignation (Crossman, 1977: 505, diary entry for 23 May to 6 June 1969).

On other occasions, while not directly alluding to resignation, Castle nonetheless acknowledged that her pursuit of industrial relations legislation 'may be the political end of me with our own people. I'm taking a terrific gamble ... My only comfort is that I am proposing something I believe in', although this did not prevent her from being 'swept with doubt from time to time as to whether I have entirely misjudged reaction. If I have, I shall have mortally damaged my political career ... but politically my conscience is clear' (Castle 1990, 296, diary entry for 7 January 1969; 299, diary entry for 15 January 1969). Her stance subsequently prompted a sharp rebuke from Callaghan, who tartly suggested that 'if she wanted to commit suicide, she was entitled to do so ... there was no reason why we should all have to commit suicide with her'.[62] Meanwhile, Crossman suggested to her that 'brinkmanship without any wisdom can bring you to catastrophe' (Crossman, 1977: 505, diary entry for 23 May to 6 June 1969).

Conclusion

When the draft of *In Place of Strife* was first presented to the Cabinet in early January 1969, outright opposition was confined to just a couple of Ministers, namely James Callaghan and Richard Marsh. The majority of Cabinet Ministers either fully supported the proposed legislative reform of industrial relations, or proffered qualified support due to reservations about specific proposals, most notably the 'penal clauses', and especially the 'conciliation pause' and associated penalties for defiance. Some of the 'qualified' Ministerial support was also offered on the basis that the draft White Paper would herald a lengthy period of consultation, during which time the contentious aspects of the proposed legislation would be moderated, or the trade unions would be persuaded to undertake their own reforms to tackle unconstitutional strikes, whereupon the 'penal clauses' could be excised from the ensuing industrial relations legislation.

However, subsequent developments served to weaken Cabinet support, to the extent that by mid-June, Harold Wilson and Barbara Castle were virtually isolated among their senior Ministerial colleagues, abandoned by some of those who had previously been the most ardent advocates of industrial relations reform, such as Chancellor Roy Jenkins and Peter Shore. Crucially, opposition emanated from Ministers on different 'wings' of the Labour party and, as such, transcended orthodox left-right ideological divisions and positions.

Some previously supportive Cabinet Ministers were surprised at the scale of opposition in the PLP, which was eventually so pronounced that both the chair of the PLP, Douglas Houghton, and the Government's new Chief Whip, Bob Mellish, warned that the imminent Industrial Relations Bill would fail to muster sufficient Parliamentary support; the Government would suffer a humiliating defeat on the floor of the House of Commons if it persevered with the legislation.

In the context of such widespread opposition among their backbench colleagues, many Cabinet Ministers also became convinced that Castle and Wilson should accept the counter-proposals for tackling unconstitutional strikes advanced by the TUC, as strongly endorsed at the latter's special conference in Croydon on 5 June 1969 (discussed in chapter 7). Given that Wilson and Castle had repeatedly urged the TUC to offer such alternative measures in return for the Cabinet abandoning or suspending the 'penal clauses', the subsequent claim by the Prime Minister and Secretary of State that the TUC's offer was not strong enough irked many senior Ministerial colleagues. Some previously supportive Cabinet Ministers now feared that sheer bloody-mindedness or brinkmanship by Wilson and Castle were affecting their political judgement, and jeopardising a credible solution which could prevent a fatal split, not only between the Labour Party and the trade unions, but within the Labour Party itself. In effect, some senior Ministers decided that the Government should take the TUC at its word; if it then failed to deliver, the Government would have a bona fide case for re-introducing legislation to tackle unconstitutional strikes in the next Parliamentary session, and the trade unions could have no complaints.

Faced with this fatal loss of Cabinet support, coupled with the parallel opposition of much of the PLP to the proposed Industrial Relations Bill (particularly the 'penal clauses'), Wilson and Castle eventually felt compelled to accept the TUC's counter-proposals, in the guise of a 'solemn and binding' agreement jointly signed by the TUC and the Government. However, any joy or relief which might have been expected when this was reported to the Cabinet was obviated by the feelings of mutual recrimination, as Castle and Wilson viewed many of their senior Ministerial colleagues as cowards, while these colleagues, in turn, bitterly resented the manner in which Wilson and Castle had risked splitting the labour movement, and pushing Ministerial loyalty and patience to the absolute limit, rather than accepting a deal with the TUC earlier.

Notes

1. NA CAB 129/139, C (68) 131, Secretary of State for Employment and Productivity, 'A Policy for Industrial Relations: Draft White Paper', 30 December 1968; NA CAB 128/44, CC (69) 1st Conclusions, 3 January 1969.
2. MRC, MSS 292B/40.2/2, Report of Meeting between the Secretary of State for Employment and Productivity, and the TUC's Finance and General Purposes Committee, 8 January 1969.
3. NA LAB 10/3478, Peart to Wilson, 'Industrial Relations', 7 January 1969.
4. MS. Castle.274, Crosland to Wilson, 14 January 1969.
5. NA CAB 128/44, CC (69) 1st Conclusions, 3 January 1969.
6. NA CAB 128/44, CC (69) 1st Conclusions, 3 January 1969.
7. NA CAB 128/44, CC (69) 1st Conclusions, 3 January 1969.
8. NA CAB 129/140, C (69) 2, Memorandum by the First Secretary of State and Secretary of State for Employment and Productivity, 'A Policy of Industrial Relations: Draft White Paper', 8 January, 1969.
9. NA LAB10/3478, Secretary of State for Employment and Productivity, 'Industrial Relations Policy – The "Conciliation Pause"', 6 January 1969.
10. NA CAB 128/44, CC (69) 1st Conclusions, 3 January 1969.
11. NA CAB 128/44, CC (69) 2nd Conclusions, 8–9 January 1969.
12. NA PREM 13/2724, Gardiner to Castle, 1 January 1969 [in the original, the year is erroneously given as 1968].
13. NA CAB 129/140, C (69) 3, Memorandum by the Paymaster General, 'Industrial Relations; The Conciliation Pause', 8 January 1969.
14. NA CAB 129/140, C (69) 7, Memorandum by the Secretary of State for Social Services and the Paymaster General, 'Industrial Relations: Draft White Paper – The Conciliation Pause Proposals', 13 January 1969.
15. NA CAB 128/44, CC (69), 3rd Conclusions, 14 January 1969.
16. NA CAB 128/44, CC (69), 3rd Conclusions, 14 January 1969.
17. NA PREM 13/2724, Peart to Wilson, 7 January 1969.
18. The committee stage in the Parliamentary legislative process is when a bill is scrutinised in detail, with a group of MPs examining it clause-by-clause, line-by-line, and proposing ('tabling') amendments to improve it. The committee stage follows the Second Reading, which is when a bill's principles and purpose have been debated and endorsed by a majority of MPs (invariably the government's MPs).
19. NA CAB 129/140, C (69) 1, Memorandum by the Lord President of the Council, 'Industrial Relations: Legislative Timetable', 7 January 1969.
20. NA CAB 128/44, CC (69), 3rd Conclusions, 14 January 1969.
21. NA PREM 13/2724, 'Note for the Record', 3 January 1969.

22 Callaghan Papers, Box 149, Personal note, 25 May 1969.
23 Callaghan Papers, Box 149, Personal note, 25 May 1969.
24 The NEC (National Executive Committee) is composed of various Ministers, MPs, members of the extra- parliamentary Labour Party and sundry trade unionists, and acted as a forum for policy development, as well as administrative and organisational oversight. It provided an institutional link, which met on a regular basis, between the different sections of the organised labour movement: the political and industrial wings.
25 MS. Wilson 1250, Harold Wilson, 'Note for the record on events following the N.E.C decision about Industrial relations legislation', undated, but *circa* early April 1969.
26 NA CAB 128/44, CC (69), 15th Conclusion, 3 April 1969.
27 NA CAB 128/44, CC (69), 15th Conclusion, 3 April 1969.
28 Callaghan Papers, Box 149, Personal note, 25 May 1969.
29 MS. Wilson 1250, Harold Wilson, 'Note for the record on industrial relations legislation', 10 May 1969.
30 MS. Wilson 1250, Harold Wilson, 'Note for the record on industrial relations legislation', 10 May 1969.
31 Callaghan Papers, Box 149, Personal note, 25 May 1969.
32 Callaghan Papers, Box 149, Letter from C. T. H. Plant to Callaghan, 26 June 1969.
33 Callaghan Papers, Box 149, Letter from Coward, Chance and Co. to Stewart-Pearson (director of Charles Knight Publishers), 4 August 1970.
34 Callaghan Papers, Box 149, Letter from Stewart-Pearson to Coward, Chance and Co., 5 August 1970.
35 MS. Castle.274, Dixon to Birdsall, 16 July 1969.
36 NA CAB 129/140, C (69) 36, Memorandum by the Secretary of State for Employment and Productivity, 'Industrial Relations', 15 April 1969.
37 NA CAB 129/140, C (69) 36, Memorandum by the Secretary of State for Employment and Productivity, 'Industrial Relations', 15 April 1969.
38 NA CAB 128/44, CC (69) 17th Conclusions, 14 April 1969.
39 MS. Wilson c.1250, 'Note for the record on industrial relations legislation', 10 May 1969.
40 NA CAB 128/44, CC (69) 17th Conclusions, 14 April 1969.
41 Callaghan Papers, Box 149, Personal note, 30 June 1969.
42 NA PREM 13/2724, Graham to Wilson, 'The White Paper on Industrial relations; A Bargain with the Unions?', 14 January 1969, emphases in original.
43 Labour Party Archives, Minutes of a meeting of the Parliamentary Labour Party, 30 April 1969.
44 MS. Wilson c.1250, 'Note for the record on industrial relations legislation', 10 May 1969.
45 Callaghan Papers, Box 149, Personal note, 30 June 1969.
46 MS. Castle.274, Hand-written note passed between Wilson and Castle, 14 April 1969.
47 MS. Castle.274, Castle to Wilson, 29 April 1969.
48 NA PREM 13/2727, 'Note of a Meeting of the Management Committee', 9 June 1969.
49 NA LAB 43/534, Crosland to Wilson, 6 June 1969.

50 NA PREM 13/2727, 'Note of a Meeting of the Management Committee', 9 June 1969.
51 NA PREM 13/2727, Ennals to Wilson, 6 June 1969.
52 MS. Castle.274, Lestor to Castle, 5 May 1969.
53 Callaghan Papers, Box 149, Personal note, 25 May 1969.
54 NA PREM 13/2727, 'Note of a Meeting of the Management Committee', 8 June 1969.
55 NA PREM 13/2728, 'Note of a Meeting of the Management Committee', 17 June 1969.
56 NA PREM 13/2728, 'Note of a Meeting of the Management Committee', 17 June 1969.
57 Callaghan Papers, Box 149, Personal note, 30 June 1969.
58 Callaghan Papers, Box 149, Personal note, 30 June 1969.
59 Callaghan Papers, Box 149, Personal note, 30 June 1969.
60 Callaghan Papers, Box 149, Personal note, 30 June 1969.
61 Labour Party Archives, Meeting of the Parliamentary Labour Party, 17 April 1969.
62 Callaghan Papers, Box 149, Personal note, 25 May 1969.

5

Increasing antipathy in the Parliamentary Labour Party

The legislative proposals foreshadowed by *In Place of Strife*, and the ensuing 'short' Industrial Relations Bill, especially its 'penal clauses', aroused strong opposition in the PLP. The first serious indication of the scale of backbench opposition – and the extent to which this transcended the usual ideological divisions in the PLP – occurred on 3 March 1969, when fifty-five Labour MPs voted against *In Place of Strife*, and forty abstained (including the PLP's chair, Douglas Houghton), following a Parliamentary debate on a motion tabled by Barbara Castle, urging that 'this House approves the White Paper ... as a basis for legislation'. The motion was carried, though, by 224 votes to 62, due to the support proffered by other Labour MPs, with the Conservative Opposition abstaining (Butt, 1969: 306; Norton, 1975: 333; Tyler, 2006: 473).

Whereas some Labour backbenchers were opposed to *In Place of Strife*, or, rather, the 'penal clauses' it contained, from the very outset, some of the Party's MPs became opposed subsequently, in response to changing circumstances and developments. Some of the MPs in the latter category initially offered tacit support for the White Paper, either in the expectation that the promised lengthy period of consultation would result in the more contentious proposals being diluted, or because of personal or political loyalty to Castle or/and Wilson, in spite of their doubts about the efficacy of the proposed legislation.

Consequently, opposition to *In Place of Strife* and the ensuing 'short' Industrial Relations Bill increased throughout the first few months of 1969, and emanated from different sections or strands of the PLP. That said, it was from the left of the PLP (especially members of the Tribune Group), and trade union-sponsored Labour MPs, that the most consistent and trenchant backbench opposition to *In Place of Strife*, and the subsequent interim Industrial Relations Bill, emanated.

The combined numerical strength of these intra-Party opponents, coupled with the vehemence of their hostility to the 'penal clauses', ensured that by the late spring of 1969, it was evident that the Government would be unable to secure sufficient support among Labour MPs to enact the legislation. With the trade unions also bitterly opposed to *In Place of Strife* and the ensuing Industrial Relations Bill – especially the 'penal clauses' (see chapter 6) – and many senior Cabinet Ministers also withdrawing their initial support, largely in response to the opinion in the PLP itself and the stance of the unions, Castle and Wilson eventually felt compelled to broker a last-ditch face-saving deal with the TUC (discussed in chapter 7), in spite of Wilson's previous claim that the Labour Government's very survival was dependent on enacting the Industrial Relations Bill.

Initial reactions within the Parliamentary Labour Party

Although the main focus of this chapter is the opposition to *In Place of Strife* (and especially the 'penal clauses') which emanated from sections of the PLP, it should be noted that while this was increasingly widespread and vocal, it was not totally unanimous: a few Labour MPs expressed their support for Castle's proposals. For example, when the House of Commons debated *In Place of Strife* in early March, Ben Ford, Labour MP for Bradford North, expressed his full support for the White Paper, arguing that it represented 'constructive steps towards a democratic socialist State', and criticised those on the left who were often heard 'muttering slogans about socialism and then saying, "It is O.K. for everybody else but me." Socialism means planning … and that involves us all' (Hansard, 1969a, Vol. 779, col. 99). A couple of months later, Ford reiterated his support for legislation to regulate industrial stoppages, arguing that this would be warmly welcomed in his constituency 'because his textile workers were sick of being thrown out of work by strikes at the dock preventing raw wool arriving'.[1]

Similarly, when Harold Wilson addressed the PLP following the mid-April announcement of the interim Industrial Relations Bill, a few Labour MPs welcomed it, arguing that many people were 'tired of continuing unofficial strikes that threatened their livelihoods', and adding that the trade unions needed to 'realise their responsibilities'.[2] Indeed, this was a common theme among the few Labour MPs who expressed support for Castle and the White Paper: 'Ordinary rank and file members of the Unions were fed up with strikes', and as such, would be aided by the Government's proposed legislation, because it would 'help them refuse to strike'.[3]

However, such support was confined to a small number of Labour MPs. In fact, at one PLP meeting, only Woodrow Wyatt spoke in support of the Government's proposed industrial relations legislation, arguing that as unofficial strikes were increasing, 'something would have to be done to stop them'.[4]

Further support at this PLP meeting was expressed by the Labour MP for Bebington (near Merseyside), Edwin Brooks, who claimed that many unofficial strikes, particularly in his region, were caused by 'Communists and Trots[kyists]'.[5]

In stark contrast to these few supportive voices, though, many Labour MPs were either critical of *In Place of Strife* from the outset, or became so in response to subsequent developments. Indeed, the scale of such backbench opposition was evidently wider, deeper and stronger than Castle and Wilson had envisaged. Certainly, Castle had initially assumed that the many pro-trade union measures enshrined in the White Paper would be warmly welcomed by most Labour MPs, to the extent that the three 'penal clauses' would be rendered more palatable or tolerable; a reasonable trade-off or *quid pro quo*. This is certainly what Castle had been led to believe by John Fraser, her PPS, at the Sunningdale weekend (Castle, 1990: 276, diary entry for 15 November).

The weekly meetings of the PLP, which all Labour MPs are entitled to attend, naturally provided a regular arena in which backbench opposition to *In Place of Strife* was articulated, with the three 'penal clauses' being the clear focus of most opprobrium. This became evident when Barbara Castle was invited to address a meeting of the PLP immediately after publication of *In Place of Strife*. Having explained the rationale of the White Paper, and reiterated that trade unions and workers already benefited from various forms of State intervention and legislation in industrial relations – the clear implication being that her proposals did not constitute a sudden departure from the *voluntarism* which the unions deemed sacrosanct – Castle heard several Labour MPs express 'very strong opposition' to the 'penal clauses', coupled with a stark warning that the pursuit of legislation based on the White Paper 'would inevitably split the Party in the House [of Commons] and in the country'. Conversely, it was emphasised that if Castle abandoned the proposals pertaining to strike ballots, a conciliation pause and attachment-of-earnings to recoup fines from trade union members, then *In Place of Strife* 'would be widely welcomed'.[6]

When the PLP met the following week, with *In Place of Strife* again being the sole item on the agenda, it was reiterated that, while the White Paper contained many constructive and desirable proposals to strengthen trade unionism and workers' rights, these would be 'entirely vitiated' by the proposals for strike ballots, a conciliation pause and fines recouped directly from wages. Castle was again warned that enacting these particular clauses 'would have a serious effect on the Party in the House and in the country, and gravely damage the Party's relations with the Trade Unions'.[7]

Although the three 'penal clauses' clearly constituted the main focus of backbench opposition to *In Place of Strife*, other concerns were variously cited by some Labour MPs, for whom 'the general tenor of the [White] Paper was disquieting'. One such concern was that once the principle of statutory intervention in industrial relations and the internal affairs of the trade unions had been established, this might prove to be 'a first step towards State control of the Trade Unions'. Certainly, there was grave apprehension that a future Conservative government might use Castle's proposed legislation as the basis for extending or strengthening statutory regulation (restriction) of trade union activities.[8]

Meanwhile, alluding to Wilson's speech attacking the 1966 strike by the National Union of Seamen, Eric Heffer wryly suggested that 'the White Paper is the product of a tightly-knit group of politically motivated men and women meeting in secret on Thursdays in a room in Downing Street' (Hansard, 1969b, Vol. 781, col. 1225).

Backbench hostility increased by the interim Industrial Relations Bill

The opposition from within the PLP was given a new focal point when the Labour Government announced, via Chancellor Roy Jenkins' mid-April Budget speech, an interim Industrial Relations Bill to be enacted in the current Parliamentary session, in advance of more comprehensive legislation in the 1969–70 session. Some Labour MPs who hitherto had tacitly supported *In Place of Strife* on the basis that it constituted the basis for discussion in development of legislation to be introduced in November, now felt that the Cabinet had reneged upon this agreement and that they were being 'bounced' into supporting an unexpected and rushed Bill. Wilson sought to pacify such concerns by explaining to the PLP that the 'short' Industrial Relations Bill was 'part of the strategy which the Government has decided must be followed … This Bill is urgent', to the extent that another major Bill, the Parliament (No.2) Bill to reform the House of Lords, had been abandoned: 'the less essential must make way for the more essential'.

Yet he also emphasised that if the TUC 'would come forward with their own measures, equally effective, equally urgent in time, to our proposals to deal with unofficial strikes, we would be prepared to consider their alternative suggestions', an olive branch which he offered on several subsequent occasions, sometimes directly to the TUC itself in the meetings which he and Castle had with its General Council, and with Vic Feather. He also extended this invitation to Labour's Trade Union Group of MPs.[9] However, more prescient Labour backbenchers recognised that if he and Castle were willing to accept effective counter-proposals from the TUC or the PLP's Trade Union Group, as an alternative to proceeding with the interim Industrial Relations Bill, then it could hardly be deemed 'essential' and 'urgent'.

Furthermore, whilst making this offer was doubtless intended to make Wilson and Castle appear reasonable and responsive, and at the same time place the impetus firmly on the TUC to respond positively, it did, unwittingly, compound the problems which he and Castle later encountered with the PLP. This was because when the TUC did subsequently offer its own substantive measures for dealing with affiliated trade unions whose members pursued unconstitutional strikes, many Labour MPs – and, crucially, several senior Cabinet Ministers who had hitherto supported industrial relations legislation – urged him and Castle to accept the TUC's offer, and abandon the Government's proposed Bill. When Wilson refused to do so, arguing that the TUC's counter-proposals were insufficiently robust, many Labour MPs (and several Ministers) judged that the TUC's General Council had skilfully called Wilson's bluff, and that it was the Prime Minister himself who was stubbornly preventing a resolution of the conflict between the Government and the trade unions. At this juncture, even some Labour MPs who had hitherto remained supportive of Wilson and Castle now made it clear that they would not vote for the interim Industrial Relations Bill if and when it was introduced to the House of Commons, and as such, the Government would fail to muster a Parliamentary majority; it would suffer a humiliating defeat, whereupon Wilson's own political credibility and authority would be seriously – perhaps fatally – damaged.

However, it was not just the contents of the interim Industrial Relations Bill, most notably the 'penal clauses', which attracted opposition from sections of the PLP, but also the manner in which the Government was pursuing it. When Wilson addressed the PLP after the announcement of the bill, he had argued that:

> [t]here is a time for discussion within the Party and within the wider Labour movement. Then there comes a time for decision. The discussion on the policy has taken place over many months. Now the Government has announced its decision to introduce this Bill. The time has come for the Party to back the Government in the action that it has decided to take.[10]

In response, some Labour MPs who had hitherto lent qualified support, or at least acquiescence, to *In Place of Strife* on the understanding that it was the basis for discussions which would not yield industrial relations legislation until November, were aghast that the Cabinet had now decided that the discussions had continued long enough, and that a Bill was to be introduced imminently, about six months earlier than originally planned. It was suggested that the Cabinet itself needed to have a 'cooling-off period' imposed on it.[11]

Meanwhile, Joan Lestor informed Castle that although *In Place of Strife* contained many commendable measures to strengthen the trade unions, the Government's approach to industrial relations reform 'is being seen as another bash at the workers', and while this was obviously not the intention, the positive proposals in the White Paper and Bill 'have got lost in the battle', to the extent that there had developed a mood of 'sheer misery and dismay within the rank and file here and in the country'. Lestor thus expressed her hope that 'we end up with a Bill that excludes the offensive parts, but is strong on the rest'.[12]

Backbench responses to pressure from the Labour whips, and the TUC's Croydon conference

Some Labour MPs who had previously proffered support to Barbara Castle and *In Place of Strife* now complained that undue pressure was being applied to them by the Government's whips, the latter seeking to maximise backbench support in the division lobbies of the House of Commons. This particular complaint was largely prompted by Wilson's appointment of the purportedly pugnacious Bob Mellish to replace the more emollient John Silkin as the Government's Chief Whip. Indeed, as we noted in chapter 4, Castle herself wrote to Wilson to complain about this appointment, noting the likelihood that some Labour backbenchers would view it as provocative, and thus likely to entrench their opposition to the proposed industrial relations legislation.

Her concerns were vindicated, for Mellish's appointment provoked a new source of opposition to the Government's bill among some Labour MPs, as previously acquiescent or supportive backbenchers now resented the pressure they were being subjected to, in order to ensure that they would vote for the imminent legislation. In effect, their resentment of the alleged conduct of the Party whips compounded their concerns about the content of the interim Industrial Relations Bill. After all, at his very first meeting with the PLP after being appointed as Chief Whip, Mellish warned that, if the Government was defeated over the Industrial Relations Bill, 'we should have no alternative but to go to the country [call a general election]. The Government's life depended upon whether they could muster support' [for the Bill].[13]

In response to such claims, and allegedly heavy-handed conduct by the Government's whips, one of Castle's former PPS, Paul Rose, complained to her that Labour MPs 'are faced with threats of votes of confidence and the resignation of the Government'. He warned that, instead of galvanising support among recalcitrant backbenchers, 'the only result [of such threats] will be to turn more of us into opposition against our own ministers'. Rose argued that 'the Government just does not seem to understand the depth of feeling and resentment on the proposed legislation', and explained that although he had, 'out of personal loyalty …refrained from voting against the White Paper', he was now likely to vote against the Industrial Relations Bill, 'rather than be treated as lobby fodder worthy only of intimidation'. In imploring Castle to reconsider her commitment to the Bill, Rose pointed out that there had developed 'a deep malaise in the Party', which was now in such 'disarray' that it was 'visibly disintegrating', and as such, 'only a compromise on this issue and/or a change of leadership can prevent a collision course leading to the destruction of our movement'.[14]

What further fuelled PLP opposition to the short Industrial Relations Bill during the spring of 1969 was the TUC's response to the Labour Government's imminent legislation. Having been invited by Wilson to develop effective measures of its own for dealing with unconstitutional and unofficial strikes, the TUC duly published a policy document called *Programme for Action*, which was then overwhelmingly endorsed at a special conference in Croydon on 5 June 1969 (see chapter 6). Although Wilson and Castle rejected some of the TUC's measures as inadequate, especially those pertaining to tackling unconstitutional strikes – although it transpired that the Prime Minister had been rather more dismissive than his Secretary of State – many others in the Labour Party believed that the TUC had shown a commendable willingness to accept much greater responsibility for tackling such industrial disputes, and that Castle and Wilson should therefore accept the TUC's counter-proposals.[15]

Consequently, by June, very many Labour MPs – and a growing number of Cabinet Ministers – wanted Wilson and Castle to reach a settlement with the TUC, based on the *Programme for Action* proposals endorsed at the specially convened Croydon conference. For example, Shirley Williams suggested that 'if the TUC can be persuaded to ask for, and can obtain, powers to become an effective arbiter in these fields', then Castle would have achieved 'an immense amount to modernise the trade union movement'. Williams therefore strongly urged Castle to 'consider the possibility of reaching an agreement on these lines', provided, of course, that 'the TUC can give you worthwhile evidence of its intention, and ability, to keep order in its own sphere'.[16]

Meanwhile, another backbench MP, Alistair Macdonald, who was generally supportive of the principle of industrial relations reform to strengthen the trade unions, and *inter alia* pave the way for a more planned and stable Socialist society, praised Castle's courage and vision, but expressed regret that 'the whole thing seems to have changed into a means of preventing unofficial strikes'.[17]

That Wilson had so swiftly and emphatically rejected the TUC's counter-proposals after their overwhelming endorsement at the Croydon conference led some Labour MPs (and Ministers) to conclude that it was the Prime Minister himself who was obstinate and intransigent, rather than the trade union leadership. Wilson seemed willing to push the Labour Party to breaking-point over the issue, in a dangerous game of brinkmanship, and in this regard, the political became personal: for some Labour MPs (and Ministers), the issue of industrial relations legislation became inextricably bound up with questions about Wilson's leadership and personality, with at least a few Labour MPs by now favouring a new leader.[18]

A significant reason for Wilson's rejection of the TUC's Croydon proposals was precisely that he was suspicious of the motives of the trade union leadership; he suspected that they were offering superficially reasonable, but ultimately cosmetic, changes to the internal governance of the unions, precisely in order to persuade sections of the Labour Party (and perhaps public opinion) that it was the unions themselves that were being reasonable and willing to make the changes necessary to improve industrial relations, and imply that it was Wilson and Castle who were unreasonable and uncompromising. In effect, Wilson suspected that the counter-proposals endorsed at the TUC's Croydon conference were subtly intended to isolate him and Castle from other sections of the PLP and the Cabinet, by depicting the trade unions as the 'good guys', and thereby secure support for the TUC's stance among Labour MPs and Ministers, a growing number of whom were increasingly keen to settle this issue swiftly, even if this meant a compromise.

Whether this really had been the intention of the TUC, or whether this apparent motive had existed solely in Wilson's suspicious mind, there is no doubt that many Labour MPs – like Shirley Williams – were suitably impressed by the counter-proposals endorsed at the Croydon conference, and consequently PLP opposition to the Industrial Relations Bill was reinforced further, a point which Roy Jenkins found 'depressing'.[19] Incidentally, even Castle's constituency Labour Party (CLP) in Blackburn had written to her on the eve of the TUC's Croydon conference, imploring her to abandon the 'penal clauses' contained within *In Place of Strife* and the Industrial Relations Bill, and warning that if the Government persevered with them, 'the basic unity of the [labour] movement could well be destroyed'. Consequently, the Blackburn CLP 'passionately recommend that you reach an agreed settlement', rather than imposing punitive legislation on the trade unions.[20]

The chair of the PLP, and the Government's Chief Whip, warn of impending defeat

In mid-June, as the negotiations between Wilson, Castle and the TUC's General Council were reaching a critical stage, the PLP's chair Douglas Houghton wrote to the Prime Minister to warn him that, since the announcement of the interim the Industrial Relations Bill and the TUC's

Croydon conference, 'opinion in the Parliamentary Party has hardened against proceeding with any Bill containing the so-called "penal clauses"', to the extent that 'the Government could not count upon enough support within the Parliamentary Party to get this Bill through the House [of Commons]'. Instead, there was now a 'widespread' desire for the Government and the TUC to reach a negotiated settlement, especially because the Government could *not* 'justify to the Parliamentary Party the final breakdown in negotiations and the inevitable devastating consequences to the Party inside and outside Parliament'. Such a settlement was now imperative 'if a grave split in the Parliamentary Party is to be averted', and to this end, it was suggested that the Government should 'take the T.U.C. at their word for the present, put them to the test of experience', to gauge how genuine and effective their counter-proposals actually were.[21]

In the context of such strong and widespread opposition in the PLP, the only way in which the proposed Industrial Relations Bill might conceivably have mustered sufficient Parliamentary support was if the dwindling number of Labour MPs who still supported the legislation had been joined in the division lobby by the Conservative Opposition, for the latter also wanted to place industrial relations and trade unionism within a clear framework of law. However, it was ultimately in the Conservative Party's political interests that Labour's Bill should fail to reach the statute book, for two reasons. First, the Conservatives could then reiterate, even more emphatically, their perennial claim that Labour was beholden to its trade union paymasters and/or in the grip of the left, and therefore intrinsically incapable of governing with due regard to Britain's economic and industrial interests, or the 'national interest' in general. Second, by not rescuing Castle and Wilson's 'short' Industrial Relations Bill, the Conservative Party's own proposals for the radical reform of industrial relations, via *Fair Deal at Work*, would almost certainly be imbued with much greater resonance and, crucially, electoral popularity. The Conservatives could claim that Labour was inherently unable and unwilling to curb trade union power and militancy, whereas the Conservative Party definitely could – and certainly would.

Houghton's warning about the lack of support in the PLP was echoed by the recently appointed Chief Whip, who informed a mid-June meeting of the Cabinet's industrial relations committee that the Trade Union Group of Labour MPs was deeply disappointed at the haste with which the TUC's Croydon counter-proposals had been rejected. In view of how far the TUC had shifted its position in recent weeks, these Labour MPs were convinced that 'it would be a tragedy to throw this achievement away'. On the assumption that 'the Government would not get the Bill through' the House of Commons, owing to insufficient support among Labour MPs, Mellish urged Wilson and Castle to 'avoid a head-on collision' with the TUC.[22] Given that Mellish had a reputation as a disciplinarian, and had apparently been appointed as the Government's Chief Whip with a brief to secure the Parliamentary passage of the interim Industrial Relations Bill, his warning proved particularly portentous.

Consequently, having previously claimed that the future of the Labour Government was dependent on enacting the Bill, Wilson found that the unity of the PLP, and the relationship between the industrial and political wings of the organised labour movement, were heavily dependent on *not* proceeding with this legislation, lest it cause deep and damaging divisions from which the Party might take a long time to recover. This was a particularly pertinent consideration in view of the proximity of the next general election, and the British electorate's perfectly understandable reluctance to vote for parties which were clearly divided internally, and therefore unlikely to be able to provide strong and stable government.

The James Callaghan–Douglas Houghton axis

Although there is no direct evidence that James Callaghan (whose strong opposition we discussed in chapter 4) actively sought to foment or orchestrate these sources of backbench opposition, it is reasonable to assume that he felt suitably emboldened by the knowledge that his antipathy to *In Place of Strife* and the interim Industrial Relations Bill was shared by many Labour MPs, particularly as he had a close professional relationship and shared background with the chair of the PLP. Douglas Houghton, who was also strongly opposed to the Government's legislative proposals, had previously served on the TUC's General Council through most of the 1950s, and then subsequently sat in the Cabinet from 1964 until becoming chair of the PLP in 1967.

Most interesting though, in the context of his and Callaghan's opposition to *In Place of Strife* and the proposed interim Industrial Relations Bill, was that back in 1922, Houghton had established the Inland Revenue Staff Federation, which he then led until 1960, and whose Assistant General Secretary from 1936 until the mid-1940s had been James Callaghan. Consequently, the two men were viewed with profound suspicion by some Ministerial supporters of *In Place of Strife* and the ensuing interim Industrial Relations Bill, with Castle herself noting bitterly that 'Jim and Houghton are playing in double harness, like a comic and his feed man' (Castle, 1990: 328, diary entry for 7 May 1969).

Houghton certainly shared Callaghan's view that the keenest Cabinet proponents of industrial relations reform, as proposed via *In Place of Strife*, were out-of-touch with the realities of life on the factory floor, and thus also with the views, or even direct experiences, of many Labour backbenchers who either represented industrial constituencies, or had themselves worked in industry prior to entering Parliament or/and had been senior trade unionists. As such, Houghton (1969: 460) argued that 'on some things – industrial relations particularly – at least a hundred Labour backbenchers claim to know better than ministerial academics'.

This allusion to 'ministerial academics' was echoed by some senior trade unionists, as we will note more fully in chapter 6: it reflected a view that, because Castle and Wilson had been educated at Oxford University and had consequently become middle class, they were now far removed and remote from their roots, and therefore out of touch with industrial workers and trade unionists out in the real world away from Westminster and Whitehall. Hence the criticism that their approach to industrial relations reform reflected an 'academic' approach to problem-solving, one which assumed that 'reason', 'logic' and 'rational argument' were sufficient to achieve policy objectives. This meant that many Labour MPs, especially those sponsored by a trade union, were 'puzzled and angered' about 'how the Government came to reach the conclusions they did. Where did the inspiration and advice to fly in the face of Donovan come from?' (Houghton, 1969: 461). Houghton thus encouraged Callaghan, a kindred spirit, 'to stand firm, secure in the knowledge that he had growing support in the parliamentary party' (Morgan, 1997: 335). Meanwhile, PLP opponents of *In Place of Strife* and the subsequent industrial relations legislation would have been greatly heartened to know that their opposition was fully reciprocated in the Cabinet by a Minister as senior as the Home Secretary.

The opposition of left-wing Labour MPs

Ideologically, it was from MPs on the left of the PLP that the most trenchant opposition to *In Place of Strife*, and the subsequent interim Industrial Relations Bill, emanated. Much, but by no means all, of the left-wing hostility towards the White Paper and ensuing legislation was articulated through the Tribune Group, which at the time comprised 33 Labour MPs, including Frank Allaun, Michael Foot, Eric Heffer, Jennie Lee, Ian Mikardo and Stan Orme. Although this was slightly less than 10 per cent of the PLP at the time, when combined with the equally consistent opposition of most of Labour's 127 trade union-sponsored MPs (discussed below), this meant that up to one-third of Labour MPs were implacably opposed to their Government's proposed industrial relations legislation, and especially the 'penal clauses'. An accurate number was difficult to ascertain, though, because a few trade union-sponsored Labour MPs were also members of the Tribune Group, thus ensuring a slight overlap among some backbenchers opposing the White Paper and the subsequent interim Bill.

However, their combined number (and thus strength) was increased further by the sundry Labour MPs who were neither members of the Tribune Group (or the left more generally), nor sponsored by a trade union, but who nonetheless also opposed *In Place of Strife*. As Labour had been re-elected with a ninety-seven-seat Parliamentary majority in 1966, the PLP opponents of the White Paper and ensuing Industrial Relations Bill were clearly numerous enough to defeat their Government if they voted in unison, and the Conservative Opposition abstained.

The Labour left bitterly resented what they perceived to be an anti-working class, anti-trade union policy being actively pursued by a Labour Government. Indeed, this antipathy was compounded by the fact that Castle was widely viewed as being on the left of the Party herself – and had evidently envisaged that this would render her proposals more acceptable – while Wilson had a reputation for having previously been on the left of the Party, at least in the 1950s. That the two of them were now actively promoting legislation which would not only curb the trade unions' ability to pursue free collective bargaining, but would empower the Secretary of State to order a cooling-off period, a pre-strike ballot and – via the Industrial Court – impose fines (possibly recouped by an attachment-of-earnings order) was tantamount to betrayal of the organised labour movement's industrial wing by its political partner.

Attributing industrial conflict to capitalism and employers

The Labour left strongly resented the implication that industrial conflict was largely or even primarily the fault of irresponsible or militant trade unions and/or their members, and the increasingly prevalent assumption that strikes were a manifestation of (excessive) trade union power (Foot, 1969b; *Tribune*, 1969c). After all, if the unions really possessed the power which their critics had previously attributed to them, or were 'running the country' as was variously claimed prior to the Thatcher Governments' anti-union legislation of the 1980s, then they would hardly need to go on strike to secure better wages, improve conditions of employment or defend members' jobs *vis-à-vis* dismissals or redundancies.

From this perspective, strikes were frequently a manifestation of the *lack* of economic power endured by ordinary working people, attributable to the structural inequalities inherent in capitalism, where the key decisions affecting ordinary people are mostly taken in company boardrooms and 'the City', yet over which workers and trade unions have no real input or influence. In effect, strikes are generally viewed by the left as a crude, defensive, response to economic or industrial decisions taken elsewhere and then imposed on working people: decisions which rarely consider the interests of, or detrimental impact on, those affected by them, and which are never subject to a ballot of those workers to gauge their support.

At one meeting of the Tribune Group, it was argued that measures to tackle unofficial strikes, regardless of whether these emanated from the Labour Government or the TUC, were likely to prove ineffective, because such industrial disputes 'arose from fundamental inequalities in the industrial and economic system, and could only be stopped when the system changed radically'.[23]

More specifically, the left (and many trade union-sponsored Labour MPs not associated with the left) insisted that industrial conflict was often caused by the unilateral and arbitrary actions and decisions of employers. For example, in a Parliamentary debate on the Donovan Report, Eric Heffer argued that:

> many ... disputes take place because employers, without due notice or discussion with the workers, dismiss a group of men or a shop steward? The reaction of the workers is immediate. They know that the only way in which they can defend their fellow workers is by taking immediate action. I suggest that the remedy lies with the employers stopping that sort of nonsense. (Hansard, 1968: Vol. 768, col. 1302)

Elsewhere, it was claimed that 'the real cause of this country's industrial problems' was 'hide-bound, nineteenth-century employers' (Turner, 1969a; see also Urwin, 1969).

What reinforced the left's antipathy to *In Place of Strife* was that the Cabinet had already attempted to hold down wage increases since autumn 1965 via increasingly stringent incomes policies; initially voluntary, but subsequently statutory. Just like the White Paper's proposals for industrial relations reform, such policies reflected and reinforced an assumption that many of Britain's economic problems were attributable to 'excessive' wage increases and the 'greed' of the trade unions, rather than to the conduct of companies and employers in seeking to maximise profits and shareholders' dividends, or even the operation of capitalism itself (for an account of these incomes polices, see Dorey, 2001: chapter four). As Eric Heffer complained, the Labour Government's incomes policies 'controlled wages only, and not the ... incomes of the rich' (Heffer, 1991: 135; see also Sinclair, 1969). Similarly, Ian Mikardo (1988: 176) argued that:

> the so-called prices and incomes policy wasn't in fact a policy for prices and incomes – it was merely a policy for restricting increases in wages at the lower end of the scale ... there was no restriction on professional earnings or managerial salaries: it was only the workers on the shop floor and in the offices, that is, those in the lowest wage-brackets, who were to suffer limitations on increases in their pay-packets.

Mikardo thus denounced *In Place of Strife* as 'a provocation to strife' (Mikardo, 1988: 176).

Although Mikardo acknowledged that there were many positive proposals in the White Paper, he insisted that these were greatly outweighed by the three 'penal clauses'. Mixing his metaphors, he described *In Place of Strife* as a mixture of 'good and bad ... the jam and ... the pills', and doubted whether 'it's worth paying the price of three swings in order to get the twenty-five roundabouts'. In objecting specifically to the proposal for a pre-strike ballot to be ordered by the Secretary of State, Mikardo pointed out that 'no employer is going to be required to hold a ballot before he's allowed to close down a factory and put a lot of people out of work', and as such, far from strengthening trade unions overall (as the White Paper purported to do), this provision would merely reinforce the inherent inequality of power between workers and employers in the workplace under capitalism.

Similarly, Mikardo denounced the proposal to impose fines on workers who refused an order to return to work when a conciliation pause was invoked, partly because he viewed this as a curb on workers' right to withdraw their labour in a supposedly free society, but also 'because it does not hold the scales fairly balanced between employer and worker, for no employer will ever be fined under these provisions'.[24] Meanwhile, a *Tribune* editorial suggested that it was the Labour Government itself which needed 'a cooling off' period' (*Tribune*, 1969a).

Many other members of the Tribune Group shared Mikardo's view that the positive measures which *In Place of Strife* included were nullified by the three 'penal clauses', which were condemned as wholly unacceptable. Heffer (1973: 103) described the contents of the White Paper as 'a barrel of honey spoilt by a spoonful of tar'. When eighteen of the Tribune Group's MPs met to discuss *In Place of Strife* almost immediately after the White Paper's publication, these clauses were branded 'the reactionary sections', whereupon it was resolved that they would constitute the main focus of *Tribune*'s opposition.[25] It was thus hardly surprising that at the end of the 3 March 1969 debate, in which Castle asked for Parliamentary approval of the White Paper 'as a basis of legislation', Tribune MPs entered the 'No' lobby to register their formal opposition (Hansard, 1969a: Vol. 779, col. 165).

A further objection, advanced by Tribunite MPs, was that once industrial relations legislation – including 'penal clauses' – had been enacted by the Labour Government, this would almost certainly be extended by the next Conservative Government, the latter likely to view Labour's measures as a foundation for much more comprehensive and repressive statutory measures against the trade unions (Tribune Group of Labour MPs, 1969).

Some on the Labour left also suspected that Castle was being unduly influenced by the allegedly anti-trade union views of her senior civil servants, with Heffer claiming that '[w]hen she entered the Department of Employment and Productivity, she was not well versed in labour relations affairs. What she learned, she learned in the Department' (Heffer, 1973: 97). Elsewhere, it was claimed that 'she has fallen under the influence of those advisers at her Ministry who [go] about under the misapprehension that penalties and restrictions … are the only way to "impose" peace in industry' (Clements, 1969).

This perspective, of course, was part of the more general left critique which explained Labour Governments' alleged abandonment of Socialism in terms of Ministers succumbing to the deadly embrace of 'the Establishment'. This then steers them back towards the perceived centre ground, and thus neutralises and nullifies any threat to existing sources and structures of power, which would be inimical to the material interests of big business.

The Labour left's furious reaction to the interim Industrial Relations Bill

Of course, the Government's subsequent mid-April 1969 announcement that it intended to introduce a 'short 'Industrial Relations Bill exacerbated the Tribune Group's antipathy to Castle's and Wilson's approach in general, and the 'penal' clauses in particular. It was again noted that a Labour Government was proposing to impose statutory curbs and sanctions on the trade unions and industrial workers, but without any corresponding limits or obligations on employers or the business community: this rendered the Government's proposals 'viciously one-sided' (*Tribune* 1969b).

The announcement of the interim Industrial Relations Bill prompted a furious response by Michael Foot, in that week's edition of *Tribune*. Under the heading 'The maddest scene in modern history', Foot asserted that 'Harold Wilson and the Labour Cabinet are heading for the rocks', having decided that the best way of demonstrating strong political leadership was 'to declare war on the trade unions'. If the labour movement was to survive, it was now essential for its supporters 'to make it as clear as possible that the anti-trade union legislation will not be tolerated', because '[s]uch a wanton, menacing, decision could threaten to break the Government and tear the [labour] movement to shreds' (Foot, 1969a). In similar vein, at the Tribune Group's April meeting, Eric Heffer warned that the 'short' Industrial Relations Bill was 'bound to wreck the labour movement', and as such, he likened the increasingly parlous political situation to that of 1931.[26] Indeed, Heffer's opposition to the proposed Bill was so strong that he suggested 'the present Prime Minister [Harold Wilson] must go', even though Heffer conceded that 'there was no clear alternative leader' at the time.[27]

Although most other Tribune Group MPs were reluctant to make public attacks on Wilson, there was broad agreement that the Prime

Minister should be summoned to a specially convened meeting of the PLP to explain the decision to introduce an Industrial Relations Bill, and that this should then be subject to a debate among Labour MPs. Moreover, it was agreed that the letter summoning Wilson to this proposed PLP meeting should be released to the press, thereby ensuring that the strength and scale of intra-Party opposition to the Labour Government's proposed industrial relations legislation was made public.[28]

The Tribune Group subsequently urged the Government to accept the counter-proposals enshrined in the TUC's policy document *Programme for Action*, and in so doing, abandon *In Place of Strife* and associated legislation.[29] It was claimed that failure to do so would 'be an act of sheer political stupidity', and would mean that the Government was stubbornly refusing to acknowledge that 'an industrial relations programme based on reason and negotiation is much more likely to produce results than one based ultimately on the bailiffs' (Turner, 1969b).

Not surprisingly, when Labour subsequently lost the 1970 general election the Labour left in general, and the Tribune Group especially, blamed the Government's economic and industrial policies, most notably incomes policies and *In Place of Strife*, for the defeat, on the grounds that many senior Ministers had spent much of their time and energy blaming the Party's own working-class supporters, and the trade unions, for Britain's economic problems, rather than senior industrialists and 'the City'. From this perspective, it was not the Labour Government's *failure* to enact *In Place of Strife*, and thus limit trade union power, which had disillusioned the Party's supporters, but the fact that the Government – with a few notable exceptions – had attempted to do so in the first place, having already spent several years curbing wage increases and cutting the social wage. To many on the left, it was yet another example of 'betrayal' by a Labour government, or, rather, its Parliamentary leadership.

The opposition of Labour's trade union-sponsored MPs

Naturally, most of the 127 Labour MPs sponsored by 25 trade unions (Silver, 1973: 139) were also vehemently opposed to *In Place of Strife*, particularly the three 'penal clauses'. These MPs were deeply concerned about the statutory powers which would be vested in the State (via the CIR and/or the Secretary of State for Employment and Productivity). This would constitute a major expansion of the law into industrial relations, whereupon the State would not only regulate relationships between workers and employers, but effectively govern relations between and within the trade unions themselves. Although some of these trade union-sponsored MPs were also members of the Tribune Group, most of them were not, which mean that opposition to *In Place of Strife* emanated from the right and centre of the PLP too, not just the left.

Indeed, it was the fact that so many of the trade union-sponsored Labour MPs who opposed *In Place of Strife* were deemed to be 'moderates' which made their antipathy so significant and, ultimately, damaging to Castle and Wilson. Had opposition been confined solely to the left of the PLP, it could probably have been contained and isolated, and ultimately 'de-legitimised'. Instead, hostility to *In Place of Strife*, and especially the 'penal clauses', spanned the PLP, and made temporary allies of many backbench MPs who normally adopted different ideological perspectives and positions on other issues.

After *In Place of Strife* was published on 17 January 1969, the PLP's Trade Union Group of MPs (one of many specialist or subject groups for Labour backbenchers) met to discuss it formally for the first time on 20 January, with seventy MPs in attendance. Castle herself also attended, to explain the purpose and objectives of the White Paper, encourage MPs to support it, and answer questions. However, according to one attendee, Eric Heffer, although she 'defended her proposals with a great deal of passion … She was not well-received'. Indeed, '[t]he atmosphere of the meeting, which lasted almost two hours, was unpleasant, the speeches were hostile', and with the exception of the ultra-loyal Jack Ashley, 'the Members' criticisms were very harsh'. Even moderate (non-left) trade union-sponsored Labour MPs bitterly denounced *In Place of Strife*, both for its proposal of 'penal clauses', and its likely damage to Labour–trade union relations. One of these in particular, ex-miner Alex Eadie, warned that, ultimately, it would be the Labour Party itself which would be destroyed by enacting *In Place of Strife*, not the trade unions (Heffer, 1973: 105, 106, 107).

Stan Orme's discussion paper

The Trade Union Group's opposition to legislative restrictions and sanctions on the unions had been foreshadowed by a discussion paper circulated to the Group's MPs before the publication of *In Place of Strife*, but with the knowledge that the Government was preparing industrial relations legislation for 1969. Drafted by Stan Orme, a member of the Tribune Group, the paper noted that the Royal Commission had been established in response to 'a great deal of pressure which came from people and organisations opposed to the British Trade Union movement', and who had expected 'to have their criticisms confirmed'. Instead, the Donovan Report had 'exonerated the Trade Union movement, and in many instances, praises and commends it', thereby confounding those who had hoped that the Royal Commission would herald a series of statutory restrictions on the unions and their activities.[30]

Ahead of the Labour Government's own proposals for industrial relations legislation being announced, Orme presciently identified five measures which he believed would feature prominently in any proposed reform, and for which the Trade Union Group needed to have a ready response or rebuttal, namely:[31]

The establishment of a Commission on Industrial Relations.
Legally enforceable collective agreements.
Sanctions against unconstitutional/unofficial strikers.
A 'cooling-off' period prior to a strike, to allow time for the cause or grievance to be investigated, and a satisfactory remedy attained.
Registration of trade unions.

Given the trade unions' inveterate commitment to voluntarism, it was not surprising that Orme's paper was either sceptical of, or outright opposed to, these five anticipated proposals. The envisaged CIR was deemed the least objectionable, although Orme was adamant that if and when such a body was established, it should operate on a voluntary and advisory basis, and not seek to impose additional obligations on the trade unions. Nor should it become a means of enforcing incomes policies.

Regarding the potential enforceability of collective agreements, Orme pointed out that employers already possessed the legal right to take action against employees who breached their contract of employment, but very few such cases were invoked, primarily because employers recognised that to do so would worsen industrial relations in their workplace or industry; any short-term gain would be greatly outweighed by the long-term damage to trust and goodwill among the workforce. As such, Orme rejected the potential option of rendering collective agreements legally enforceable, both because it would signify a sharp break with voluntarism – an industrial relations framework, he reiterated, in which collective agreements were usually 'by word of mouth, and … custom and practice built up within the industry' – and because of the almost inevitable problems of enforceability and sanctions which would be raised when such agreements were broken.

It was the issue of sanction against workers engaging in unconstitutional or unofficial strikes, however, which Orme believed represented 'the nerve centre of much of the agitation which is going on against the trade unions'. He argued that the impact of such strikes was being grossly exaggerated or misunderstood, for while it was true that 95 per cent of industrial stoppages were unofficial (or unconstitutional), the vast majority were of much shorter duration, and involved far fewer workers, than official strikes.

Yet although there was almost universal hostility to *In Place of Strife*, and particularly its proposed 'penal clauses', among Labour's trade union-sponsored MPs, not all of them actually voted against the White Paper after it had it been debated in the House of Commons at the beginning of March. On the contrary, a few voted in favour, but on the strict understanding that (as Charles Pannell explained):

> The Motion, for which I shall vote '... invites Her Majesty's Government to continue consultation with view to preparing legislation'. My support is based on that pledge. Consultation does not just mean listening – it means taking some action. It means that if the Minister is to get her legislation in due course she will have to give way on some points, and will make not a political judgment but a judgment based on facts. (Hansard, 1969a: Vol. 779, col. 143)

Although Labour's trade union-sponsored MPs were vehemently opposed to all three of the 'penal clauses', some of them tended to focus on a specific clause in opposing *In Place of Strife* and the subsequent Industrial Relations Bill. For example, in the Parliamentary debate on the White Paper, Charles Pannell was especially scornful of the proposal to impose fines on workers who continued engaging in industrial action after being ordered to return to work under the auspices of the conciliation pause. He took issue with Castle's claim that, under this scheme, no trade unionist would end up in prison for non-payment of a fine, because any monies deliberately withheld would be recouped directly from their wages through an attachment-of-earnings order. Pannell cited a recent report into the collection of child maintenance payments from absent fathers, which revealed that 34 per cent of them eventually went to prison for non-payment. The implication of his argument was that, although an attachment-of-earnings order might be invoked to recoup monies owed, the non-payee might already have been imprisoned as a civil debtor, and thus lost their job anyway.

Yet even if this was not the case, and an attachment-of-earnings order was successfully imposed to recoup an unpaid fine, Parnell emphasised that he, and many other Labour MPs, were bitterly opposed to this aspect of the White Paper as a matter of fundamental principle; some other sanction ought to be applied to deal with cases where workers, for whatever reason, refused to return to work, although he declined to suggest an alternative: 'It is not for me to say what should be done, because I did not initiate the legislation. It is for my Right Honourable Friend [Castle] to bring forward a piece of machinery which will stand up to examination' (Hansard, 1969a: Vol.779, col. 144).

Opposition strengthened in response to the 'interim' Bill and TUC's Croydon conference

The Government's subsequent mid-April announcement of the imminent Industrial Relations Bill provided the Party's Trade Union Group (as with other PLP critics) with a new focus for criticism and opposition, with one complaint being that the Group had not been consulted before the Government's intention was made publicly known on Tuesday 15 April.[32] It was not alone in this regard, because neither the trade unions nor the TUC had been consulted or informed either, even though the TUC's leadership had met Wilson and Castle on Friday 11 April, when no indication had been given of the Government's intention. The Cabinet was also urged to pay more attention to 'the vast experience of Members [of Parliament] in the field of industrial relations',[33] another allusion to the fact that Ministers such as Castle and Wilson had no first-hand experience of working in industry, and the struggles which many workers routinely endured.

The opposition of the PLP's Trade Union Group (to the Government's planned interim bill) was compounded by the TUC's counter-proposals in *Programme for Action,* for these were deemed to constitute a credible set of measures for tackling inter-union disputes and unconstitutional strikes, thereby addressing the very problems which Wilson and Castle were so concerned about. Accordingly, a 20 May meeting of the Trade Union Group unanimously endorsed *Programme for Action*, thereby adding to the growing pressure on the Labour leadership to abandon *In Place of Strife* and the Industrial Relations Bill, and instead trust the TUC to tackle the main forms of industrial disruption.[34]

As noted earlier, although organisationally distinct, there was some overlap between members of Labour's backbench Trade Union Group and the Tribune Group, because some of the Party's MPs belonged to both. Moreover, some of these 'dual members' were the most active or vocal participants in the weekly meetings of the PLP. For example, at the six meetings of the PLP for which *In Place of Strife* was the sole item on the agenda,[35] the main participants (and critics) were members of the Trade Union Group or/and the Tribune Group, such as Norman Atkinson, Alex Eadie, James Hamilton (chair of the Trade Union Group), Eric Heffer, Michael Foot, John Horner, Roy Hughes, Ian Mikardo, Stan Newens, Stan Orme and Trevor Park. As ever, it was the three 'penal clauses' which were the prime target of their objections.

The strong and well-organised opposition of these Labour MPs was clearly integral to the PLP's rejection of *In Place of Strife*, and the subsequent Industrial Relations Bill, but it was supplemented, and therefore, further enhanced by the growing opposition from other Labour MPs during the spring of 1969; MPs who were neither on the left of the Party, nor sponsored by a trade union, but who had become convinced either that the proposed legislation was inherently flawed, or that it posed a serious risk to the unity of the labour movement. As such, by May and June 1969, opposition to *In Place of Strife* and the interim bill emanated from all sections of the PLP, thereupon transcending traditional ideological divisions and identities, while also incorporating sundry Labour MPs who were not directly associated with a trade union. Many of these Labour MPs had modified their stance in response to intra-Party arguments, developments and warnings, and/or the response of the TUC at its Croydon conference. Indeed, by early June 1969, it was evident that PLP opposition to the Labour Government's proposed industrial relations legislation was so widespread that it would fail to muster a Parliamentary majority to enact that legislation.

Conclusion

The Labour Government, and Barbara Castle especially, clearly failed to foresee the breadth and depth of the opposition which *In Place of Strife* would arouse in the PLP. While some initial antipathy was naturally anticipated, it was assumed that this would dissipate once backbench MPs became more familiar with the objectives (philosophy) and content of the proposed industrial relations legislation, particularly as the vast majority of the measures would grant the trade unions and workers a range of statutory rights. Furthermore, Castle was supremely confident that she could convince many of the White Paper's backbench sceptics or critics of its alleged virtues, this feat to be achieved through reasoned argument and patient persuasion. She also assumed that many Labour MPs would be impressed by the fact that the Prime Minister fully supported *In Place of Strife*, thereby further enhancing the authority and credibility of the White Paper – and of Castle herself.

Yet far from abating in the months following publication of *In Place of Strife*, opposition in the PLP steadily increased, until it extended far beyond the serial rebels who might have been discounted as 'the usual suspects'. It was little surprise that opposition initially emanated from two discrete sources on the backbenches, namely the left (particularly Tribunite MPs), and trade union-sponsored MPs, but instead of constituting an instinctive or knee-jerk reaction which soon dissipated, this opposition actually became stronger and more entrenched in subsequent months, and proved impervious to Castle's, and Wilson's, arguments, exhortations and, eventually, dire warnings about the political consequences of rejecting industrial relations legislation.

Worse still for Castle and Wilson was that opposition to *In Place of Strife* and the subsequent interim Industrial Relations Bill steadily spread to other parts of the PLP, to the extent that some Labour MPs who had previously been supportive subsequently changed their minds, and became opposed to the continued pursuit of industrial relations legislation. Some of these MPs had originally professed support for *In Place of Strife* on the basis that it would be followed by a lengthy period of consultation, whereupon they hoped that some of the more contentious aspects, most notably the 'penal clauses', would be diluted or discarded. Many of these MPs were thus antagonised by the mid-April announcement of imminent legislation and the appointment of Bob Mellish as the Government's Chief Whip; some of them felt that they were being 'bounced' or even coerced into supporting the interim bill, and that their loyalty was being taken for granted.

Other Labour MPs effectively withdrew their erstwhile support when the TUC advanced its own proposals for tackling unofficial strikes, but on condition that Castle and Wilson abandoned their proposed legislation. To some of these 'switching' Labour MPs, it was the TUC which now appeared constructive and reasonable, and keen to avoid a crisis or even a schism between Labour and the trade unions, whereas Castle and Wilson, by (initially) rejecting the TUC's counter-proposals, were increasingly perceived to be intransigent and bloody-minded, to the extent of seriously risking a fatal split in the labour movement.

Notes

1 MS. Wilson 1250, Harold Wilson, 'Note for the record on industrial relations legislation', 10 May 1969.
2 Labour Party Archives, Minutes of PLP Meeting held on 17 April 1969.
3 Labour Party Archives, Minutes of PLP Meeting held on 14 May 1969.
4 Labour Party Archives, Minutes of PLP Meeting held on 7 May 1969.
5 MS. Wilson 1250, Harold Wilson, 'Note for the record on industrial relations legislation', 10 May 1969.
6 Labour Party Archives, Minutes of PLP Meeting held on 29 January1969.
7 Labour Party Archives, Minutes of PLP Meeting held on 5 February 1969.
8 Labour Party Archives, Minutes of PLP Meeting held on 19 February 1969.
9 Labour Party Archives, Minutes of PLP Meeting held on 17 April 1969.
10 Labour Party Archives, Minutes of PLP Meeting held on 17 April 1969.
11 Labour Party Archives, Minutes of PLP Meeting held on 30 April 1969.
12 MS. Castle.274, Lestor to Castle, 5 May 1969.
13 Labour Party Archives, Minutes of PLP Meeting held on 30 April 1969.
14 MS. Castle.274, Rose to Castle, 30 April 1969.
15 Labour Party Archives, Minutes of PLP Meeting held on 14 May 1969.
16 MS. Castle.274, Williams to Castle, 4 May 1969.
17 MS. Castle.274, Macdonald to Castle, 18 June 1969.
18 Labour Party Archives, Minutes of PLP Meeting held on 14 May 1969.
19 NA PREM 13/2727, 'Note of a Meeting of the Management Committee', 8 June 1969.
20 MS. Castle.274, Roberts [Acting Secretary of Blackburn CLP] to Castle, 4 June 1969.
21 NA PREM 13/2728, Houghton to Wilson, 16 June 1969. See also NA PREM 13/2727, Houghton to Wilson, 13 June 1969.

22 NA PREM 13/2728, 'Note of a Meeting of the Management Committee', 17 June 1969.
23 RICH/3/1/5 (Jo Richardson Papers), Minutes of Tribune Group Meeting, 21 April 1969.
24 MS. Castle.274, Ian Mikardo, '*In Place of Strife*: A Critique', undated, but *circa* May 1969.
25 RICH/3/1/5 (Jo Richardson Papers), Minutes of Tribune Group Meeting, 20 January 1969.
26 In 1931, the Labour Prime Minister, Ramsay MacDonald, facing dire economic circumstances and leading a minority Labour Government, formed a National Government with the Conservatives and the Liberals. Although a few Labour MPs and Ministers followed MacDonald, the majority of Labour MPs remained loyal to the Party. The new National Government then proceeded to impose major cuts in the 'social wage', and the Labour Party was out of office for the next fourteen years. For the left, MacDonald thereafter became synonymous with betrayal (see, for example, Eatwell and Wright, 1978).
27 RICH/3/1/5 (Jo Richardson Papers), Minutes of Tribune Group Meeting, 14 April 1969.
28 RICH/3/1/5 (Jo Richardson Papers), Minutes of Tribune Group Meeting, 14 April 1969.
29 RICH/3/1/5 (Jo Richardson Papers), Minutes of Tribune Group Meeting, 19 May 1969.
30 NA LAB 16/618, Stan Orme, 'The Donovan Report', undated, but *circa* late 1968, p. 1.
31 NA LAB 16/618, Stan Orme, 'The Donovan Report', undated, but *circa* late 1968, pp 2–9.
32 Labour Party Archives, Minutes of PLP Meeting held on 17 April 1969.
33 Labour Party Archives, Minutes of PLP Meeting held on 17 April 1969.
34 NA PREM 13/2726, R. J. D [Roger Dawe, Wilson's Private Secretary] to Wilson, 20 May 1969.
35 The dates of the six PLP meetings at which *In Place of Strife* was the sole item on the agenda were: 29 January 1969; 5 February 1969; 19 February 1969; 17 April 1969; 30 April 1969; 14 May 1969.

6

The trade unions' implacable hostility

The trade unions constitute the industrial wing of the organised labour movement, while the Labour Party is the political wing, but from the start of the twentieth century the two have been inextricably linked and bound together. Indeed, the trade unions were instrumental in creating the Labour Party, in order to ensure Parliamentary representation for ordinary working people, and *inter alia* defend the unions themselves from political (Conservative) attacks and hostile judicial decisions. As such, the decision by senior Ministers in a Labour Government to introduce industrial relations legislation which would include curbs on strike action, accompanied by financial penalties in particular circumstances, caused astonishment and anger through much of the trade union movement during the first half of 1969. It seemed tantamount to an act of betrayal by their Cabinet comrades.

In fact, there were four discrete reasons why the trade unions exuded such antipathy towards *In Place of Strife* and the ensuing short Industrial Relations Bill, namely: the trade unions' traditional commitment to voluntarism in industrial relations; the fact that In *Place of Strife* included 'punitive' measures, especially as these had been rejected by the Donovan Commission; the context and manner in which the subsequent 'short' Industrial Relations Bill was announced; sexism towards Barbara Castle, manifesting itself in the outrage which many (male) trade union leaders felt when a woman presumed to intervene in 'their' affairs.

The trade unions' commitment to 'voluntarism'

As was clear in the TUC's written submission to the Royal Commission on Trades Unions and Employers' Associations (discussed in chapter 2), Britain's trade unions were strongly wedded to the philosophy of 'voluntarism' or 'collective *laissez-faire*' in industrial relations, and as such, bitterly resented attempts by the State either to impose a legal framework on relationships between management and unions, or to legislate to regulate the internal affairs of the unions themselves. Of course, trade unions regularly welcomed (even lobbied for) legislation which would guarantee certain rights – both for themselves as corporate entities and in the form of basic employment rights for workers – and, in turn, provide a degree of legal parity between employers and employees. With this in mind, Ackers has recently referred to '[t]he TUC's *voluntarist myth*' which 'involved a high degree of self-perception', for much of the trade unions' increased post-1945 bargaining power 'was heavily shaped and sponsored by the corporatist state and employers' (Ackers, 2018: 262, emphasis in original). However, governmental initiatives to place the general conduct of industrial relations within a statutory framework, such as stipulating that ballots should be held prior to strike action, or to curb the 'closed shop' (compulsory union membership), were invariably opposed by the trade unions, for whom industrial self-government was sacrosanct.

The trade unions' staunch support for voluntarism was itself derived from four main sources: the principle of industrial and institutional self-government; an empiricist tradition which prioritised 'custom-and-practice', coupled with notions of what was deemed practicable; suspicion of the motives of those who promoted industrial relations legislation, pertaining to the question of whose interests would ultimately be served by statutory restrictions or regulations; and scepticism about the impartiality of the judiciary.

The principle of voluntarism

Britain's trade unions have been strongly wedded to the belief that good industrial relations cannot be secured through Acts of Parliament or statutory stipulation. Instead, it has long been a conviction of British trade unionism that more harmonious relationships in the workplace can only be attained through the long-term development of mutual trust and regular dialogue between the so-called 'two sides of industry'. Writing in the mid-1970s, one academic expert on industrial relations suggested that if Britain's trade unions could be characterised by 'any common ideology ... it is not socialism or the class struggle, but a devotion to what is called the voluntary system' (Flanders, 1974: 352). In elaborating on this key point, Flanders explained that trade unions:

> want to order their own affairs according to their preferences with as little outside interference as possible. This applies at all levels of trade union organisation, to union affairs within a plant, to their relations with district or higher union authorities, as well as to national unions and their relations with the state. Self-government is the essence, and

a concern for it can hardly be treated as of ephemeral or trivial value. (Flanders, 1974: 362)

Or as an American industrial relations expert explained, 'the unifying theme of voluntarism was that workers could best achieve their goals by relying on their own voluntary associations. Voluntarism defended the autonomy of the ... union against the coercive interference of the state' (Rogin, 1962: 522).

This voluntarist perspective had been strongly emphasised, in 1963, by the future TUC leader Victor Feather,[1] when he asserted that '[w]hatever government may be in power, *trade unions must be free to follow their collective policies, independently reached,* towards their basic aim', namely 'higher real wages, shorter hours and better working conditions'. These objectives were generally attained via *'the voluntary agreements and arrangements reached in industry* between the organised employers on the one hand, and organised workers on the other' (Feather, 1963: 38, 39, 41, emphases added).

He reiterated this perspective five years later, after the publication of the Donovan Report, insisting that:

> [g]ood relations cannot be imposed by a statutory body. Relationships by statute would be a move towards sanctions, and this would entail the creation of a whole legalistic labour code, with the state deciding the substantive terms of employment; party politics would thus be pushed deep into the heart of industrial relations. (Feather, 1968: 345)

The same year also heard John Edmonds, a future leader of the General, Municipal, Boilermakers and Allied Trade Union, argue that 'governments have little understanding of trade union organisation', and as a consequence '[t]he idea that a government should undertake the reform of a movement of 150,000 [shop] stewards, 20,000 branches and 200 complex rule books is beyond expectation'. Edmonds was therefore adamant that '[n]or *should* the government interfere ... it ought not to interfere in the detailed internal affairs of a voluntary organisation. That way lies ... perversion of the union movement's democratic purpose' (Edmonds, 1968: 52, emphasis in original).

Meanwhile, a future leader of the National Union of Mineworkers, Joe Gormley, insisted 'you can't legislate for these things. Industrial relations have to be on a voluntary basis if they are to be any good at all' (Gormley, 1982: 73).

An empiricist tradition

The principle of voluntarism was reinforced by a strong empiricist tradition within British trade unionism, in which great emphasis was placed on addressing industrial relations problems in an incremental, piecemeal and practicable manner, displaying due respect to the particular features of each industry or workplace. This entailed a strong commitment to evolutionary development and pragmatic adaptation as industrial circumstances changed, or new problems emerged. Ultimately, therefore, improvements in industrial relations needed to develop organically within each workplace or industry.

This perspective clearly militated against most attempts at invoking industrial relations laws, for most Westminster politicians and Whitehall mandarins were unlikely to have direct or practical experience of daily life on the factory- or shop-floor, and as a consequence, were prone to have a naïve or greatly exaggerated faith in the ability of governmental legislation to procure more constructive or cordial relationships between management and workers. Of course, some Labour MPs did emanate from industrial backgrounds prior to entering the House of Commons, but these were precisely the Party's Parliamentarians who – along with those of their colleagues who were either sponsored by trade unions, or themselves had backgrounds as union officials (like James Callaghan, whose major – and controversial – role in opposing *In Place of Strife* was discussed in chapter 4) – were most implacably opposed to Barbara Castle's proposed 'penal clauses'. They deemed these measures to be wrong in principle and/or likely to prove unworkable in practice, for according to George Woodcock (who was the TUC's General Secretary until the end of February 1969, when he was appointed chair of the newly established CIR), 'litigation led to trickery and legal manoeuvring'.[2]

Suspicion of the motives of would-be reformers

Although voluntarism was a fundamental principle *per se* for the trade unions, it was underpinned by suspicion of the motives of those politicians who advocated industrial relations legislation. After all, advocacy of statutory curbs on the activities of trade unions was rarely accompanied by proposals for similar limits on the conduct or power of the business community or corporate management. On the contrary, the advocacy or active pursuit of industrial relations legislation has often been ultimately concerned to secure the confidence of the business community and/or enhance managerial authority in the workplace, and thus the subordination of workers and their material interests, along with the suppression of sundry trade union activities.

Consequently, trade unions have instinctively been fearful that the main objective or motive is to tilt the balance of power in industry even further away from workers towards employers, and thereby firmly subordinate employees and unions to the interests and authority of companies and their managers. As such, 'any government intervention in union affairs will always be treated with suspicion' by trade unions' (Flanders, 1975: 292).

Scepticism towards the judiciary

This deep scepticism about the motives of those who advocate industrial relations legislation has been compounded by trade union doubts about the professed impartiality or/and class background of Britain's judiciary. Indeed, Flanders suggested that what often underpinned the trade unions' commitment to voluntarism was 'not so much a distrust of legislation as a distrust of courts of law' (Flanders, 1974: 354). After all, if statutory curbs or obligations were imposed on the trade unions or their members then, in the last instance, alleged breaches of these were liable to result in referral to the courts for adjudication. As such, voluntarism entailed a strong trade union commitment to 'keeping industrial disputes out of the courts by preserving our non-legalistic type of collective bargaining ... Their attitude to the courts has ... been the hard core of the unions' attachment to voluntarism' (Flanders, 1975: 289, 292).

The trade unions' profound scepticism towards the judiciary derived both from the class (socio-educational) background of many, if not most, of Britain's senior judges, and the actual experience of the trade unions from the nineteenth century onwards, when judicial decisions in key legal cases were rarely in the unions' favour (Kahn-Freund, 1959: 241).

With regard to the former of these sources of trade union suspicion, it has often been noted that many of Britain's senior judges tend to emanate from privileged backgrounds, having often been educated at the country's top public schools and Oxbridge, prior to embarking upon a career in law. Consequently, they are very unlikely to have any direct experience of the day-to-day working lives of ordinary people, and hence are instinctively inclined to make judicial decisions which uphold the stance or interests of employers and managers, rather than those of workers and trade unions.

If the judiciary did occasionally decide in favour of workers, it was invariably in cases where aggrieved employees were pursuing legal action against a trade union, rather than against an employer or company. In such instances, although the judiciary could cite such verdicts as clear evidence that they were not intrinsically anti-working class (as the left claimed), the ultimate result would almost certainly be detrimental to the trade unions *qua* institutions – as exemplified by the *Rookes v Barnard* case described in chapter 1.

Moreover, although the judiciary could claim to be politically independent, critics claimed that the privileged socio-educational background of many senior judges, and their narrow socio-cultural milieu or social networks – members-only 'gentlemen's clubs', dining with each other at top restaurants, attending exclusive or elite annual sporting or cultural events, etc. – almost inevitably inculcated them with deeply conservative attitudes and Conservative politics. As such, although they might claim that they merely interpreted the law in the cases which appeared before them, critics would argue that such interpretation was not value-free nor strictly neutral, but was often influenced by the innately conservative views and values of many senior judges (see, for example, Griffith, 1991: 30–7; Miliband, 1973: 124–30); what is today recognised as the phenomenon of 'unconscious bias'.

Yet even if the judiciary genuinely exercised (or sought to exercise) greater impartiality, many of the cases where they were called upon to adjudicate involved laws which were intended to uphold the rights of individuals or property, or enforce contracts, and which, as a consequence, were ultimately inimical to the interests of institutions based on collectivism – trade unions. Of course, the greater the number of landmark legal cases decided on this basis, the greater became the volume of 'case law' upon which judges draw, whereupon the conservative perspective of the judiciary became self-perpetuating. This aspect was candidly noted, in 1911, by Winston Churchill while he was a Minister in Herbert Asquith's Liberal Government, when he informed the House of Commons that:

> [i]t is not good for trade unions that they should be brought into contact with the courts, and it is not good for the courts … The courts hold justly a high, and I think, unequalled prominence in the respect of the world in criminal cases, and in civil cases between man and man, no doubt, they deserve and command the respect and admiration of all classes in the community but where class issues are involved, it is impossible to pretend that the courts command the same degree of general confidence. On the contrary, they do not, and a very large number of our population have been led to the opinion that they are, unconsciously no doubt, biased. (Hansard, 1911: Vol. 26, col. 1022)

This perspective was effectively endorsed nine years later by a senior judge, Lord Justice Scrutton, when he candidly confessed that:

> [t]he habits you are trained in, the people with whom you mix, lead to your having a certain class of ideas of such a nature that, when you have to deal with another set of ideas, you do not give as sound and accurate judgements as you would wish. This is one of the great difficulties at present with Labour. Labour says 'Where are your impartial Judges? They all move in the same circle as the employers, and they are all educated and nursed in the same ideas as the employers. How can a labour man or a trade unionist get impartial justice?' It is very difficult sometimes to be sure that you have put yourself into a thoroughly impartial position between two disputants, one of your own class and one not of your own class. (Quoted in Wedderburn, 1971: 26)

For all of these four reasons, therefore, Britain's trade unions were strongly wedded to a voluntarist perspective, and accordingly insisted that the 'two sides of industry' should be free to determine terms and conditions of employment between themselves, with little or no intervention (interference) by governments. Of course, the unions were firmly in favour of State intervention when it was intended to guarantee the rights of employees *vis-à-vis* employers, and protect the unions from apparently hostile decisions by the courts (perhaps by enacting legislation which restored the *status quo ante*), but overall British trade unionism was loath to permit governments or the law to regulate either collective bargaining between unions and employers, or the internal affairs and activities of the trade unions themselves.

As such, throughout the 1950s, the 'two sides of industry' had strongly subscribed to this system of 'collective *laissez-faire*' (Kahn-Freund, 1959: 224) or 'legal abstentionism' (Hyman, 2003: 39) in industrial relations; a system of 'collective bargaining [between management and trade unions] from which the state was only too ready, during peacetime, to exclude itself' (Fox, 1985: 439). Indeed, so prominent and prevalent was this voluntarist paradigm during the 1950s that '[t]he non-interventionist framework of labour law came to be regarded as part of the natural order of British industrial relations' (Lewis, 1983: 367). Or as Fox expressed it, '[t]his role of holding the ring ... entered into the state ideology of the impartial ruler' (Fox, 1985: 439).

This, in turn, became an integral component of the pluralist theory of political power, which perceives the state to be a neutral umpire or referee 'holding the ring' or mediating between competing societal interests – 'the free play of collective forces in society' (McCarthy, 1992: 6) – albeit with these interests broadly or tacitly accepting the 'rules of the game'. Consequently, there was a strong inclination to secure policies (or changes of policy) through negotiation and compromise: what Charles Lindblom (1965: *passim*) termed 'partisan mutual adjustment'. Until the early 1960s, this broadly neutral, 'holding the ring' or 'umpire' role was readily adopted by the Ministry of Labour itself.

The TUC's reaction to the Donovan Report

In view of the trade unions' unequivocal commitment to voluntarism, as reaffirmed in the TUC's written evidence to the Donovan Commission's inquiry, it was not surprising that the TUC warmly welcomed the Report's general endorsement of the voluntarist system of industrial relations in Britain. In so doing, the TUC reiterated that '[a] collective bargain was between employers and trade unions, and its content could not be determined and imposed by a statutory body' (Trades Union Congress, 1968a: 304).

Yet even when the Donovan Report did comment unfavourably on specific aspects of industrial relations, most notably the quantity of unconstitutional and/or unofficial strikes, the TUC argued that many if not most of these were concentrated in just a few industries and, as such, the Royal Commission had exaggerated or over-generalised the nature and scale of industrial disputes.[3] In effect, '[w]ell-founded generalisations about particular industries became generalisations about the whole field of collective bargaining', and as such, the Donovan Report 'could in some respects be said to present a picture which was somewhat larger than life' (Trades Union Congress, 1968a: 302).

Nonetheless, the TUC's General Council acknowledged that the trade unions could not be complacent, for their critics would be deeply be disappointed at the overall stance of the Donovan Report; the demands for legislative reform would continue from hostile quarters in spite of – or, rather, because of – the Royal Commission's overall rejection of statutory measures. In this context, it was vital that the trade union movement seize the initiative by pursuing reforms of collective bargaining and industrial relations which would obviate the need for government legislation. Indeed, the General Council readily acknowledged that '[w]ithout exaggeration, it can be said that this is the last chance for reform on the basis of voluntary action'.[4]

Shortly after the publication of the Donovan Report, Castle asked the TUC to provide a written response to its recommendations by mid-October. This deadline would not only provide the trade union leadership with three months during which to craft a considered and comprehensive response, it would also ensure that this could be endorsed by the TUC's annual conference in September, while still leaving time for any post-conference revisions.

In the meantime, the TUC's General Council, or sometimes the smaller Finance and General Purposes Committee, had various meetings with Castle and her senior DEP officials during the summer and early autumn of 1968, as an integral component of her post-Donovan consultations with the two sides of industry; she also held meetings with leaders of the CBI during this period. At the first post-Donovan meeting between Castle and six representatives from the TUC's General Council, the latter immediately queried whether the proposed CIR would be entitled to make proposals which the Secretary of State then deemed 'mandatory'. Even at this initial stage, the TUC leaders warned that '[t]he TUC attitude to the CIR would depend on the answer to that question', adding that it was highly unlikely that 'the General Council would favour the establishment of a CIR if it was to be based on the use of sanctions'.[5]

Following its own deliberations on the Donovan Report during the summer and early autumn of 1968, which had been interspersed with these consultative meetings with Barbara Castle, the TUC subsequently published an 'interim statement' on the Donovan Report, entitled *Action on Donovan*. This also constituted the trade unions' response to a questionnaire which the DEP had issued to the TUC and the CBI in the summer, in order to elicit their responses to specific aspects of the Donovan Report.

The TUC utilised *Action on Donovan* to reiterate the trade unions' commitment to voluntarism, which the Donovan Report itself had mostly endorsed. In particular, *Action on Donovan* emphasised that '[t]he General Council share the Royal Commission's view that the legal enforceability of collective agreements would be both undesirable and impracticable', not least because of the need for procedures 'to be tailor-made to the circumstances of the industry'. This, of course, again reflected the extent to which voluntarism placed immense importance on custom-and-practice in the conduct of industrial relations, and a highly pragmatic approach to problem-solving in industry and the workplace.

Thus did the TUC's General Council 'share the Royal Commission's view that relevance and flexibility are the two essential characteristics of procedures', and this need for flexibility would be strongly reinforced in an era of accelerating industrial and technological change which would yield significant 'changes in the pattern of work'. In this context, 'the notion of a binding legal contract becomes more and more unacceptable' (TUC, 1968b: 17, paras 38 and 39). The same unwavering commitment to voluntarism also meant that the TUC strongly endorsed the Donovan Report's rejection both of compulsory strike ballots and a statutory 'cooling-off' period (Trades Union Congress, 1968b: 29, paras 74 and 75).[6]

The TUC was not entirely dismissive of the need for change in industrial relations, but was adamant that these needed to be developed from within industry itself, rather than being imposed by the State: 'the TUC and the CBI accept that considerable improvements need to be made in our *voluntary* system … and that these depend primarily on the initiative of management, employers' associations and trade unions' (Trades Union Congress, 1968b: 47, para. 2, emphasis added).

As we noted in chapter 3, at the very end of 1968 and in early 1969, and before she had formally unveiled her proposals to the Cabinet, Castle held two meetings, first with senior members of the TUC's General Council and then with the Finance and General Purposes Committee, to discuss the draft (and still unnamed) White Paper. Given the trade unions' unwavering commitment to voluntarism, it was inevitable that they would offer a mixed response to Castle's proposals for reforming industrial relations. The TUC naturally welcomed the many proposals which sought to strengthen the roles and rights of trade unions *qua* institutions, in tandem with a corresponding strengthening of employment protection for individual workers. However, not only was the TUC aghast that a Labour Government was intending to depart from the hitherto voluntarist system of industrial relations and trade union self-government, it was also aggrieved that Castle was going much further than the Donovan Commission had proposed in its recommended reforms of collective bargaining and industrial relations.

In particular, the TUC's General Council was deeply concerned about those aspects of the draft White Paper which aimed to grant the Secretary of State for Employment various powers over the activities of trade unions, most notably potentially requiring a ballot prior to a strike, invoking a 'conciliation pause' or cooling-off period for unconstitutional strikes, and imposing fines in cases where a trade union or its members defied an order to return to work pending 'peace talks'. The latter was to prove particularly contentious, because of TUC fears that if fines were imposed on individual workers, a subsequent failure to pay them would ultimately run the risk of imprisonment. In effect, some workers would effectively be made criminals for going on strike.

The TUC's concerns were expressed by the TUC representatives at the second of two meetings with Castle which preceded the (3 January 1969) presentation of the draft White Paper to the Cabinet. The first of these meetings was primarily an outline by Castle of the main proposals, with only a cursory response by the TUC, owing to both lack of time and a natural need for the General Council to consider more carefully what Castle was proposing.[7] The second meeting, though, was effectively a question-and-answer session, with Castle and some of her senior officials responding to the sundry concerns and queries raised by various trade union leaders. Not surprisingly, many of the questions asked by trade union leaders at this second meeting were about the statutory powers which Castle intended to award herself in relation to various types of industrial dispute, and the tenor of these specific queries made it quite clear that they were strongly opposed by the TUC leadership.

In response to the specific trade union concern that non-payment of fines might result in some trade unionists being sent to prison, Castle emphasised that she was determined to avoid such an outcome, although the precise details of how financial penalties would be retrieved in cases of non-payment or arrears were still being developed. On this issue, one of her Departmental officials intervened to suggest that Parliament could decree that certain types of debt should be exempt from the penalty of imprisonment, thereby ensuring that payment of outstanding fines was achieved though non-custodial methods.[8]

That such an important issue had not already been resolved by Castle and her legal advisers merely exacerbated the TUC's anxieties, and meant that the trade union leaders were unconvinced by Castle's professed determination to avoid the imprisonment of union members who failed (for whatever reason) to pay fines. Besides, TUC leaders emphasised that '[p]enalties were not an effective way to make people behave.'[9]

Furthermore, when Castle subsequently suggested that fines could be paid via an attachment-of-earnings order, and thus deducted directly from an employee's wages, Jack Jones pointed out that this 'would mean that workers were having money deducted by the very people with whom they had been in dispute', a scenario which was very likely to cause 'the most intense resentment' (Jones, 1969).

There was little progress between Castle and TUC leaders when they held a further meeting with Castle and her senior DEP colleagues on 8 January, by which time the Cabinet had discussed the draft White Paper, albeit without actually endorsing it at this stage. At this third meeting to discuss Castle's legislative proposals, the TUC's opposition to the conciliation pause was reiterated, both because of strong opposition to the fines which would be imposed on workers who defied an order to return to work, and because, in some instances where 'unconstitutional' strikes were called, the union's apparent failure to adhere to disputes procedures was because no such procedural agreements existed.

Castle's stance on this issue served to provide the TUC with further evidence of her lack of real understanding of industrial relations and life on the factory floor. The TUC leadership asked her bluntly 'how a procedure could be broken when there was no procedure?' The TUC's perspective was that the emphasis should be on establishing, clarifying or strengthening procedural agreements, rather than focusing on imposing financial penalties in cases where such agreements had allegedly been breached. As such, the TUC leaders insisted that it was 'premature to be talking about sanctions' while warning that, if Castle persevered, the Government would, in effect, be moving 'towards the imposition of criminal sanctions in the field of industrial relations'.[10]

While the trade unions naturally abhorred the Labour Government's apparent criminalisation of industrial relations and trade union activities, *pace* the 'penal clauses' proposed in the draft White Paper, and the extent to which these proposals departed from the recommendations of the Donovan Report, three other contextual factors compounded trade union antipathy. The first was that, since 1965, the Labour Government had resorted to a series of increasingly stringent, and statutory, incomes policies to curb wage increases. Yet in the 1964 election Labour had decried such incomes policies, committing itself instead to 'a policy for incomes' whose objective was *not* 'to keep increases down to a minimum, but up to the maximum possible', as determined by a dual policy of industrial planning and expansion to secure steady and sustainable economic growth. This was supposed to ensure that 'incomes policy is not wage restraint. It should allow real wages to rise.'[11]

The subsequent recourse to a succession of increasingly strict incomes policies designed to hold down wage increases (Dorey, 2001: chapter four) naturally created tensions between the Labour Government and the trade unions. These were not just because of the impact on workers' living standards and prosperity, but because such policies were effectively a negation of *free* collective bargaining, a mode of pay determination which the trade unions viewed as sacrosanct and inextricably linked to their commitment to voluntarism. Yet from the trade unions' perspective, recourse to *statutory* incomes policies, with legal sanctions and penalties liable to be imposed on those who breached them, was tantamount to criminalising workers who sought a pay rise in excess of that decreed acceptable or affordable by the Government. As one industrial relations expert noted a few years later, '[i]n terms of abstentionist legal policy, the statutory incomes policy was a revolutionary development, as it interfered with free collective bargaining'. Even during the exceptional exigencies of the Second World War, Ministers had baulked at such direct and draconian intervention (Lewis, 1976: 11).

The second contextual factor which strained relations between the Labour Government and the trade unions during this period, well before the publication of *In Place of Strife*, was the implementation of deflationary policies from 1965 onwards, initially as an alternative to devaluation (of sterling), and then persevered with in order to ensure the success of devaluation. Of course, deflation entailed sundry cuts in public expenditure, and thus in the 'social wage'. These measures, in tandem with incomes policies to curb wage increases, clearly constituted an abandonment of the progressive economic and social policies which the Party had pledged in the 1964 election, and consequently fuelled a strong sense of betrayal among many erstwhile Labour supporters and trade unionists. Thus it was that when these measures were subsequently accompanied by proposed legislation to curb strikes, the patience and loyalty of much of the labour movement was pushed to the absolute limit.

The third contextual factor which compounded trade union hostility to *In Place of Strife* was sundry prominent criticisms of the unions which had been expressed by some senior Labour politicians in the latter half of the 1960s. The most notable of these was Harold Wilson's bitter condemnation of a strike, ostensibly concerning working conditions and hours (the amount of time spent at sea), by the National Union of Seamen in the middle of 1966. The Prime Minister alleged, in the House of Commons, that this dispute was actually being fomented by a:

> tightly knit group of politically motivated men who, as the last General Election showed, utterly failed to secure acceptance of their [Communist] views by the British electorate, but who are now determined to exercise backstage pressures, forcing great hardship on the members of the union and their families, and endangering the security of the industry and the economic welfare of the nation. (Hansard, 1966: Vol. 730, cols 42 and 43)

Following the twin assault of incomes policies to restrain wage increases in tandem with deflationary economic measures entailing cuts to the 'social wage', naturally such condemnation of trade union activities by a Labour Prime Minister further soured relations between the Government and the unions, and ensured that the latter were *not* favourably disposed towards the legislative reforms and statutory curbs heralded by *In Place of Strife*. In fact, a few weeks before the White Paper was published, a weekly meeting of the PLP heard Norman Atkinson, a member of the left-wing Tribune Group, complain about 'attacks on the Trade Unions by Members of the Party', with two former Cabinet Ministers being named (George Brown and Ray Gunter, the latter being Castle's predecessor).[12]

In short, the economic and political circumstances in which the Labour Government announced its plans to 'reform' industrial relations were also the very circumstances which ensured the hostility of the trade unions, who resented being made 'scapegoats' for the sundry problems afflicting British industry and the economy.

The TUC's hostile response to *In Place of Strife*

Although Barbara Castle sought to depict *In Place of Strife* as a balanced package of proposals for reforming industrial relations, containing many positive proposals intended to benefit trade unionism, it was the 'punitive' or prescriptive aspects which attracted the most prominence, and provided the main target for the unions' hostility. While union leaders readily acknowledged that much of the White Paper was favourable to the trade unions and working people, this was nonetheless viewed as 'sugar coating on a very bitter pill' (Jones, 1986: 202); or as Frank Cousins expressed it, whilst *In Place of Strife* contained many proposals which would greatly benefit the trade unions and their members, 'it would be absolutely stupid to believe that putting the proposals in the form of a package deal will compensate for the introduction of restrictive clauses affecting strikes, and relationships between members and their own trade unions' (quoted in *The Sunday Mirror*, 19 January 1969).

The trade unions harboured several objections to *In Place of Strife*, these constituting a blend of general and specific concerns. The first, and most general, objection was that the White Paper heralded a clear break with the voluntarist tradition of British industrial relations which had prevailed since 1946, when the 1927 Trades Disputes and Trade Union Act, which was despised by the unions, had been repealed. Thus was the voluntarist tradition variously cited or invoked when trade union leaders condemned the punitive measures or 'penal clauses' which *In Place of Strife* advocated.

For example, the TUC's official response to *In Place of Strife*, agreed at a special meeting of the General Council on 7 January 1969 and issued ten days later, on the same day that the White Paper was published, declared its commitment to 'strengthening voluntary collective bargaining', and added that this objective had been 'the test by which the General Council have examined both the Report of the Royal Commission and the Government's proposals'. The General Council reiterated that 'voluntary action ... is at the same time the foundation of free trade unionism, and the essential prerequisite if the men and women who together make up the trade union movement are themselves to accept such changes willingly'. Consequently, although *In Place of Strife* contained several proposals which 'could in principle help to improve industrial relations and to promote trade union objectives', the TUC was 'opposed to, or at least have reservations about, the Government's other proposals', so much so that the General Council wanted the Government to be 'in no doubt about the nature of these reservations and the strength of their objections' (Trades Union Congress, 1969a: 205).

Second, the trade unions were aggrieved that it was a Labour government that was intending to place statutory controls on their activities and internal affairs. Such prescriptive or punitive measures would have been expected had they been announced by a Conservative government, but for a supposedly left-wing Labour Minister (Castle) to announce such legislation beggared belief. Joe Gormley recalled that '[a]s we went into 1969, it became more and more apparent that the Labour Party was bent on some form of legislation to curb the power of the trade unions' (Gormley, 1982: 72) yet, when *In Place of Strife* was published, he was still shocked that a government would be prepared to go so far: 'It was an attempt to shackle the unions by bringing legislation into the field of industrial relations. What was worse, it proposed to back up that legislation with the threat of punishment by the courts.' Such was Gormley's outrage at *In Place of Strife* that 'I doubt if any politician or trade union leader was more furious than I' (Gormley, 1982: 73).

Some trade union leaders suspected that it was her Department's civil servants who were advising Castle to place statutory curbs or obligations on the trade unions (Silver, 1973: 130). This suspicion relates to the point we noted in chapter 3, namely the hardening of attitudes towards trade unions (or, rather, unofficial strikes) among some senior officials in the Ministry of Labour, a shifting stance which was then reinforced by the influx of new (pro-legislation) officials from the DEA when the two Ministries were merged to establish the DEP in April 1968. Indeed, at one meeting, Jack Jones asked Castle why she and Wilson were allowing a Labour Government to adopt 'the anti-trade union ideas of top civil servants', ideas which meant that 'the fate of the Labour Movement was at stake' (Jones, 1986: 204).

This last point reflected a deep concern that the 'penal' or prescriptive measures which *In Place of Strife* proposed were likely to jeopardise the relationship between the Labour Party and the trade unions. As such, the TUC warned that '[a]ny attempt ... to impose unreasonable and therefore unworkable constraints on the freedom of working people to pursue their legitimate objectives could only harm the relationships between the trade union movement and the Government' (Trades Union Congress, 1969a: 206).

Third, trade unions bitterly resented the implication of *In Place of Strife* that it was they, rather than employers and workplace management, that were largely to blame for many, if not most, of Britain's industrial relations problems. Such blame was often inextricably linked to claims that the unions were 'too powerful', as evinced by the extensive disruption often caused by strikes. Yet, as one senior union official argued, unions 'can only shut down factories for temporary periods, and then through the sacrifices of their members', whereas large employers and industrialists – likened to feudal barons – 'can close whole factories permanently, and throw thousands of people out of work, simply to improve profit margins' (Urwin, 1969).

Meanwhile, trade unions suspected that the legislative measures foreshadowed in the White Paper were motivated less by a genuine desire to improve Britain's industrial relations by tackling injustices and inequities in the workplace, and more by a concern both to pacify 'the City' (*pace* the announcement of the short Industrial Relations Bill by Chancellor Roy Jenkins during his 1969 Budget speech) and impress both the electorate and pro-Conservative newspapers that a Labour government was willing to 'take on' the trade unions.

Fourth, there was concern that once industrial relations were placed firmly within a statutory framework, vesting particular powers in the hands of the Secretary of State for Employment, these were likely to be extended and strengthened, especially by future Conservative governments; it would the thin end of a wedge, or the start of a slippery slope, leading ultimately to State control of trade unions redolent of a totalitarian regime. This is partly why Barbara Castle's insistence that the 'penal clauses' would only be enacted sparingly, as a last resort, failed to overcome the trade unions' implacable opposition. Quite apart from the break with voluntarism which these clauses represented, the unions were deeply concerned that, regardless of how restrained *Castle* might prove to be in invoking these measures, a Conservative successor was very unlikely to practice similar reticence. As such, Castle's repeated claim that her proposals were much less legalistic or restrictive than those which would almost certainly be introduced by a Conservative government failed to assuage the TUC: the latter was convinced that, once statutory curbs and penalties had been imposed by a Labour government, they would almost certainly be extended by a Conservative government.

Fifth, some trade union leaders believed that Ministerial advocates of industrial relations legislation based on *In Place of Strife* lacked any real or direct understanding of factory-floor or internal trade union politics. According to Jack Jones, for example, 'Wilson and Castle were basically academics, and it was difficult to persuade them to see things from a shop-floor angle … they revealed a lack of understanding of working conditions', having never 'lived through the rough and tumble of life on the shop-floor' (Jones, 1986: 204, 203). Joe Gormley was even more scathing when he remarked: 'God knows who advised her, but to my mind she [Castle] was utterly stupid' (Gormley, 1982: 73). Meanwhile, Frank Cousins' biographer (Goodman, 1984: 573) noted that, by the end of 1968, after the Sunningdale weekend, 'the legislative hawks had captured her', adding that 'Harold Wilson took the same view as the civil service advisers around Barbara Castle'.

Consequently, senior trade union leaders repeatedly warned Castle and Wilson that the penal aspects of *In Place of Strife* were not only unacceptable to the unions in principle, but would also ultimately be unenforceable in practice. Furthermore, some of them were likely to exacerbate the very problems they were intended to solve. For example, it was argued if the Secretary of State acquired the right to order a ballot prior to a strike, then this was 'likely to militate very strongly against confidence in union leadership', whereupon 'unofficial action would be encouraged, not reduced, as a result'. Moreover, 'to force an Executive, against its judgement, to hold a ballot, under the threat of financial penalties, would worsen, not improve, the situation' (Trades Union Congress, 1969a: 207).

Meanwhile, with regard to the proposed 'conciliation pause' *vis-à-vis* unconstitutional strikes, the TUC's antipathy was not assuaged by the statement that this would only be invoked on a discretionary basis. On this particular point, during the drafting of the White Paper, senior civil servants had envisaged that, by granting the Secretary of State *discretionary* power to order a conciliation pause in particular circumstances, the proposal would appear less draconian or rigid: 'it is deliberately designed to avoid the need for criteria justifying its use.'[13] Instead, the conciliation pause would only be invoked on a case-by-case basis – or 'selectively' according to Castle herself[14] – depending on the character and circumstances of an unconstitutional or unofficial strike.

However, from the trade unions' perspective, its discretionary basis actually made it potentially more draconian, because it would be for the Secretary of State to decide when, and on what basis, to order a conciliation pause, and thus an immediate return to work. Had explicit criteria been adopted, then such decisions might have been imbued with a degree of objectivity or transparency, although they would almost certainly still have been opposed by the trade unions. Instead, their discretionary nature had potential, at least, to significantly increase the scope for direct, but arbitrary, Ministerial intervention, for she would decide if circumstances warranted an order to return to work. Moreover, sooner or later, it would be a Conservative Secretary of State wielding such discretionary power, cognizance of which reinforced trade union opposition.

Yet even if the Secretary of State did successfully order an immediate return to work pending conciliation talks or an inquiry into the source of a dispute, the General Council was adamant that 'it would not be possible to prevent them [strikers], if they so chose, from working without enthusiasm', something which no law could effectively tackle.

Ultimately, the TUC insisted, the objective should be to tackle the underlying causes of the majority of unconstitutional strikes, and thereby minimise their occurrence, rather than invoke prescriptive or punitive measures to solve them after they had begun (Trades Union Congress, 1969a: 208). What the TUC was alluding to in this last point was that unconstitutional strikes were frequently an immediate response by unions or workers to arbitrary, unjust or otherwise provocative decisions or actions by management, and as such, the Government ought to be directing its legislative efforts at bad employers. If it did so, then unconstitutional strikes were almost certain to diminish significantly in any case.

Trade unions and their senior leaders instead sought to persuade Castle and Wilson that the TUC should be permitted to devise its own policies and procedures for tackling unofficial and unconstitutional strikes, and inter-union disputes, thereby obviating the need for government legislation. It was emphasised that such an approach would both prevent a damaging schism between the trade unions and the Labour Party/Government, and be fully in accordance with the British tradition of voluntarism and self-government in the realm of industrial relations. In fact, Castle and Wilson did subsequently pledge that, if the TUC devised its own credible counter-proposals for tackling strikes, the Government would withdraw the 'penal clauses' from the Bill, or at least place them in 'cold storage' while the effectiveness of the TUC's measures was evaluated.

Although the punitive aspects of *In Place of Strife* dominated the ensuing discussions between Castle, Wilson and TUC leaders, there was broad agreement on the timetable for consultations over, and the drafting of, legislation based on the White Paper. Following an invitation, on 21 January 1969, from Castle to the TUC's General Council, to consider this specific issue, it was agreed that the consultative process would be completed by the end of May, whereupon a Bill would be drafted in readiness for the next [1969–70] Parliamentary session, with its First Reading tentatively scheduled for November 1969.[15] However, the DEP acknowledged that consultations between the Government and the TUC (via its General

Council) would not actually cease at the end of May, but would almost certainly continue during the drafting stage of the ensuing industrial relations legislation.

Yet this agreement, that legislation should entail a lengthy gestation between publication of the White Paper and the formal introduction of legislation, belied the differences in motive or expectation between Castle and the TUC's General Council. Castle anticipated that a lengthy period of consultation would enable her (and Harold Wilson, who usually accompanied her in meetings with the TUC) to persuade the trade union leaders to accept the proposed reforms, especially if she could also convince them that the statutory powers she was intending to acquire (to intervene in certain types of dispute in particular circumstances) would be used only rarely and sparingly. By contrast, the TUC's amenability to a long period of pre-legislative consultation derived from its calculation that this would give it time to persuade Castle to abandon the 'punitive' aspects of *In Place of Strife*, especially if the TUC could, in the meantime, devise its own measures to tackle the types of industrial dispute that Castle was targeting. Furthermore, the TUC's General Council would immediately have been aware that the longer the period of pre-legislative consultation, the more likely it was that opposition to the 'punitive' aspects of *In Place of Strife* would widen and deepen, not just inside the trade unions themselves, but also among Labour MPs – many of whom were sponsored by a trade union (as noted in chapter 5).

Of course, as we noted in chapter 4, it was the likelihood of growing opposition to, rather than gradual acceptance of, *In Place of Strife* which had led some Cabinet Ministers, most notably Crossman and Jenkins, to urge immediate industrial relations legislation when the White Paper was published in January. They had presciently foreseen that the longer the delay, the greater the mobilisation against the White Paper's proposals, and thus the stronger would be the opposition to the planned Bill.

The TUC's reaction to the short Industrial Relations Bill

Having thus assumed, on the basis of the timetable agreement with Castle, that legislation based on *In Place of Strife* would not be introduced until the 1969–70 Parliamentary session, the trade unions were inevitably furious at the announcement, in the mid-April Budget, that a 'short', interim, Industrial Relations Bill would actually be introduced imminently, to precede a more comprehensive bill in the 1969–70 session. In fact, there were two aspects of this short Bill which annoyed the trade unions, and thus further strained the relationship between them and the Labour Government. The first was that, whereas *In Place of Strife* had proposed a Bill in which three out of twenty-five clauses would be punitive or prescriptive (from the trade unions' perspective), what was suddenly being proposed was a Bill in which two out of just six clauses were of a penal character.

The second reason why the interim Industrial Relations Bill antagonised the trade unions was the manner of its announcement, which took the trade unions by surprise and left them feeling angry and betrayed by what they perceived as Castle and Wilson's duplicity. This was because, on Friday 11 April, just four days before Roy Jenkins announced the Bill in his Budget Speech, senior TUC leaders had attended one of their (by now) routine meetings with Castle and Wilson to discuss the Government plans concerning *In Place of Strife* and the content of proposed legislation. At this meeting, Vic Feather had referred directly to sundry press reports that the Government was intending to introduce industrial relations legislation immediately, rather than waiting until November, as previously planned. If this speculation proved correct, Feather warned, and legislation containing 'penal clauses' was introduced now, then the TUC would not only come under strong pressure from affiliated unions to organise a Special Conference, rather than leave the issue until the annual conference in September, it was also likely that such a conference would vote to reject *In Place of Strife* altogether.[16]

In response, Wilson had claimed the Government had made no decision on the timing of industrial relations legislation, albeit adding that the Cabinet naturally reserved the right to decide whether and when to introduce such a Bill. As such, Wilson asserted that he could not give any indication about the timing of legislation on this issue. The TUC had assumed that this was a rebuttal of the rumours of imminent industrial relations legislation but, upon closer reading, Wilson's answer seems to have been deliberately mired in ambiguity – if not deliberately evasive. Strictly speaking, the Cabinet had not yet made a decision on introducing an Industrial Relations Bill, but Wilson and Castle would surely have been aware that it was likely to do so at its next meeting, which took place on Monday 14 April 1969.

When Castle and Wilson next met the same TUC leaders the following Wednesday, the day after the formal announcement of the 'interim' Industrial Relations Bill, the Prime Minister explained that the decision to introduce a short Industrial Relations Bill had only been taken at the Cabinet meeting on Monday morning, the implication being that there had been nothing disingenuous or deceitful in not informing the trade union leaders at the previous Friday's meeting; they had not been informed because the Cabinet had not taken a decision at that time, and so there had been nothing to report.

It was at this meeting, though, that Wilson tried to assuage the understandably aggrieved and deeply sceptical TUC leaders by offering an olive branch of sorts. He promised that, if they could put forward convincing and credible counter-proposals to tackle unofficial and unconstitutional strikes, the Government would reconsider the 'penal clauses' pertaining to this aspect of the interim Industrial Relations Bill, which it intended to have drafted by the end of May. He even intimated that the Bill could be modified during its Parliamentary legislative stages (beyond May) if the TUC could offer equally effective measures of its own to deal with members or affiliated unions who engaged in strikes which were unconstitutional or unofficial.

The TUC leaders retorted that, by bringing legislation forward from November, the Government was depriving them of the necessary time to consult with affiliated trade unions over reforming the TUC's internal rules and procedures for tackling unofficial and unconstitutional strikes. It had been the TUC's intention to continue conducting such consultations over the summer, with a view to putting forward clear counter-proposals for ratification at its annual conference in September. Now the TUC was being expected to 'make proposals to over 150 affiliated unions, who would have to discuss them through their own machinery, and get decisions in so short a time'. As such, the Government's precipitate action now seriously jeopardised the likelihood of 'constructive reform'.

Besides, the TUC suggested that Wilson's exhortation that the trade unions should advance 'equally effective' counter-proposals rather assumed that the Government's own proposals would be 'effective', an assumption which the TUC most certainly did not share; such effectiveness was 'conjectural'.[17] Incidentally, although obviously he was not a participant in these negotiations, this objection was strongly shared by James Callaghan: 'it is begging the question to ask that the TUC should produce a solution as effective as the Government's, because no-one knows how effective the Government solution is going to be.'[18]

In the meantime, the Government's announcement of the interim Industrial Relations Bill increased pressure on the TUC to hold a Special Conference to discuss the trade unions' response to the Government's legislative proposals. Several trade unions had recently held spring conferences, which had passed motions calling for a Special Conference rather than waiting until the usual September seaside gathering. Many of these conferences had been held in March, a few weeks *before* the Government's announcement of the 'interim' Industrial Relations Bill: when this was announced, the pressure on the TUC to accede to such demands became virtually irresistible. In fact, some trade unions wrote to urge a Special Conference *after* (but precisely because) the interim bill had been announced.[19]

The TUC's General Council acceded to these demands at a meeting on 23 April, when it was readily acknowledged that not only was the content of the interim Bill a major cause of concern to the trade unions, but also 'the precipitate way in which the Government is acting'. In announcing the decision to hold a special conference in Croydon on 5 June 1969, the trade union leaders reiterated the extent to which they 'fundamentally disagree with the idea that it is possible to promote good industrial relations by punitive measures'. The TUC's General Council warned that, instead of securing such an improvement in industrial relations, the Labour Government's proposals would not merely prove unworkable, they would 'embitter, not alleviate, industrial difficulties, would impair, not strengthen, the authority of trade unions and their representatives, and would sap, not reinforce, the procedures for avoiding and settling disputes'. That the Government seemed so determined to persevere with such legislation merely illustrated, once again, its 'misunderstanding of the nature of the industrial relations system'.[20]

Sexism towards Castle

Before discussing the TUC's special Croydon conference, we need to acknowledge a fourth reason for the unions' hostility towards *In Place of Strife* and the interim Industrial Relations Bill, namely the degree of sexism and chauvinism towards Barbara Castle which many senior trade unionists harboured at this time. Indeed, sexism was widely prevalent in Britain during the 1960s, not least in many workplaces and male-dominated trade unions. For all the trade unions' rousing rhetoric about equality, fairness and Socialism, and the Labour Government's own legislation formally outlawing sexual and racial discrimination, blatant sexism was rife during this time. Sexist comments, sexual innuendo and even crude sexual propositions addressed to women in the workplace, were invariably defended by the chauvinistic perpetrators as mere 'banter', some lighthearted levity to lighten up a dull day in a dead-end, low-paid job.

Similarly, in some workplaces, what would today be recognised as 'inappropriate touching', and thus as sexual assault, was widely tolerated as 'harmless fun'. Needless to say, women who complained about such sexism were likely to be denounced as kill-joys who had no sense of humour or sense of fun, and could not take a joke; or be accused of being 'one of those Women's Libbers'.

After all, in this era, the law did not recognise the concept of 'rape in marriage' (incredibly, it did not do so until the early 1990s), and domestic violence was usually ignored by the police, either treated as a private incident in which others should not interfere, or because it was often assumed that the wife had somehow 'provoked' her husband into losing his temper and hitting her; apparently, it was six-of-one, half-a-dozen of the other: a classic case of blaming the victim.

In an era characterised by such widespread and deeply ingrained sexism, it is sadly not surprising that Barbara Castle was herself subject to considerable male chauvinism from some senior trade unionists, virtually all of whom were men. Moreover, many of them emanated from heavy industry (iron and steel, manufacturing, ship-building, coal-mining, car-making, etc.), with its associated notion of hard, physical work undertaken by 'real men', and accompanying 'macho' attitudes; a prolier-than-thou perspective. As such, she was contemptuously viewed not only as a middle-class, Oxford-educated intellectual trying to impose her apparently airy-fairy, high-falutin' ideas on the hard-grafting working class, but also as a woman who had the audacity to decree how men should conduct their industrial affairs and trade union activities, something of which she had no personal experience. Even though *In Place of Strife* was fully endorsed by Harold Wilson, such sexism meant that it was Castle who bore the brunt of the opprobrium from trade union leaders.

According to Marie Patterson, tellingly one of only two women on the TUC's General Council, the attitude of many male trade union leaders was 'the statutory woman politician was alright as Minister for Education or something, not interfering in things they knew nothing about, like the horny-handed sons of toil' (quoted in Martineau, 2011: 218). Similarly, Wilson's Press Secretary, Joe Haines, recalled that the TUC leaders 'were anti-feminist ... so macho. She would lecture them, and some of them would say that was the sort of thing that happens when you go home. Your wife might tell you off, but you're not going to be told off by Barbara Castle. They really were pretty dreadful' (quoted in Martineau, 2011: 218).

Meanwhile, Nicholas Davenport, who was a pro-Labour City banker (a very rare breed indeed) who occasionally met or dined with senior Labour Ministers in the latter half of the 1960s, suggested that 'it was a mistake to leave these critical negotiations to a strident Amazon. Barbara really upset the old trade union boys who hate nagging women always trying to get their own way', adding that, in terms of impact, *In Place of Strife* 'was like a bomb thrown by a Women's-Lib fanatic into a quiet front parlour while Dad was having his high tea' (Davenport, 1974: 221). In trying to characterise the sexist attitudes of many senior trade unionists, Davenport seems also unwittingly to have revealed his own.

The TUC's Croydon conference

The 5 June special conference was the first such TUC gathering for almost fifty years, and thus clearly conveyed the immense importance attached to this episode. The general purpose of this conference was to endorse *Programme for Action*, a policy document written by the TUC's General

Council in response to the Government's announcement of the interim Industrial Relations Bill. This reaffirmed the trade unions' commitment to voluntarism, and thus their unequivocal opposition to State intervention in the internal affairs and activities of the trade unions. It did, however, put forward alternative proposals whereby the TUC would amend some of its own rules concerning the governance of inter-union disputes and unconstitutional strikes. It was intended that these measures would render the Government's proposed 'penal clauses' unnecessary.

When he had first been informed of this special conference, Harold Wilson had suggested, to Vic Feather, that he should be invited to address the delegates, in order that they could 'hear the truth'. Feather gently but firmly rebuffed Wilson's suggestion, explaining that if the delegates at Croydon voted against the Government's proposed industrial relations legislation, particularly the 'penal clauses', after he had delivered a speech, this would be widely construed as a personal rebuff. Indeed, the Prime Minister's presence might be perceived by some delegates as provocative, and thereby harden opinion trade union opposition to the Government's planned bill even further. As to informing union delegates of 'the truth', Feather retorted 'with a broad grin, that ... he was intending to put the truth anyway to the TUC in his opening speech', to which Wilson replied 'truth was not only a many splendoured thing, but a many sides thing'. Nonetheless, Wilson accepted Feather's advice that addressing the TUC's Croydon conference might be unwise in the circumstances and context.[21]

The delegates at the TUC's special Croydon conference were asked to endorse three 'recommendations', namely:

1. To affirm that the TUC is 'unalterably opposed' to the Government's proposal, via the Industrial Relations Bill, to acquire a statutory right to impose financial penalties, either on trade unions or their members, in connection with their pursuit of particular kinds of industrial action.
2. To affirm that various other proposals advanced via *In Place of Strife* and the Industrial Relations Bill 'could in principle help to improve industrial relations and to promote trade union objectives'.
3. To grant the General Council further power to improve procedures and resolve disputes. (Trades Union Congress, 1969b: 23)

In opening proceedings, the TUC's chair, John Newton, argued that some people 'are suffering from industrial relations hallucinations and delusions which have been brought about by the excessive burden of four years of unprecedented political endeavour'. It was therefore necessary for the TUC 'to rid them of their delusions and save them from themselves' (Trades Union Congress, 1969b: 25). Shortly after Newton's introductory peroration, Vic Feather addressed the Special Conference in his role as the TUC's Acting General Secretary, and again reiterated the unions' commitment to voluntarism by insisting that:

> the pedantic precision of law cannot settle industrial issues which of their nature require for their solution a feeling for a situation, a recognition that people are involved as well as machines, an acceptance of flexibility, and often a willingness to compromise, which is the basis of most bargaining. To try to solve such issues by the threat of legal punishments will be to introduce an element of rigidity which will break under its own weight ... Each particular problem has got to be dealt with very much in the light of its own circumstances: no two situations are exactly alike ... Trade union rules are infinitely more effective instruments for promoting good industrial relation than any legal regulations. Our rules, and the way they are operated, must and can take account of the light and shade of industrial life in a way that Courts of Law, bound by form and precedent, never can. (Trades Union Congress, 1969b: 30, 34, 35)

Feather also explained that the TUC had:

> been surprised by the suggestion that in return for the right to join a trade union, and the right for a trade union to be recognised, we ought to accept the imposition of penal clauses. Some of us have thought that the right to belong to a trade union, and freedom of association, were inherent rights in a modern democracy – a birthright – and not something for which we have to pay extra in 1969 ... we reject the idea that we must accept penal sanctions as the price to pay for those rights. We thought we already had those rights. (Trades Union Congress, 1969b: 28)

He further expressed his bewilderment that the Cabinet had agreed to introduce a short Industrial Relations Bill before Parliament's summer recess, in contravention of the hitherto agreement that legislation would be introduced in the autumn, by which time extensive consultations would have been conducted, both within the trade union movement (under the auspices of the TUC), and between the TUC and Ministers. Deferring legislation until the autumn would also have enabled the annual conferences of the TUC and the Labour Party to have debated any firm proposals for the reform of industrial relations, and possible offered their respective endorsements (Trades Union Congress, 1969b: 29).

Of course, as we noted in chapter 4, some Ministers had anticipated that delaying the introduction of an industrial relations bill would gift opponents, both in the trade unions and the Labour Party itself, ample time to mobilise against such legislation, and then use the respective conferences to pass resolutions against such legislation. Hence the haste with which some Ministers sought to introduce the Bill, which seemingly perplexed Feather.

As well as continued hostility to the proposal to fine workers or trade unions which defied an order to return to work when a conciliation pause was invoked, there was trenchant opposition to empowering a government minister to intervene in industrial disputes depending on their perceived seriousness or scale. On this issue, Frank Cousins was adamant that:

> [w]e are not prepared to have a Government taking these unprecedented powers to pick out the disputes they want to intervene in – not on the merits of it, but on the consequences. We do not take strikes because of the consequences. We take strikes on the merits and the cause. (Trades Union Congress, 1969b: 41)

This distinction between the causes of industrial disputes and their consequences, and the extent to which the TUC was interested in the former whereas the Government was seemingly concerned solely with the latter, was subsequently reiterated in the speech delivered by Norman Stagg, the leader of the Union of Post Office Workers (Trades Union Congress, 1969b: 43). Stagg also derided Castle's attempt at proving her Socialist credentials in naming her White Paper *In Place of Strife*, in homage to Aneurin Bevan's *In Place of Fear*. Stagg accused her of seeking to exploit the legacy and phrases 'of great Socialists to promote polices which those Socialists, were they were still with us, would have been the first vehemently to oppose' (Trades Union Congress, 1969b: 43).

Meanwhile, Clive Jenkins, leader of the Association of Scientific, Technical and Managerial Staffs, advanced two other objections in his address to the delegates. First, he argued that the Government's proposed legislation actually had nothing to do with genuinely improving industrial relations, but was motivated by electoral expediency: 'a General Election strategy ... that is what it is all about. This is an attempt to rob the Conservatives of their electoral clothing' (Trades Union Congress, 1969b: 56).

His second objection pertained to the proposed fines on workers who defied an order to return to work in the context of the 'conciliation pause'. He noted how the legislation only intended to impose fines on workers, whereas 'the management would not be fined, the shareholders would not be fined'. In this regard, he warned that the Government's proposed industrial relations legislation, and especially its 'penal clauses', would effectively 'divide British society into two classes, the fineable and the unfineable, and this must be really a derogation of all the principles of British jurisprudence' (Trades Union Congress, 1969b: 58).

However, while there was strong and widespread condemnation of the Government's proposed legislation, and in particular the 'penal clauses' and proposed fines, a few trade union leaders at the Croydon conference expressed reservations about endorsing the third of the three recommendations proposed by the TUC's General Council, namely that which proposed vesting greater power in the TUC itself in order to tackle various types of industrial dispute. The objections expressed to this specific recommendation reflected a particular aspect of voluntarism noted earlier in this chapter, namely the jealously guarded autonomy of individual trade unions not only *vis-à-vis* the State, but also from umbrella or federal organisations like the TUC.

This objection was most cogently expressed by George Doughty, of the Draughtsmen's and Allied Technicians Association, who argued that '[t]o suggest internal disciplinary measures as an alternative to Government punitive measures is plain bad tactics. It reduces the disagreement to a question of the type of interference which is necessary, and what kind of sanctions are likely to work' (Trades Union Congress, 1969b: 61). A similar perspective was advanced by T. Thomas, the leader of the Clerical and Administrative Workers' Union, who confessed that his union was 'apprehensive in conceding additional powers to the Trades Union Congress' (Trades Union Congress, 1969b: 78).

Thus it was that all three recommendations were endorsed by large majorities, albeit the third of these attracting the highest number of opposing votes (Trades Union Congress, 1969b: 84):

Recommendation 1. For: 8,252,000 – Against: 359,000. Majority = 7,893,000.
Recommendation 2. For: 8,608,000 – Against: 144,000. Majority = 8,464,000.
Recommendation 3. For: 7,908,000 – Against: 846,000. Majority = 7,062,000.

Harold Wilson summarily dismissed the TUC's counter-proposals for tackling unconstitutional strikes as inadequate and insufficiently robust. This, of course, imbued the subsequent meetings between Castle, Wilson and the TUC leaders with additional *frisson*, and increased the likelihood that no agreement would be reached between the two 'sides'. Wilson was adamant that the Government would not withdraw the 'penal clauses' unless or until the TUC put forward stronger and more credible measures for tackling unconstitutional strikes. The TUC maintained that it had already done so, and that the Croydon conference had emphatically endorsed these; if the Government persevered with the interim Industrial Relations Bill, including the 'penal clauses', then the TUC would withdraw its counter-proposals altogether. A stalemate seemed to have been reached.

Conclusion

Given that voluntarism had long been a sacrosanct principle for Britain's trade unions, it was inevitable that the Labour Government's intention to invoke legislation which contained penal clauses and financial penalties would provoke strong union opposition. Of course, Barbara Castle could legitimately point to the fact that the trade unions actually welcomed, and indeed often demanded, legislation which strengthened trade unionism and workers' rights, but as far as the unions were concerned, such statutory intervention was qualitatively different to laws which concerned themselves with the internal affairs and governance of trade unions, particularly the conditions or circumstances in which they could engage in strike activity.

The trade unions had reiterated their commitment to collective *laissez-faire* in their written evidence to the Royal Commission on Trade Unions and Employers' Associations, and this had then broadly endorsed voluntarism in its June 1968 Report; this seemingly vindicated the trade unions' philosophy and perspective. As such, the Labour Government's January 1969 publication of *In Place of Strife*, followed three months later by an interim Industrial Relations Bill, infuriated the trade unions, and seriously threatened to cause immense damage to the relationship between the Party and the unions. From the trade unions' perspective, the Cabinet was ignoring both their long-standing and deep-rooted commitment to voluntarism, and the Donovan Report's overall rejection of industrial relations legislation.

That it was a Labour Government which was planning to legislate, and impose statutory curbs on strikes, compounded the anger and hostility of the trade unions; it was tantamount to an act of betrayal by their political comrades. It was as if Wilson and Castle were accepting a quintessentially Conservative narrative that the problems facing the British economy were almost entirely the fault of the trade unions, rather than the poor quality of industrial management, or even capitalism itself.

What compounded trade union antipathy to the Government's proposed industrial relations legislation was the belief that Wilson and Castle did not really understand British trade unionism and industrial relations. On the contrary, they were viewed, rather contemptuously, as middle-class Oxbridge graduates and quasi-academics who totally lacked experience of life on the factory floor, in a shipyard or down a coal mine. Moreover, there was a suspicion among some trade union leaders that Castle especially was being unduly influenced by pro-legislation officials in her Department, although some of the hostility directed towards her by some union leaders was also a manifestation of blatant sexism: how dare a woman presume to tell predominantly male trade union leaders how to conduct their affairs, and to show more regard for the wider community?

Trade union resentment increased further during the spring and very early summer of 1969, both because of the mid-April decision to introduce a short, interim Industrial Relations Bill, which effectively reneged on the original plan to introduce a Bill only in November following lengthy consultations with the trade unions, and because of Wilson's and Castle's apparent obstinacy in refusing to accept the counter-proposals which the TUC put forward, via *Programme for Action*, for tackling unconstitutional strikes. When Wilson and Castle repeatedly insisted that these were neither sufficiently robust (due to the apparent lack of explicit sanctions to be imposed on affiliated unions or union members who refused to comply with a TUC instruction to return to work), nor in the right format (not in the form of an explicit rule change – see chapter 7), the TUC strongly suspected that the Prime Minister and Secretary of State were not genuinely interested in reaching an agreement, but were looking for an excuse to persevere with the planned Industrial Relations Bill.

Thus, the period from mid-April to mid-June entailed a series of increasingly fraught meetings between Wilson, Castle and the TUC leadership, which were often characterised by a marked lack of trust, with a strong suspicion that neither side was genuinely committed to a negotiated compromise settlement, albeit wanting to blame the 'other' side for the apparent lack of progress.

Notes

1 Feather was generally known as 'Vic Feather'.
2 NA LAB 28/610, The Royal Commission on Trade Unions and Employers' Associations, Minutes of the 109th meeting, 30 January 1968.
3 NA LAB 16/618, 'Summary of TUC comments on main recommendations of the Royal Commission on Trade Unions and Employers' Associations', 6 November 1968. /618
4 MRC, MSS 292B/40.2/2, 'Royal Commission on Trade Unions and Employers' Associations – the Trade Union Response', 24 June 1968.
5 NA LAB 16/618, 'First Secretary's Meeting with the TUC to discuss the Report of the Commission on Trade Unions and Employers' Associations', 2 July 1968.
6 NA LAB 16/618, 'Summary of TUC comments on main recommendations of the Royal Commission on Trade Unions and Employers' Associations', 6 November 1968.
7 NA LAB 10/3478, Meeting between the Secretary of State for Employment and Productivity, and the TUC's Finance and General Purposes Committee, 30 December 1968.
8 MRC, MSS 292B/40.3/1, Report of Meeting between the Secretary of State for Employment and Productivity, and the TUC's Finance and General Purposes Committee, 2 January 1969.
9 MRC, MSS 292B/40.3/1, Report of Meeting between the Secretary of State for Employment and Productivity, and the TUC's Finance and General Purposes Committee, 2 January 1969.
10 MRC, MSS 292B/40.2/2, Report of Meeting between the Secretary of State for Employment and Productivity, and the TUC's Finance and General Purposes Committee, 8 January 1969.

11 Labour Party Archives, Labour Research Department, 'A Policy for Incomes', RD.433, March 1963.
12 Labour Party Archives, Minutes of PLP Meeting held on 12 December 1968.
13 NA LAB 10/3478, Burgh to Bayliss, 'Definition of Strikes in which the Conciliation pause would be used', 9 January 1969.
14 NA LAB 10/3478, Barbara Castle, 'Industrial Relations Policy – The Conciliation Pause', 6 January 1969.
15 The 'First Reading' of a bill is its formal presentation to Parliament for the first time. Its title is merely read out, but no actual debate takes place on this occasion. Instead, a date is then announced for the bill's Second Reading, which is when its objectives and principles are subject to debate by MPs (or peers, if the bill has been introduced in the House of Lords).
16 MRC, MSS. 292B/40.2/4, Meeting between the TUC's Finance and General Purposes Committee, and Harold Wilson and Barbara Castle, on 11 April 1969.
17 MRC, MSS. 292B/40.2/4, Meeting between the TUC's Finance and General Purposes Committee, and Harold Wilson and Barbara Castle, on 16 April 1969.
18 Callaghan Papers, Box 149, Personal note, 25 May 1969.
19 MRC, MSS. 292B/40.2/5, K. Graham to Feather, 'Government Proposals on Industrial Relations', 21 April 1969.
20 MRC, MSS. 292B/40.2/5, Minutes of 12th Meeting of the TUC General Council, 23 April 1969.
21 MS. Wilson, 936, Harold Wilson, Record of a Meeting between the Prime Minister and Mr Victor Feather at No. 10, Downing Street on Friday 25 April 1969.

7

A 'solemn and binding' agreement

Faced with implacable trade union hostility towards the 'penal clauses' in both *In Place of Strife* and the subsequent 'interim' Industrial Relations Bill, coupled with inexorably growing opposition both from within the Cabinet and on the Labour backbenches, Castle and Wilson spent two months, from mid-April until mid-June 1969, holding numerous meetings with senior TUC figures in an increasingly desperate attempt at securing a settlement. What Castle and Wilson were hoping for was a solution which would simultaneously provide the Cabinet (but in effect, Wilson and Castle themselves) with a pretext for abandoning the Bill, while enabling the TUC to depict itself as responsible and innovative rather than backward-looking and intransigent. If such an agreement could be brokered, then a *rapprochement* could be secured between the Labour Party/Government and the trade unions. Initially, though, such an agreement appeared unlikely, as both sides strongly defended their stance, and each insisted that the other would have to yield.

Yet Castle's and Wilson's increasingly frantic search for a compromise served to reveal the limited authority which the TUC was able or willing to exercise over its affiliated member unions. It was ironic that industrial relations legislation which was widely viewed as a long overdue initiative to curb the more irresponsible aspects of trade union power struggled, in large part, because the TUC's power was limited – something of which most Ministers had not previously been aware. This, of course, further reflected the extent to which the main proponents of industrial relations legislation had the least experience of life on the factory floor or of trade unionism *per se*. The key source of disagreement during the period from mid-April to mid-June concerned the extent to which the TUC would itself accept responsibility for tackling inter-union disputes, and both unconstitutional and unofficial disputes, thereby obviating the need to retain the 'penal clauses' in the Industrial Relations Bill.

However, as explained in chapter 6, the TUC's antipathy had been intensified by the manner in which the Industrial Relations Bill had been announced, for many trade union leaders viewed this as an act of bad faith by the Labour Government. When they had met TUC leaders on 11 April, Wilson and Castle had given no indication that a Bill was to be announced just four days later, although when he next met the TUC leaders, the Prime Minister claimed that the decision had only been taken by the Cabinet on 14 April. The clear implication was that, as no decision had been formally taken about introducing the 'short' Industrial Relations Bill prior to the 11 April meeting with TUC representatives; Wilson had not withheld such information or been dishonest.

Yet the TUC leaders were convinced that Wilson and Castle must have known that the 'interim' Industrial Relations Bill was going to be presented for Cabinet approval on the following Monday, not least because of a Prime Minister's key role (in tandem with the Cabinet Secretary) in drafting the agenda for Cabinet meetings. Needless to say, the frustration and impatience that Castle and Wilson had increasingly felt towards the TUC over its apparent intransigence in accepting the need for legislation, which *inter alia* placed certain curbs or conditions on particular forms of strike action, was now fully reciprocated by the TUC's distrust of Castle and Wilson and its perception of duplicity in them.

During this two-month period, there were eight meetings between Castle, Wilson, and the TUC's General Council at 10, Downing Street, five meetings between Castle, Wilson and a smaller group of TUC leaders (delegated to pursue discussions on the organisation's behalf and report back), and approximately twelve 'bilaterals' between Wilson and Vic Feather (Silver, 1973: 142), some of the latter meetings taking place over a late-night glass of brandy upstairs at 10, Downing Street.

Both 'sides' viewed the other as bloody-minded, obstinate and stubborn, yet at the same time each 'side' was convinced that if it held its ground and refused to yield, the other 'side' would eventually concede in order to avoid fatal damage to the organised labour movement. Each 'side' was therefore convinced that it could, with patience and perseverance, compel the other 'side' to back down. As a consequence, from mid-April to mid-June 1969, Castle and Wilson, and the TUC leadership, were effectively engaged in a game of political brinkmanship, each adamant that they could 'go no further' in meeting the demands of their counterparts.

The role of Vic Feather

According to his biographer, Feather was a key figure in these negotiations, not merely because of his official position – he had become Acting General Secretary of the TUC on 1 March 1969, when George Woodcock became chairman of the new CIR – but because he was perceived to be a naturally more conciliatory character than other senior (and left-wing) TUC members, such as Hugh Scanlon and Jack Jones, and thus potentially more amenable to compromise. After all, Feather was 'a machine politician, a scarred and decorated hero of the smoke-filled room and the midnight formula' (hence the convivial late-night brandies with Wilson). Or as another writer characterised him, he was 'a tireless negotiator and consensualist' (Dorfman, 1979: 39).

On one occasion, following one of the several dinners he had with Feather during this period to discuss the 'penal clauses', Wilson recalled that it had 'as always, been very friendly', regardless of their differences over this crucial aspect of the Industrial Relations Bill.[1] Denis Healey, meanwhile, deemed Feather to be 'more helpful' than many other TUC leaders, most notably Jack Jones and Hugh Scanlon: 'the position of the two of them was so rigid'.[2]

In fact, Jack Jones was subsequently somewhat critical of Feather's apparent affability in this context, suspecting that Feather was inclined 'to agree with all men', whereas '[w]e might have made more progress had he presented our case strongly, as though it was his own'. As it was, Jones lamented that Feather sometimes 'acted as a messenger rather than an advocate' (Jones, 1986: 205). Jones also noted, tartly, that Feather was subsequently 'attracted to establishment figures like a moth to a candle' (Jones, 1986: 215).

Feather fully conceded that the trade unions needed to 'modernise', particularly with regard to tackling inter-union, unofficial and unconstitutional strikes, but in accordance with voluntarism, he remained convinced that such reform should be undertaken directly by the trade union movement itself, rather than be imposed from above by a government – even if it was a Labour government. Yet Feather privately hoped that Castle's proposed industrial relations legislation would galvanise the trade unions into reforming themselves, thus obviating the need for a bill containing 'penal clauses'. In effect, '[h]e was certain that the law was not the answer, but the distant crackle of court summonses might drive the unions his way' (Silver, 1973: 136, 137).

The TUC's *Programme for Action*

As we noted in chapter 6, the TUC claimed that the Labour Government's decision to bring industrial relations legislation forward from November to spring 1969 left the trade unions with too little time to devise alternative measures. Yet in May, the TUC did draft a policy document entitled *Programme for Action*, which was emphatically endorsed at the 5 June Croydon conference. This document provided the main basis of the discussions between Wilson, Castle and the TUC leaders from mid-April onwards, with paragraph 42, and Rules 11, 12 and 13 of the TUC's Congress, constituting the main focus and reference points throughout. To understand the significance of these, and their centrality to the search for an agreement – Roy Jenkins (1991: 289) described the negotiations as being 'of almost Byzantine complication ... so convoluted that I ceased to follow them' – it is necessary to outline paragraph 42 and the three specific TUC Rules which it cited.

Paragraph 42 of 'Programme for Action'

Of the seventy-eight paragraphs which collectively comprised *Programme for Action*, it was paragraph 42 which was repeatedly cited, particularly by Harold Wilson, during these two months of intense negotiations. Given its importance in these negotiations, it is worth quoting the bulk of this paragraph:

> The General Council would also require [affiliated] unions to satisfy them that they had done all that they could reasonably be expected to do to secure compliance with a recommendation ... including taking action within their own rues where necessary. They recognise that a few unions may need to review their own rules to ensure that they are in a position to comply with recommendations ... by the TUC. The General Council also consider that it should be made clear in Rule 11 (as is already implicit in that Rule, and is explicit in Rule 12) that in the unlikely event of a union refusing to abide by a decision of the T.U.C., the General Council can take action under Rule 13. (Trades Union Congress, 1969b: 236–7)

Rule 11 – Industrial disputes

This delineated the TUC's procedures with regard to industrial disputes involving trade unions affiliated to it. Rule 11 required such unions to keep the TUC's General Council informed of industrial disputes, especially unconstitutional and unofficial strikes involving or affecting large numbers of workers. Beyond this requirement, though, the TUC's general policy was not to intervene if and when there was a prospect of the dispute being 'amicably settled by means of the machinery of negotiation existing in the trades affected'.

However, in some instances, most notably when a strike impinged upon a wider range of workers or unions, the TUC's General Council was entitled to 'take the initiative by calling representatives of the organisation into consultation, and use their influence to effect a just settlement of the difference'. In so doing, and having ascertained the relevant facts, the General Council might offer its advice or opinion on the situation, and suggest how it could or should be resolved. Should the union(s) or workers involved disregard the General Council's advice or recommendation, then it would be entitled to take further action, which could, ultimately, be of a disciplinary nature, as decreed by Rule 13 (discussed below).

Rule 12 – Disputes between affiliated organisations

This concerned disputes between affiliated trade unions over issues such as membership (to which specific union should a worker or group of workers belong?) and 'demarcation disputes' (which occupational group of workers should perform a particular task?). In such circumstances, the trade unions involved should allow the TUC's General Council to investigate before commencing strike action, and if a stoppage had already started, the unions concerned should secure a return to work while the issue was investigated. Such an investigation might entail the General Council establishing a 'Disputes Committee', which could summon the disputants to submit evidence, either oral (appearing in person) or written, and possibly both. The General Council would then make a decision. Any affiliated trade union which failed to abide by this decision would, again in the last instance, be liable to disciplinary action, as stipulated in Rule 13.

Rule 13 – Conduct of affiliated organisations

If the conduct of any affiliated trade union was deemed detrimental to the interests of the trade union movement overall, or incompatible with the principles and policies of the TUC's General Council, then the latter would be entitled to investigate the alleged or apparent misconduct. If such misconduct was proven, the TUC would be entitled to order the union(s) to desist immediately. If the union(s) failed or refused to abide by such an instruction, the TUC's General Council could have the recalcitrant union(s) temporarily suspended from the TUC, or *in extremis*, excluded permanently.

The negotiations

Of these three Rules, it was Rule 11 which proved most problematic, particularly from Castle's and Wilson's perspective.

When, on 12 May, Wilson, Castle and the TUC's General Council met to discuss a draft of *Programme for Action*, Wilson offered warm words of praise, and suggested that in some respects, the TUC was seeking to adopt 'powers and influence [over affiliated unions] over a wider scope than the Government's proposed legislation, and indeed, in some respects, than would ever be appropriate for any legislation'. As such, Wilson deemed this proposal to constitute 'a viable and equally effective alternative to the Government's proposals'. In particular, Wilson was deeply impressed with the TUC's proposal for tackling inter-union disputes, which 'appeared to be very effective'.

This meant that the remaining source of disagreement concerned the TUC's proposals for dealing with unconstitutional strikes, which Wilson argued were not 'copper-bottomed', and fell significantly short of providing a viable alternative to the Government's proposals. This was, he claimed, the 'missing link' between the TUC's welcome proposals for tackling inter-union disputes, and its failure to offer equally credible measures for addressing unconstitutional stoppages of work.[3] What Wilson and Castle were seeking was a clear and convincing statement from the TUC's General Council of what action it would take, when an unconstitutional strike occurred, to ensure that affiliated members returned to work while talks were conducted to resolve the dispute, and what sanctions it would invoke against trade unionists or unions which defied a TUC order to return to work. Until or unless the TUC could provide a credible explanation of how it would ensure the compliance of its members when ordering a return to work in the context of an unconstitutional strike, then the TUC's proposal on this specific issue, Castle claimed, 'could at best be regarded a pious hope'.[4]

At the next meeting, on 21 May, the TUC's General Council explained that in instances of unconstitutional strikes, it would take the same action as it would when a union refused to obey an order to return to work in the context of an inter-union dispute, namely reporting it to the full Congress, which was deemed to be 'a serious matter and one which the unions treated seriously'. The General Council emphasised that '[u]nions and union members generally accepted the judgement of their peers'. Furthermore, the General Council insisted that, as in most other aspects of industrial relations, 'flexibility' was the key to tackling problems in order to secure greater order and stability, whereas the 'major fallacy of the Government's thinking was the belief that the imposition of automatic sanctions would solve disputes'.

Besides, the TUC leaders had earlier observed pointedly, they were 'not trading sanctions with the Government', alluding to Wilson's pledge that the 'penal clauses' would be dropped from the forthcoming Bill if the TUC offered equally effective proposals for tackling unconstitutional strikes.[5] The TUC's General Council did, however, propose a rather different trade-off, namely that unless the Government abandoned the 'penal clauses', the counter-proposals in *Programme for Action* would be withdrawn entirely.[6]

In opposing the Government's proposals, the TUC insisted that 'it was no good saying that unofficial strikers ought to be disciplined without knowing the details of particular cases'. Furthermore, 'it would be impossible for the General Council to attempt to say how they would deal with every hypothetical situation, particularly as it was always necessary to take into account the attitude of the employer'. Consequently, rather than acting in accordance with prescriptive or punitive legislation, the TUC's leadership was adamant that 'the method which unions would adopt to deal with particular situations would, as at present, be discussion and persuasion. This is how trade unionism worked.'[7]

Following directly on from this last point, the TUC leaders again reminded Castle and Wilson of the voluntarist tradition in Britain industrial relations, namely that:

> The affairs of trade unions were for the TUC to look after, and they ought to be allowed to do the job unhampered by unnecessary and restrictive legislation. It was wrong for the Government to ask the TUC to pay for long overdue rights in respect of trade union organisation by penal provisions on trade unions and workpeople ... penal clauses should not enter the employer/employee relationship.[8]

Wilson remained adamant, though, that the Government would not contemplate the withdrawal of the 'penal clauses' unless the TUC provided a much clearer, convincing indication of how it would deal with workers who defied instructions to return to work after starting an unconstitutional strike. What was needed from the TUC, Wilson explained, was an unequivocal statement of what sanctions would be invoked against 'recalcitrants who refused to resume work'. In particular, the Government wanted 'a guarantee that ... fines or, in the last instance, expulsions, would be imposed [either by the relevant trade union or by the General Council] on union members who refused to return to work'.[9]

This, though, was not the only disagreement aired at this 21 May meeting, and which therefore made an agreement seem even more remote. On the core issue of unconstitutional strikes, the TUC's General Council emphasised that its objective was to expedite a negotiated settlement when such disputes occurred, in order to remedy the source of the dispute, and thereupon secure a return to work. By contrast, Castle and Wilson appeared to be adamant that a return to work, based on the *status quo ante*, was vital *before* such negotiations could be conducted. This prompted the TUC leaders to complain that '[t]he continued emphasis on getting people back to work, rather than on securing an agreed settlement of a dispute, underlined the fallacies in the Government's whole approach: the aim must be to prevent disputes and, if they arose, to settle them'. In response, Castle argued that whereas the TUC seemed more concerned with 'judging the merits of disputes', the Government's prime objective was 'securing a resumption of work and ensuring the continuation of discussion through procedure'.[10]

In some respects, this respective intransigence and resultant *impasse* reflected a clear lack of trust between the two sides, with each suspecting the other of acting in bad faith, and of not genuinely wanting to reach a negotiated settlement. Certainly, the manner in which the interim Industrial Relations Bill had been announced had led the TUC leadership to view Wilson and Castle with grave suspicion. According to one writer, by this stage '[t]he question of trust ... dominated the discussion far more than the substance of the disagreement' (Dorfman, 1979: 38–9).

By late May, Wilson deemed there to be five options available to the Government:[11]

1. Defer industrial relations legislation until the next Parliamentary session.
2. A bill which tackled inter-union disputes and established an Industrial Board (to adjudicate in industrial disputes and make recommendations for their resolution), but which did not contain penal clauses *vis-à-vis* the conciliation pause. Instead, in the last instance, fines would be imposed on trade unions who failed to comply with a decision of the Industrial Board.
3. A bill similar to the proposed interim Industrial Relations Bill, but with the conciliation pause and 'penal clauses' to be deferred, possibly for six months, and then only invoked by the Secretary of State with Parliamentary approval. This would provide the TUC with time in which to develop its own proposals for tackling unconstitutional strikes, and to gauge their effectiveness.
4. A variant of the previous option, but with the conciliation pause to be invoked only after the TUC's own attempts at tackling an unconstitutional strike had manifestly failed.
5. Place the responsibility for collecting fines on the trade union itself, in instances when workers refused to obey an Industrial Board order to return to work after an unconstitutional strike had begun.

These proposals failed to elicit a consensus among senior Ministers and the Chief Whip, with Wilson and Jenkins firmly rejecting the first option (deferral), whilst Bob Mellish, 'whose nerve had obviously been shaken by interviews with TU [Trade Union] Group Members', clearly favoured it. Wilson and Jenkins were strongly inclined towards the third option, whereas Fred Peart and Richard Crossman (hesitantly) favoured the second. Denis Healey also preferred the third option, while conceding that 'we might have to fall back on two'.[12]

Wilson was initially adamant that abandoning the proposed 'penal clauses' was out of the question; they were non-negotiable. If the TUC failed (or refused) to take tougher measures to tackle unconstitutional strikes, the Government's proposed 'penal clauses' would be wholly justified and the short Industrial Relations Bill would be introduced. If, however, the TUC did adopt stronger measures which the Government judged to be sufficiently robust and credible in dealing with such industrial disputes, then the 'penal clauses' need never be invoked, but would instead be placed in 'cold storage'. Yet this apparent olive branch, far from being welcomed by the TUC, actually weakened their trust in Wilson even further, for it appeared that he was now reneging on the original pledge to abandon the 'penal clauses' if the TUC adopted sufficiently strong counter-measures to tackle unconstitutional and unofficial strikes; now he was saying that even if the TUC did what was asked of them, the 'penal clauses' would effectively lie dormant, rather than be discarded altogether. In the meantime, the Prime Minister promised that no 'final decisions' over the proposed legislation would be taken by Ministers until he and Castle had met with the General Council after the forthcoming Croydon Conference.[13]

The 1 June Chequers meeting

A few days before the Croydon conference, there was an attempt at brokering a solution, via a dinner at Chequers (the Prime Minister's official country residence) on the evening of 1 June 1969, attended by just six people: Wilson, Castle, the three most senior figures from the TUC (Vic Feather, Jack Jones and Hugh Scanlon) and John Newton, the TUC's chair. There is some confusion about whether Castle was intending to attend this meeting. She had already booked a holiday, on a boat off the Italian coast, for late May into early June, and Wilson claimed that 'I would be totally opposed to her cancelling her holiday, and would indeed order her to go away'. In her place, it was intended that 'the Chancellor, certainly no less hawkish than Barbara – indeed much more – would be present'.[14] Yet on 21 May, Castle told Wilson that she was 'willing to fly back from my holiday for the secret talks' (Castle, 1990: 335, diary entry for 21 May 1969), whereupon Wilson 'agreed to bring her back from her holiday in Italy' (Wilson, 1971: 653). Castle herself told Richard Crossman, who was also on the Italian holiday with her (and their respective spouses), 'that she had to fly back on Sunday, June 1st, to Chequers for secret talks with a few trade union leaders' (Crossman, 1977: 503, diary entry for 23 May to 6 June 1969).

So that Wilson could communicate confidentially with Castle during her holiday absence, everyone involved, however marginally, was ascribed an animal-themed code-name, presumably lest their conversations were overheard or eavesdropped (whether this was an entirely sensible precaution, or a manifestation of paranoia on Wilson's part, will forever remain a matter of conjecture). This compounded the confusion over whether Castle was expected to attend the Chequers dinner; why would Wilson make such convoluted or conspiratorial plans to communicate with her in Italy, during negotiations with the three TUC leaders, if she was going to be present anyway?

The code-names obliquely referring to senior Ministers and the Cabinet were as follows:

Eagle – Harold Wilson
Peacock – Barbara Castle
Starling – Roy Jenkins
Owl – Richard Crossman
Magpie – Fred Peart
Thrush – Bob Mellish
Pigeon – Denis Healey
Robin – Michael Stewart
Sparrow – James Callaghan
Canary – Judith Hart
The Aviary – The Cabinet

However, the code-names ascribed to senior trade union leaders and the TUC itself were notably less quixotic, namely:

Rhino – Vic Feather
Bull – Frank Cousins
Bear – Hugh Scanlon
Horse – Jack Jones
Panda – John Newton
Elephant – Danny McGarvey
The Zoo – TUC General Council
The Herd – TUC Finance and General Purposes Committee
The Jamboree – TUC's Croydon Conference
The Bible – TUC's *Programme for Action*
The Teeth – The 'penal clauses'
Brawls – Inter-union disputes
Riots – Unofficial strikes
False Teeth – TUC penalties against unions
The Break – Conciliation pause.

The secret memo also stipulated that if Castle's boat was required to enter port, the phrase 'Aunty has mumps' would be deployed, and if a specific port was required, then this would be indicated thus: 'Aunty has mumps in Naples'.[15]

Regardless of whether Castle had originally intended to attend, her arrival, having flown back from Naples to the RAF base at Benson, Oxfordshire, and then been driven straight to Chequers (just under 20 miles/32 kilometres away), was an unwelcome surprise to the three TUC leaders. Indeed, when Jack Jones arrived shortly after Castle, he was immediately intercepted by Vic Feather, who warned him: 'She's here. Don't be difficult!' Jones recalled that he was 'fuming' throughout dinner, because he had relished the opportunity to negotiate with Wilson alone, doubtless reflecting a view among many senior TUC leaders that Wilson was slightly less intransigent than Castle: 'Barbara's presence ... would inhibit the chances of getting an understanding' (Jones, 1986: 204). Wilson was aware of this perception, but strongly denied its veracity.[16]

Wilson himself naturally conferred with Castle before dinner to agree on their approach, which entailed pressing the TUC leaders 'very hard on Paragraph 42', with particular regard to how the TUC proposed to tackle unconstitutional strikes, and how it would deal with trade unions or their members who defied an order to return to work while talks were held to seek a resolution to the dispute.

With no civil servants present, the 'official' record of this meeting was that written immediately afterwards by Wilson himself. He described the overall tone as 'genial and reasonably friendly throughout', but acknowledged that 'the talking did get pretty tough at one or two points', more particularly after dinner, when discussions continued for three hours, and 'became very much harder hitting', but with no new arguments advanced. When Wilson pressed the trade union leaders on the need for the TUC to strengthen its counter-proposal on tackling unconstitutional strikes, as outlined in paragraph 42 and with reference to Rule 11, both Jones and Scanlon insisted that they could not agree to any further transfer of sovereignty from their unions to the TUC beyond that already agreed, and even this was too much in Scanlon's view. Indeed, he confessed that he had been 'in total opposition to any transfer of power in the matter of disputes affecting his members, *either* to the Government *or* to the T.U.C.'[17]

The discussions also heard a reiteration of the key distinction between the Government's and the trade unions' stance towards resolving unconstitutional strikes. Whereas Wilson and Castle were adamant that the priority was a return to work while 'peace talks' were conducted, the TUC leaders were equally emphatic that, in many instances, unconstitutional strikes 'were due to action by management, whether in terms of a dismissal or a change in working practices', and in some cases, 'particularly if great bitterness had had developed, the men would not go back to work without some decision about the merits of the dispute itself'. In other words, a resolution of the dispute was often a pre-requisite of a return to work, rather than vice versa, as Wilson and Castle were insisting.

Wilson reiterated that unless the TUC was willing to go further in strengthening its own procedures for tackling unconstitutional strikes, and taking disciplinary action against recalcitrant unions or their members who defied an order to return to work, the Labour Government would be obliged to persevere with introducing the Industrial Relations Bill. It was vital to curb unconstitutional strikes. In response, Jones and Scanlon repeated the TUC's warning that if the Government proceeded with the Bill, then the counter-proposals offered by the TUC in the draft of *Programme for Action*, namely those pertaining to tackling inter-union and unconstitutional strikes, and confidently expected to be endorsed at the Croydon conference in four days' time, would be withdrawn altogether: 'everything the T.U.C. was trying to do would be nullified if the Government went ahead … the T.U.C. plan would be dead'.[18]

This threat prompted Wilson to warn the TUC about the grave constitutional implications of their stance: they were, in effect, acting as 'a state within a state', and 'putting itself above the Government in deciding what a Government could and could not do'. In so doing, Wilson complained, the TUC was effectively challenging 'the right and possibility of a Labour Government to govern, and the very essence of democracy in this country'. In response, the TUC leaders insisted that, in a democracy, the trade unions were fully entitled to resist legislation which would restrict their ability to pursue free collective bargaining, and defend their members against bad managerial decisions or actions.[19]

By 12.30 am, it was evident that an *impasse* had been reached, and so the discussions were brought to an end, it being agreed that Wilson and Castle would meet the TUC's General Council again on Monday 9 June, when the discussions could focus on the outcome of the TUC's Croydon conference to endorse *Programme for Action*. Wilson did promise, though, that the Government would not make a final decision about the timing or content of its Industrial Relations Bill until it had held this post-Croydon meeting with the TUC leadership, although 'we would expect a further move by the TUC itself, involving a readiness by constituent unions to discipline those responsible for unconstitutional action' (Wilson, 1971: 654). Given the extent to which the TUC deemed employers and management frequently to be 'those responsible for unconstitutional action', through arbitrary action and decisions affecting workers, Wilson's expectation seemed doomed to disappointment, and so it proved.

The Government's response to the TUC's Croydon conference

As noted in chapter 4, Castle was 'astonished to learn on my return from holiday that in my absence, and without consulting me, Harold Wilson had issued a statement over my name rejecting the [Croydon] proposals on unconstitutional strikes as inadequate'. Consequently, when she returned home from Italy, she was confronted by a *Daily Telegraph* headline declaring that 'Mrs Castle snubs unions', and as such, she was 'furious' because Wilson's declaration (ostensibly on her behalf) had 'reduced our room for manoeuvre' (Castle, 1990: 339, diary entry for 6 June 1969).

Wilson sought to assuage Castle by explaining that he had wanted her to be informed of the statement before it was published, but that her Private Office had been unable to contact her off the Italian coast. Had he waited until she was contactable, he claimed, the press would probably have chosen to interpret the Government's silence as an indication that its resolve was weakening. On balance, therefore, he had judged it best to release the statement sooner rather than later, although he did concede that, in hindsight, maybe some other Cabinet colleagues ought to have been consulted in Castle's absence before the statement was released.[20]

When Wilson, Castle and senior members of the TUC's General Council met four days after the Croydon conference 'for a ritual baring of fangs' (Silver, 1973: 155), Vic Feather argued that: '[t]here was no difference between the Government and the trade union movement about the aim, which was to minimise strikes. Their differences were about means.'[21] As Jack Jones explained, whereas the Government seemed wholly concerned with securing an immediate return to work when unconstitutional strikes occurred, the TUC was convinced that 'the essential problem was to deal with the *causes* of industrial disputes'.[22]

Of course, *apropos* Feather's remark, Castle and Wilson remained unconvinced that the 'means' being proffered by the TUC would prove effective. Moreover, while not demurring from the need to tackle the underlying causes of many industrial disputes and improve procedural agreements, as emphasised by Jones, Wilson and Castle were adamant that these were essentially longer-term objectives, although obviously the process could and should be started immediately. In advance of such improvements, though, the Government's immediate concern was to tackle the unconstitutional strikes which currently afflicted British industry, and accordingly discussions continued to focus on the extent to which the TUC could, or would, strengthen paragraph 42, and in particular, Rule 11 (pertaining to unconstitutional strikes). According to Castle, strengthening Rule 11 'was the breaking point for her … this was essential to for the Government's credibility'.[23]

Wilson pointed to the satisfactory manner in which the TUC's General Council had strengthened its position with regard to intervening in interunion disputes, but was perplexed as to why it could not similarly strengthen its stance towards unconstitutional strikes. He pointed out that, while paragraph 42 of *Programme of Action* declared that the TUC would 'require' affiliated trade unions to abide by a General Council instruction to return to work in the case of an unconstitutional strike, it was still unclear what action it would take if it was flagrantly defied. Wilson wanted to know precisely what sanctions the TUC would invoke against trade unions, or their members, if they ignored an order to resume work while conciliation talks were conducted. As it was currently worded, he considered paragraph 42 'to represent an expression of hope, rather than of resolve', although he seemingly offered a glimmer of hope that a compromise was attainable by acknowledging that it 'might merely be a matter of drafting'.[24]

Wilson's (and Castle's) exasperation at the TUC's unwillingness to strengthen paragraph 42 and/or Rule 11 was fully matched by the General Council's frustration at Wilson and Castle's apparent inability to understand the dynamics of trade unionism. This, of course, was again attributed to their seemingly academic approach to industrial relations, which reflected their total lack of understanding or direct experience of the realities of daily life in industry. These 'realities' involved inherent conflicts of interest, and concomitant power struggles, between workers and employer, even though the introduction to *In Place of Strife* had acknowledged that '[c]onflict in industrial relations is unavoidable'.

The most hopeful sign of a breakthrough occurred when one of the General Council's members asked Wilson: 'If we strengthen paragraph 42, will you definitely drop the penal clauses?', to which, with 'barely a moment's hesitation', he answered 'Yes' (Castle, 1990: 340, diary entry for 9 June 1969).[25] Thus it was that Wilson, Castle and the TUC's General Council met two days later, to discuss how paragraph 42 of *Programme for Action*, coupled with Rule 11, could be redrafted and strengthened sufficiently to enable the Industrial Relations Bill's 'penal clauses' to be withdrawn. Or as Wilson himself expressed it, to ensure the 'effectiveness and saleability to the country of the General Council's proposals'.

Yet an agreement on how precisely to strengthen Rule 11 continued to prove highly problematic and thus elusive, with repeated disagreements over the wording of various redrafts, coupled with re-iteration by the General Council that Wilson and Castle did not understand the dynamics of the trade unions, or the operational relationship between the TUC and affiliated unions. Wilson complained that Rule 11 was too equivocal in its stance towards tackling unconstitutional strikes; it 'used words like "may" instead of "shall", "advice and guidance" instead of a positive directive, and there was nothing in it which carried through ... condemnation of some unauthorised stoppages'.[26]

The TUC retorted that Castle and Wilson were seeking to introduce uniformity and rigidity into its approach towards tackling unconstitutional strikes, when what was needed was flexibility and pragmatism, in order to take into account the context and circumstances of each dispute: 'It was neither possible nor desirable to define in Rules every permutation of every type of dispute'. As a consequence, the TUC could not seriously be expected to issue a blanket condemnation of every unconstitutional strike, and automatically order its members to return to work immediately, especially because many such strikes were a response to provocative behaviour or precipitate decisions by management. It was mainly for this reason, the General Council explained, that Rule 11 could not be re-written with the same clarity or specificity as Rule 12; 'the latter related exclusively to domestic disputes, i.e., between unions', which meant that the TUC could impose a settlement on the unions concerned.

In stark contrast, Rule 11 was concerned with the resolution of unconstitutional strikes which derived from disputes between workers and management, many of which occurred as a direct consequence of the (allegedly) unreasonable conduct or decisions of the latter. This sometimes took the form of seemingly deliberate 'protracted ... negotiation' by managers, wholly intended to frustrate employees by causing the maximum delay in resolving an issue. In such circumstances, the TUC leaders claimed, an unconstitutional strike was entirely understandable, such that it would be 'unrealistic' to order the workers involved to return to work.

The General Council also explained to Wilson and Castle that in trade union parlance, the words 'advice and guidance' were viewed as the equivalent of an instruction or recommendation, so that the phrase carried much more authority than when used by a lay-person. Wilson was unconvinced. The union leaders emphasised that since Rule 11 had originally been endorsed by the TUC's annual conference in 1929, 'there had never been a case where unions refused the advice of the General Council'. As such, the TUC could not understand why Wilson and Castle kept insisting on redrafting Rule 11.

In an attempt at pacifying Wilson and Castle, however, the General Council proposed that, rather than directly re-writing Rule 11, which would then require approval (which might not be granted) by delegates at the TUC's conference in September, a circular could instead be sent to all trade unions, clearly explaining how Rule 11 should be interpreted and applied. This would stipulate that when an unconstitutional stoppage occurred, the TUC, via its Disputes Committee, would swiftly ascertain the facts, and then make a recommendation. In cases 'where they find that the negotiations should proceed on the basis of a return to work, they will place an obligation on the organisation or organisations concerned to take immediate and energetic steps to obtain a resumption of work'.

This, though, was still insufficient to satisfy Wilson and Castle, partly because it implied that that, in some instances, the TUC would *not* seek or recommend a return to work when an unconstitutional strike occurred, but also because there was still no clear indication of what action the General Council would take against trade unions or their members who failed or refused 'to take immediate and energetic steps to obtain a resumption of work'. Once again, the TUC was deemed to be relying too much on its perceived powers of persuasion or moral authority, and so failed to stipulate what penalties or sanctions it would impose when its advice, guidance or recommendations were ignored. To address the first of his two objections, Wilson suggested a redraft of this proposed 'circular of clarification', to include the statement 'in cases where … they find that there has been an unconstitutional stoppage, and therefore that negotiations should proceed on the basis of a return to work …'.[27] He refrained, however, from including any reference, in his redraft, to sanctions or penalties to be imposed by the TUC.

This time it was the TUC which objected, because Wilson's redrafting seemingly implied that the General Council would almost always be expected to promote a return to work when an unconstitutional strike occurred; its discretion to evaluate each case on its merits, according to the specific context and circumstances, would be seriously restricted. Such a requirement or restriction could not be accepted.

Wilson and Castle were naturally dismayed at the TUC's apparently obstinate stance, and the continuing *impasse*, although a few days earlier the Prime Minister had acknowledged that 'we were dealing with people who had spent all their life negotiating, and were masters of brinkmanship'.[28] Yet with hindsight, there was another discrete indication of the subsequent breakthrough which finally occurred the following week, albeit this was barely perceptible at the time. When the TUC's General Council proposed circulating this clarification to affiliated unions, explaining how Rule 11 was to be interpreted and applied, Wilson enquired what status or authority this would have. Would it, the Prime Minister asked, constitute a *'binding statement of intent'*?[29]

Nonetheless, when Wilson and Castle met with the TUC's General Council the next day (12 June), the 'two' sides reiterated their previous position and perspectives. Wilson and Castle were still insisting on a re-writing of Rule 11 to make explicit that the TUC would ordinarily intervene to secure a return to work when unconstitutional disputes occurred, and would impose sanctions against recalcitrant trade unions or their members. The TUC countered that some unconstitutional strikes were justified, and as such, it was unreasonable to place the onus on the TUC to compel a return to work, particularly when such a stoppage had been provoked by an employer or management.

Castle and Wilson also reiterated their insistence that when unconstitutional strikes occurred, the prime objective should be a cessation of the stoppage and a return to work, whereupon negotiations could be conducted to secure a peaceful resolution. The TUC responded by again insisting that the priority should be securing a settlement through negotiation, which would then facilitate a return to work. From the TUC's perspective, Wilson and Castle seemed to be far more concerned with stopping unofficial strikes when they occurred, than with improving industrial relations – and the conduct of management – so that there were far fewer unconstitutional strikes in the first place; prevention was better than cure. Such was the apparent stalemate at this stage that Wilson informed the Cabinet's industrial relations committee that 'there was no suggestion that we were in sight of a breakthrough, but nor were we in sight of an inevitable breakdown.'[30]

Crucially, by this time, as we discussed in chapter 4, Cabinet support for the 'short' Industrial Relations Bill, and particularly its 'penal clauses', had virtually ebbed away, with Michael Stewart, the Foreign Secretary, proving to be the only senior Minister still urging Castle and Wilson to stand firm in the context of the TUC's apparent failure to offer credible and effective measures for tackling unconstitutional strikes and disciplining recalcitrant members.[31] Nonetheless, in their meetings with the TUC leaders, Wilson and Castle maintained the pretence that they had the Cabinet's backing. After all, they could hardly enter tough negotiations with the TUC's General Council or (smaller) Finance and General Purposes Committee by admitting, at the outset, that they had lost the support of most of their senior Ministerial colleagues, so that even most of the Ministers who had previously been strongly supportive of the proposed legislation were now convinced that Wilson and Castle should accept the TUC's counter-proposals. At the same time, opposition to the proposed legislation had also been growing in the PLP, as we noted in chapter 5.

In this context, even some of those who had previously supported Wilson on this issue now viewed him (and Castle) as the main source of obstinacy and intransigence, whereas the TUC had – by Wilson's own admission – moved a long way towards what the Government had demanded, even though he deemed it not far enough. In effect, the TUC seemed to be winning the moral and tactical arguments in the eyes of many Ministers and Labour MPs, thereby placing Wilson and Castle on the defensive. This naturally increased the pressure on them to accept what the TUC was offering in *Programme for Action*, accompanied by the proposed 'circular of clarification' of Rule 11. As Crossman noted following the Croydon conference, 'the T.U.C. has completely outmanoeuvred the Prime Minister and Barbara. The T.U.C. has made concessions at the right time, and put themselves in the right with the Parliamentary [Labour] Party' (Crossman, 1977: 504, diary entry for the period 23 May to 6 June 1969).

Although none of the TUC leaders was sufficiently indiscreet to allude to the isolation of Wilson and Castle in the Cabinet during (what proved to be) the final meeting – or, rather, series of increasingly urgent meetings – on 18 June, the General Council would almost certainly have been aware, if not through any communication with James Callaghan, then by the public warnings of Douglas Houghton, as chair of the PLP, or/and reports provided the Chief Whip Bob Mellish, that the Government would not muster sufficient Parliamentary support to secure the Bill's passage through the House of Commons. In fact, Wilson had informed the previous day's meeting of the Cabinet's industrial relations committee that he had 'evidence from a reliable source that a member of the Cabinet was having direct contact with the T.U.C. leaders, and telling them not to worry about the proposed legislation because it would not be introduced'.[32]

There were also, almost inevitably, a plethora of press reports about the divisions in the Cabinet and PLP, and the extent to which opposition to the Bill had increased among Labour's Parliamentarians. Yet Wilson was adamant that 'it was not right that a Labour Government should be dictated to by those Labour Members [of Parliament] who took their orders from the Trade Union Movement'. To take such dictation was tantamount to conceding 'that Government should always give in against pressures from the Party and unions. This was in effect saying that the T.U.C. should govern.'[33]

Wilson and Castle were under immense political pressure to reach an agreement with the TUC's General Council, although the two senior Labour Ministers initially maintained their previous stance that Rule 11 need to be re-written, and that a circular of clarification would not suffice. Wilson's and Castle's intransigence was seemingly intended to belie their isolation in the Cabinet, and thereby maintain pressure on the TUC to move beyond its extant position, so that a compromise settlement could then be announced which would publicly benefit both 'sides'. As one junior Minister recalled, at the crucial meeting with the TUC leaders on 18 June, 'Harold Wilson weaved and ducked with the General Council, but they knew they had him on the ropes' (Owen, 1992: 157).

Yet most of the TUC leaders were keen to avoid completely humiliating Wilson and Castle, because this would further weaken the Prime Minister's and Secretary of State's political authority, and consequently make an election defeat to the Conservatives more likely the following year. As such, the TUC's General Council was keen to broker a deal which would simultaneously ensure that the trade unions attained most of what they had fought for in opposing *In Place of Strife* and the interim Industrial Relations Bill, but allow Wilson and Castle the face-saving claim that they had secured concessions from the TUC which met many of the Government's own objectives. Needless to say, it was a very delicate and nuanced balancing act.

Initially on 18 June, Castle and Wilson, and the TUC's General Council, merely reiterated the arguments they had advanced, and held the positions they had adopted at the previous week's meetings. Again, Wilson challenged the TUC to incorporate the wording in its proposed 'circular of clarification' into Rule 11, the Prime Minister insisting that '[a] piece of paper is not sufficient'. The TUC retorted that it did not have the authority to make rule changes unilaterally; any changes would have to be endorsed at the September conference. Not only would this be incompatible with the

Government's insistence that the issue needed to be settled now, it could not be assumed that the TUC's annual conference would agree to another rule change in the early autumn, particularly so soon after endorsing *Programme for Action* at the Croydon conference. Indeed, 'there was a danger that all the progress made would be overturned at Portsmouth'.

As the negotiations threatened to become repetitive, with the two sides seemingly going round in circles, it became apparent just how much of the disagreement was *not* over the actual words stipulating how the TUC would respond to unconstitutional strikes, but the format in which these words would be enshrined – a revision to Rule 11, as demanded by Wilson and Castle, or a 'circular of clarification', as offered by the TUC. Wilson himself acknowledged that 'the difference in real terms was so narrow that it had become a procedural point',[34] while the TUC's General Council conceded that, by this stage, 'the issue was not one principally of wording, but stemmed from a divergence between them and the Government about their respective interpretations of the implementation of T.U.C. policy' (Trades Union Congress, 1969a: 223).

What proved to constitute the breakthrough – although it was not immediately apparent – occurred when Feather explained, to Wilson and Castle, that in terms of TUC governance, 'Congress policy was the important part, the rules were incidental', a distinction he highlighted by alluding to the Bridlington Agreement.[35] In accordance with this landmark agreement in trade union history, Feather explained that the 'note of clarification' which the General Council was proposing to circulate, with regard to the application of Rule 11, 'would be just as binding on the affiliated unions as the Bridlington Principles',[36] a crucial point which was then reiterated by Jack Jones (Wilson, 1971: 659).

Initially, Wilson continued to insist that nothing less than a revision of Rule 11 would suffice, reiterating that the proposed 'note of clarification' was merely 'a piece of paper ... not sufficient', in response to which the TUC pressed him over why he continued to believe that a change of rule would be more 'binding' than the proposed circular to be applied to Rule 11. On this point, the TUC leadership was adamant that, in terms of practicability and effectiveness, it 'could not see the difference between a rule change and a solemn undertaking', to which Wilson replied that a change to Rule 11 could be presented, to the public, as the TUC 'legislating. That would make all the difference.' This purported presentational advantage would not be gained from a mere note of clarification.[37]

However, 'Barbara was clearly attracted by the thought of a Bridlington-type binding agreement' (Wilson, 1971: 659), to the extent that during the lunchtime adjournment her senior Departmental officials perused the 1939 Bridlington Agreement, to ascertain just how authoritative it had proved to be among trade unions. After Conrad Heron had explained to Castle just how much authority it had enjoyed since 1939, and how effective it had proved to be, she persuaded Wilson to consider a 'binding undertaking' between the Government and the TUC, *'provided that our words were approved'* (Castle, 1990: 345, diary entry for 18 June 1969, emphasis in original).

When Wilson, Castle and the TUC leaders reconvened after lunch, the General Council reiterated, once again, their total opposition to amending Rule 11, but readily agreed to the Prime Minister's new suggestion that 'a solemn and binding undertaking'[38] be discussed, which could then be jointly issued. This, Wilson, explained, would be instead of the amendment to Rule 11 which the Government had hitherto insisted upon, but would nonetheless 'in the annals of the Congress, be comparable in standing to the Bridlington Declaration'.[39] It was this status which would, in effect, render it 'binding' on the TUC.

Following a series of redrafts between the two 'sides' (Wilson and Castle had been joined at this stage by the Attorney-General), what transpired was a statement which declared that '[t]he General Council [of the TUC] have agreed unanimously to a solemn and binding undertaking', the substance of which was delineated as an annex. The General Council confirmed that:

> this undertaking will forthwith govern the operation ... of Congress Rule 11, as recommended by the General Council to the Special Congress on June 5. This undertaking unanimously given by the General Council will have the same binding force as the T.U.C. Bridlington Principles and Regulations. (Trades Union Congress, 1969a: 224)

The TUC thereupon agreed to a four-point 'solemn and binding undertaking' that:

a) where a dispute has led, or is likely to lead, to an unconstitutional stoppage of work which involves, directly or indirectly, large bodies of workers or which, if protracted, may have serious consequences, the General Council shall ascertain and assess all the facts, having regard to paragraph 20 to 27 of *Programme for Action.*

b) in cases where they consider it unreasonable to order an unconditional return to work, they will tender the organisation or organisations concerned their considered opinion and advice with a view to prompting a settlement.

c) where, however, they find there should be no stoppage of work before procedure is exhausted, they will place an obligation on the organisation or organisations concerned to take energetic steps to obtain an immediate resumption of work, including action within their rules if necessary, so that negotiations can proceed.

d) should an affiliated organisation not comply with an obligation placed on it under (c) above, the General Council shall duly report to Congress or deal with the organisation under [the relevant Clauses in] Rule 13. (Trades Union Congress, 1969a: 225)

Wilson then demanded that *all* of the members of the TUC's General Council should sign this agreement, in order that there was an official and public record of their unanimous endorsement, but on this too, he was compelled to back down, as the TUC refused to accede to this final demand. Instead, Feather and John Newton (the TUC's chair) signed the 'solemn and binding' agreement on behalf of the General Council (Silver, 1973: 161).

The Cabinet's response

The 'solemn and binding' agreement fell somewhat short of what Wilson and Castle had demanded from the TUC during the previous two months, but with Cabinet support having ebbed away in recent weeks, leaving them isolated and with no realistic prospect of securing sufficient support from the PLP to pass the proposed Industrial Relations Bill, the two senior Labour Ministers were in a significantly weakened bargaining position. Even Wilson's occasional hints, or even explicit threats, of resignation over the issue had failed to secure Cabinet support for his – and Castle's – unyielding stance towards the TUC.

Indeed, Crossman recalled that by mid-June the Cabinet had, in effect, called Wilson's bluff over his threats to resign: if he did stand down he would almost certainly be replaced by Callaghan or Jenkins, and the Government would continue until the general election – it might even enjoy a boost in the polls, just as a football team can enjoy a sudden fillip when it appoints a new manager. Yet if he resolved to remain as Prime Minister, Crossman reasoned, then Wilson would have to compromise with the TUC, rather than continuing to insist that the proposed 'penal clauses' would only be abandoned if the General Council offered counter-proposals which were likely to prove equally robust and effective. If the TUC were offering something else, albeit sufficiently credible and workable, then Wilson would be obliged to accept it; 'he must stay and settle' (Crossman, 1977: 527, diary entry for 18 June 1969).

Nonetheless, because the 18 June negotiations with the TUC's General Council proved so protracted, due initially to the brinkmanship involved on both sides and then, when a breakthrough was finally achieved, owing to the need to agree on the precise wording of the 'solemn and binding' agreement with the TUC, the rest of the Cabinet was kept waiting all day, not knowing when Wilson and Castle would reappear. When they finally did so, at 17.00, the ensuing Cabinet meeting, while formally endorsing the agreement which Wilson and Castle had just reached with the TUC, was characterised by understandable relief that such a vexatious issue had finally been resolved, and *inter alia* that this obviated the need for industrial relations legislation during the remainder of the Parliamentary session.

Beyond this, accounts diverge over the response of Cabinet Ministers when informed of the 'solemn and binding' agreement. Wilson himself claimed that there was 'great excitement, even cheers' (Wilson, 1971: 661), whereas Richard Crossman recalled that, whilst the Cabinet offered perfunctory congratulations and 'a series of little odious speeches', there was 'no enthusiasm'. For his part, Wilson was 'very abrasive, very tough, very furious with the Cabinet' (Crossman, 1977: 529, diary entry for 18 June 1969), or 'truculent', according to Tony Benn (1988: 188, diary entry for 18 June 1969). Castle claimed that she and Wilson were 'oozing contempt for the cowards from every pore' (Castle, 1990: 347, diary entry for 18 June 1969), while Wilson recalled that Castle 'dressed down the whole Cabinet for placing me in this position: they had left me without a card in my hand, and I had taken the ace, she said' (Wilson, 1971: 661).

A few Ministers offered congratulations – George Thomas displaying his Welsh Methodist roots by joyously proclaiming 'Hallelujah, Harold', followed a little later by 'Dare to be a Daniel'[40] – but these were insufficient to overcome the overall sense of bitterness and betrayal that Castle and Wilson felt towards most of their Cabinet colleagues for failing to support them collectively and consistently. Shortly after this Cabinet meeting George Thomas sent an obsequious telegram to Castle, declaring '[o]h you beautiful doll. I am proud to serve with you. Full marks for courage and steadfastness.'[41] There is no record of her response.

The immediate aftermath

The immense relief which Ministers naturally felt after the 'solemn and binding' agreement with the TUC was tinged, in some instances, with regrets and recrimination at the way the whole episode had been handled by Wilson and Castle. The most trenchant criticism emanated from Richard Crossman, who feared that '[t]he scars will take some time to heal, and I suspect that after this searing experience, things will never be the same in this Cabinet'. Crossman attributed much of the acrimony, not merely to the Industrial Relations Bill itself (clearly important though this was), but to Wilson's and Castle's crucial role in pursuing it in spite of growing opposition and dire warnings from all levels of the Labour Government and the Party: 'The prime cause of the ever-growing split between you and the Cabinet on the I. R. Bill was the way you and Barbara put it over us last January', resulting in a 'catastrophic relationship between yourself and us'.

According to Crossman, when the Cabinet formally endorsed *In Place of Strife* back in January, it did so largely because 'you [Wilson] deliberately bounced us into accepting the White Paper and the appalling risks that it implied', and that suspecting the opposition it would have aroused if it had been presented to the Cabinet *before* being shown to the TUC, 'you decided to present us with a virtual *fait accompli*', and then securing 'a majority vote in which none of the Trade Union members were on your side'. On this basis, Crossman alleged, the Labour Government 'had been committed to … a reckless and possibly disastrous policy without any consultation', which left many senior Ministers in 'the role of anxious spectators watching two colleagues performing an exercise in brinkmanship which involved all of us in the risks'. Crossman lamented that '[w]hat has happened since January in the I. R. Bill is only the latest example, of a relationship between Prime Minister and colleagues which leaves Cabinet solidarity very weak and liable to break in a crisis'.[42]

Also greatly irked by Wilson's and Castle's conduct over *In Place of Strife* and the aborted interim Industrial Relations Bill was the Chancellor, Roy Jenkins, who subsequently bemoaned the manner in which Wilson and Castle 'had got themselves deeply involved in a series of negotiations of almost Byzantine complication with a variety of trade union leaders'. Indeed, 'so convoluted' did the issues and associated talks become, Jenkins claimed, that 'I ceased to follow them' (Jenkins, 1991: 289). Yet Jenkins considered this episode to be symptomatic of Wilson's own personality and political style in general, whereupon '[t]he real count against Wilsonism was that it was opportunistic and provided leadership by manoeuvre and not by direction' (Jenkins, 1991: 288).

Another member of the Cabinet, Peter Shore, subsequently noted that *In Place of Strife* had been 'a brave new policy … pressed with reckless courage by Barbara Castle, with Harold Wilson's total support', albeit 'to the point where it was painfully clear that there was no majority for it in either the PLP or the Cabinet', whereupon it resulted in a 'major defeat for Harold Wilson' (Shore, 1993: 102). As a consequence, 'Prime Minister Wilson's sense of his own importance suffered a severe knock' (Crosland, 1982: 205).

Six years earlier, Richard Crossman had written an Introduction to a new edition of Walter Bagehot's *The English Constitution*, which had originally been published in 1867, the year of the second Reform Act which extended the franchise (the right to vote in elections) to much of the male population; women were not granted the vote until 1918 and 1928. In this Introduction, Crossman had lamented that, since the democratisation of British politics, power had actually been continually centralised, to the extent that not only had the Cabinet superseded Parliament as the real source of political power, but that the Cabinet itself had seen much of its power abrogated by Prime Ministers. Thus did Crossman complain that '[t]he post-war epoch has seen the final transformation of Cabinet Government into Prime Ministerial Government' (Crossman, 1963: 51). This perspective was ostensibly borne out by Wilson's conduct in pursuing, albeit in tandem with Castle, *In Place of Strife* and then the interim Industrial Relations Bill, in spite of the growing opposition both in the Cabinet and on the Labour Government's backbenches.

Yet Crossman's 1963 thesis about the rise of Prime Ministerial Government prompted a trenchant refutation, two years later, by G. W. Jones, who argued that any Prime Minister was ultimately dependent on the support or acquiescence of their Parliamentary and Ministerial colleagues, and as such '[i]t would be fatal for a Prime Minister to set himself apart from his Parliamentary party ... the Prime Minister is not the master of his party. Leaders can lose their parties' support and be toppled', so that '[a] Prime Minister is only as strong as his party, and particularly his chief colleagues, lets him be' (Jones, 1965: 177, 178). From this perspective, the fact that Wilson eventually felt obliged to abandon *In Place of Strife* in the face of mounting backbench and Cabinet opposition seemed to vindicate Jones' perspective; Wilson could not pursue his clear policy preference and the associated legislation, due to dwindling support among his Parliamentary and Ministerial colleagues. Ultimately, it was the Prime Minster who was effectively compelled to back down, not the Cabinet or backbench Labour MPs.

Conclusion

The 'solemn and binding' agreement ostensibly represented a last-minute, face-saving deal between Wilson, Castle and the TUC's General Council, which could then be presented to the Cabinet, and *inter alia* the country as a mutual solution to the prevalence of unofficial and unconstitutional strikes. Even so, it was widely, but often tacitly, recognised that Wilson (and Castle) had ultimately yielded more than the TUC. The latter had not introduced the rule change demanded by Wilson, which he had insisted was essential if industrial relations legislation was to be avoided. He had even threatened his resignation if he did not secure the enactment of either the interim Industrial Relations Bill or the change to Rule 11 by the TUC, the Prime Minister staking his personal authority on achieving one of these objectives. Yet Wilson ultimately failed to secure either.

This failure reflected both his lack of understanding of the internal dynamics and politics of the TUC, whose General Council enjoyed only limited authority over its affiliated members, and the haemorrhaging of support in the Cabinet and on the Labour backbenches which ultimately left Wilson and Castle isolated. Cognizance of Wilson's weakened political position, in turn, enabled the TUC leadership to stand firm against his demand for a change to Rule 11, and effectively call his bluff.

At the same time, Wilson presented the 'solemn and binding agreement' to a mostly lukewarm Cabinet, in which many previously supportive Ministers had grown impatient with his apparent brinkmanship, and the extent to which he had jeopardised the unity of the labour movement in doggedly pursuing industrial relations reform, regardless of the growing opposition and despair in the Labour Party at all levels. He had ignored the exhortations of many Ministers and MPs to accept the proposals enshrined in the TUC's *Programme for Action*, insisting that these were inadequate, yet the 'solemn and binding' agreement which he and Castle eventually signed with the TUC leadership, and which he sought to depict as a victory, as well as a testimony to his tough negotiating skills, was not much different in substance to the TUC proposals he had spent several weeks rejecting. In the process, instead of illustrating the predominance and supremacy of the contemporary Prime Minister, Wilson unwittingly highlighted the constraints and contingent character of Prime Ministerial power, and the extent to which the occupant of 10, Downing Street is ultimately reliant on Ministerial and backbench support, or, at least, acquiescence.

Notes

1 MS. Wilson 1250, Harold Wilson, 'Note for the Record on Industrial Relations Legislation', 10 May 1969. See also MS. Wilson 1250, Harold Wilson, 'Record of a meeting between the Prime Minister and Mr. Victor Feather at No. 10, Downing Street on Friday 25 April 1969', undated, but *circa* late April 1969.
2 NA PREM 13/2727, 'Note of a Meeting of the Management Committee', 9 June 1969.
3 MRC, MSS. 292B/40.2/5, Meeting between Harold Wilson, Barbara Castle and the TUC's General Council, on 12 May 1969.
4 MRC, MSS. 292B/40.2/5, Meeting between Harold Wilson, Barbara Castle and the TUC's General Council, on 12 May 1969.
5 MRC, MSS. 292B/40.2/5, Meeting between Harold Wilson, Barbara Castle and the TUC's General Council, on 12 May 1969.
6 MRC, MSS. 292B/40.2/5, Meeting between Harold Wilson, Barbara Castle and the TUC's General Council, on 21 May 1969.
7 MRC, MSS. 292B/40.2/5, Meeting between Harold Wilson, Barbara Castle and the TUC's General Council, on 21 May 1969.
8 MRC, MSS. 292B/40.2/5, Meeting between Harold Wilson, Barbara Castle and the TUC's General Council, on 21 May 1969.
9 MRC, MSS. 292B/40.2/5, Meeting between Harold Wilson, Barbara Castle and the TUC's General Council, on 21 May 1969.
10 MRC, MSS. 292B/40.2/5, Meeting between Harold Wilson, Barbara Castle and the TUC's General Council, on 21 May 1969.
11 MS. Wilson 936, Harold Wilson, 'Note for the Record on Industrial Relations Legislation', undated but *circa* late May 1969.
12 MS. Wilson 936, Harold Wilson, 'Note for the Record on Industrial Relations Legislation', undated but *circa* late May 1969.
13 NA PREM 13/2726, Note of a Meeting with Representatives of the Trades Union Congress, 21 May 1969; MRC, MSS. 292B/40.2/5, Meeting between

Harold Wilson, Barbara Castle and the TUC's General Council, on 21 May 1969.
14 MS. Wilson 936, Harold Wilson, 'Note for the Record on Industrial Relations Legislation', undated but *circa* late May 1969.
15 MS. Castle.274, 'Whereabouts of First Secretary – 23rd May to 6th June', undated but *circa* mid-May 1969.
16 MS. Wilson c.1250, 'Note for the Record on Industrial Relations Legislation', 10 May 1969.
17 NA PREM 13/2726, Note of Discussion at Dinner, Chequers, 1 June 1969, emphasis in original.
18 NA PREM 13/2726, Note of Discussion at Dinner, Chequers, 1 June 1969.
19 NA PREM 13/2726, Note of Discussion at Dinner, Chequers, 1 June 1969.
20 NA PREM 13/2727, Note of telephone conversation between Harold Wilson and Barbara Castle on 6 June, 9 June 1969.
21 MRC, MSS. 292B/40.2/5, Meeting between Harold Wilson, Barbara Castle and the TUC's General Council, on 9 June 1969.
22 NA PREM 13/2727, Note of a Meeting with Representatives of the Trades Union Congress, 9 June 1969.
23 NA PREM 13/2727, 'Note of a Meeting of the Management Committee', 12 June 1969.
24 MRC, MSS. 292B/40.2/5, Meeting between Harold Wilson, Barbara Castle and the TUC's General Council, on 9 June 1969.
25 MRC, MSS. 292B/40.2/5, Meeting between Harold Wilson, Barbara Castle and the TUC's General Council, on 9 June 1969.
26 MRC, MSS. 292B/40.2/5, Meeting between Harold Wilson, Barbara Castle and the TUC's General Council, on 11 June 1969.
27 MRC, MSS. 292B/40.2/5, Meeting between Harold Wilson, Barbara Castle and the TUC's General Council, on 11 June 1969.
28 NA PREM 13/2727, 'Note of a Meeting of the Management Committee', 8 June 1969.
29 MRC, MSS. 292B/40.2/5, Meeting between Harold Wilson, Barbara Castle and the TUC's General Council, on 11 June 1969, emphasis added.
30 NA PREM 13/2727, 'Note of a Meeting of the Management Committee', 9 June 1969.
31 NA PREM 13/2728, 'Note of a Meeting of the Management Committee', 17 June 1969.
32 NA PREM 13/2728, 'Note of a Meeting of the Management Committee', 17 June 1969.
33 NA PREM 13/2728, 'Note of a Meeting of the Management Committee', 17 June 1969.
34 MRC, MSS. 292B/40.2/5, Meeting between Harold Wilson, Barbara Castle and the TUC's General Council, on 18 June 1969.
35 The Bridlington Agreement had been reached at the TUC's 1939 conference in the east-coast town, and constituted a code of practice regulating inter-union competition for members. This was widely respected and adhered to by the unions, because although it 'was not a rule … it had the same authority' (Silver, 1973: 160).
36 MRC, MSS. 292B/40.2/5, Meeting between Harold Wilson, Barbara Castle and the TUC's General Council, on 18 June 1969.

37 MRC, MSS. 292B/40.2/5, Meeting between Harold Wilson, Barbara Castle and the TUC's General Council, on 18 June 1969.
38 The phrase soon became subject to mockery, as it was widely referred to as 'Solomon Binding', which Denis Barnes, the DEP's Permanent Secretary, suggested '[s]ounds like a character out of George Eliot' (quoted in Perkins, 2003: 322).
39 MRC, MSS. 292B/40.2/5, Meeting between Harold Wilson, Barbara Castle and the TUC's General Council, on 18 June 1969.
40 Callaghan Papers, Box 149, Personal note, 30 June 1969.
41 MS. Castle.274, Thomas to Castle, 1 June 1969.
42 MS Wilson c.1250, Crossman to Wilson, 19 June 1969.

Conclusion

The Labour Government's travails over *In Place of Strife* and the ensuing Industrial Relations Bill have variously been blamed, by some of those most closely involved, for the Party's defeat in the 1970 general election. Their critiques are outlined below, but given the controversy surrounding the White Paper and associated legislative proposals, it is worth considering why Harold Wilson decided to call the general election in 1970 anyway. At that time, there was no Fixed Term Parliament Act, and hence a Prime Minister was entitled to call a general election at any time *within* five years of the previous election. Having been re-elected in 1966, the Labour Government could have deferred an election until 1971, by which time, the controversies and bitterness engendered by the proposed, and then abandoned, industrial relations legislation might have abated.

According to Wilson's Press Secretary, Joe Haines, a major reason for *not* opting to serve the full five-year term was that in early 1971, Britain would be adopting a new currency – 'decimalisation' (BBC, 2011). Some Ministers feared that this might prove so controversial and unpopular (even if only temporarily until people became accustomed to it), that the Government could suffer an electoral backlash. Consequently, a 1970 general election became the default option, the main discussion being over whether it should be held in the early summer (before the schools closed, and many families went away on holiday) or the autumn. Haines acknowledged that '[i]n favour of waiting until the autumn was the fact that the wounds inflicted upon Labour voters between 1967 and 1969 – devaluation, the wage freeze, tax increases, the battle with the unions – would take a little longer to heal' (Haines, 1977: 170).

However, June was chosen for several reasons, one of the most influential being Labour's improved performance in May's local government elections, coupled with a concomitant increase in the Party's support in opinion polls (Wilson, 1971: 778). This naturally buoyed the confidence of many Cabinet Ministers, and seemingly convinced them that the bitterness aroused by the previous year's industrial relations proposals had largely dissipated. In fact, Wilson subsequently confessed that he had 'virtually decided', on 13 April 1970, that the general election should be held on 18 June, although he naturally wanted first to analyse the mid-May local election results, to gauge the scale and strength of Labour's electoral recovery, and then consult with senior colleagues, before making a final decision and announcement (Wilson, 1971: 778). In fact, only two senior Ministerial colleagues were consulted by Wilson before he informed the Cabinet of his decision, namely the Chancellor – who had no strong preference concerning the date – and Peter Shore, who definitely favoured June (Haines, 2003: 23–4).

A further factor alluded to by Wilson, when he informed the Cabinet that he was going to call a June election, was international affairs. Indeed, Wilson deemed that:

> [o]ne of the most important considerations was the uncertainty of the international prospect in relation to such issues as European security ... and the need for the Government to be able to speak for the United Kingdom with authority in the forthcoming negotiations for entry into the European Communities.[1]

He also referred to the heightened expectations of the electorate regarding a June election. Moreover, Wilson pointed out that if the Government deferred the election, it 'would find it progressively more difficult to control events and would increasingly lose the power of initiative'.[2]

This last observation highlighted a perennial dilemma facing governments and Prime Ministers in the era long before the 2011 Fixed Term Parliament Act. If a Government had faced difficulties or/and unpopularity during the third or fourth year in office, the natural temptation was to serve the full five years, in the Micawberish hope that its fortunes would improve in the final year, sufficient to secure re-election. Yet this offered a hostage to fortune by placing the Government at the mercy of unforeseen events, which might perpetuate or even exacerbate its unpopularity, and therefore further damage its electoral prospects at the end of the five-year term.

A further reason cited for choosing June, according to Haines, was that the Conservatives were expecting an autumn election, and were thus planning to pursue a major advertising campaign over the summer: 'A June election would put a stop to that'(Haines, 1977: 170; see also Haines, 2003: 23).

Finally, it was acknowledged that an autumn general election would be conducted in the context of less clement weather, darker evenings and an electoral register which was almost a year out of date (Haines 2003: 23), although such objections did not dissuade Wilson from later calling

Table 3 Results of the 1970 general election, with corresponding figures for 1966

	Votes	Share (%)	Seats
Conservative	13,145,123 (11,418,455)	46.2 (41.4)	330 (253)
Labour	12,208,758 (13,096,629)	43.9 (48.9)	288 (364)
Liberal	2,117,035 (2,327,457)	7.6 (8.6)	6 (12)
Others	873,882 (422,206)	2.3 (1.1)	6 (1)

(http://www.bbc.co.uk/news/special/politics97/background/pastelec).

a general election for October 1974, albeit under rather different political circumstances.

The result of the 1970 general election is in Table 3, with the corresponding figures for 1966 in brackets to show the scale of the changes.

What these figures do not show was the proportional decline in turnout between 1966 and 1970, from 75.8 per cent to 72 per cent, although the actual number of people who voted in 1970 was somewhat higher than four years earlier. This apparent discrepancy is explained by the fact that, in 1969, the minimum age of voting had been reduced from 21 to 18, thereby increasing the total electorate from 36 million people to 39.3 million. However, although more than 3 million new voters had been added to the electoral register only just over 1 million additional votes were cast in 1970, hence the drop in turnout in percentage terms.

Accounts of Labour's defeat

It was almost inevitable that *In Place of Strife*, and the subsequent abandonment of the proposed industrial relations legislation, would feature prominently in much of the debate about why Labour lost the 1970 general election, in spite of the strong lead which the Party had enjoyed in several opinion polls during the campaign. However, there emerged two markedly different perspectives about the manner in which *In Place of Strife* and the Industrial Relations Bill allegedly contributed towards Labour's electoral defeat, these contrasting interpretations depending on whether the commentator had supported or opposed the White Paper and the subsequent proposed legislation.

To the proponents and supporters of *In Place of Strife* and the subsequent Industrial Relations Bill, it was the failure to enact the intended reform of industrial relations and trade unionism which contributed significantly to Labour's electoral defeat a year later. According to Michael Stewart, who had been Foreign Secretary in 1969 and remained supportive of *In Place of Strife* throughout, even while other senior Minister were withdrawing their support in the face of opposition from the trade unions and much of the PLP, the failure to enact the proposed industrial relations legislation cost Labour electorally. Had the Government persevered, and shown firm leadership, it 'would have made a most favourable impression in the country, and gone a long way towards winning us the approaching Election' (Stewart, 1980: 253).

Meanwhile, the biographer of Chancellor Roy Jenkins claims that the Labour Government's 'ignominious surrender to the unions over *In Place of Strife* probably contributed more than anything else to Labour's defeat the following year', in the 1970 general election (Campbell, 2014: 346). Similarly, Joe Haines averred that '[t]he failure of *In Place of Strife* indirectly cost Labour the election' (Haines, 2003: 17). This critique held that a growing number of voters, including many trade union members, had become exasperated by the industrial disruption caused by strikes, particularly those of an unconstitutional or unofficial character which were, by definition, unpredictable. Consequently, these voters were deemed to be deeply disappointed at the Labour Government's perceived capitulation to the trade unions in June 1969, and were not remotely convinced that the 'solemn and binding' agreement with the TUC would have any discernible or enduring impact on strikes. In this context, the Conservatives' pledge to enact clear and comprehensive industrial relations legislation, based on *Fair Deal at Work*, was deemed likely to have persuaded some erstwhile Labour voters to switch to the Conservative Party in the June 1970 general election.

Against this perspective, critics and opponents of *In Place of Strife* and the Industrial Relations Bill claimed that it was the stubborn pursuit of such legislation during the first half of 1969, rather than its subsequent failure *per se*, which seriously damaged Labour's electoral performance in 1970. According to this interpretation, Wilson and Castle especially had alienated many erstwhile Labour voters as a consequence of their desire to place statutory obligations and restrictions on the trade unions and their members, especially after several years of enforced wage restraint via a succession of incomes policies. The Labour Government had seemingly been pre-occupied with curbing workers' pay and collective bargaining, and cutting the social wage, in order to impress the City and international financiers with its economic and fiscal probity; no corresponding curbs were placed on the business community or boardroom pay.

For example, when Wilson opted for a June 1970 election, even though constitutionally he could have waited another year, Joe Gormley warned him that it was too soon, because '[t]he scars of your industrial relations policy haven't healed yet … You've soured your supporters …. You've hurt that trade union support.' Not only was this likely to reduce Labour's support on polling day, Gormley explained, it also meant that during the election campaign itself the Party would struggle to muster sufficient activists to mobilise support: 'In Lancashire …where I used to be able to get three or four hundred miners out on to the streets and the hustings – well, I'd be hard pushed to … rake up a dozen at the moment' (Gormley, 1982: 74). Similarly, Eric Heffer believed that June was too early, because 'we needed a little longer to regain our support', and as such, he 'felt that we could win in October, but had grave doubts about June' (Heffer, 1973: 168).

When Heffer's doubts about Labour's electoral prospects in June were subsequently vindicated, he claimed that (election night) conversations with members of his constituency [Liverpool Walton] Labour Party convinced him that 'one of the factors contributing to our defeat … had been the attitude adopted by the Labour Government to industrial relations issues. In particular, the Prices and Incomes Policy, and *In Place of Strife*, came under heavy criticism' (Heffer, 1973: 169). The erstwhile Chancellor, Roy Jenkins, meanwhile, candidly conceded that '[i]t was broadly my policies on which Wilson had chosen to fight, and on which we had lost' (Jenkins, 1991: 303).

Of course, it was not necessarily an either/or issue: it is perfectly plausible to assume that some erstwhile or potential Labour voters declined to vote for the Party due to disappointment at the failure to enact industrial relations legislation, while others withheld their votes because of disapproval that the Government had devoted so much time and energy to attempting to place statutory obligations and restrictions on trade union activities. If this was the case, then the issue might have cost Labour votes from supporters *and* opponents of *In Place of Strife* alike.

However, attributing blame for Labour's defeat to the Government's troubles over industrial relations legislation is over-simplistic, for two reasons. First, hardly any political phenomenon can be adequately or accurately explained by a mono-causal account which attributes an occurrence or event to just one factor. Of course, a particular factor or event might be highly influential, and indeed, be the most important variable, but even when this is the case, other factors will have contributed to the significance of the 'key' factor, and thereby contributed towards, or enhanced, its impact. As such, rather than identify a single, causal, factor when explaining a political occurrence, it is essential to adopt a somewhat broader approach, or dig a little deeper, in order to examine the event more holistically.

In the case of Labour's 1970 election defeat, this means looking at the Party's overall record in government, the problems it encountered and its policy responses, of which *In Place of Strife* was just one – albeit obviously a significant one. To express it another way, Labour's electoral woes did not begin in the first half of 1969, when the battle over *In Place of Strife* was being waged, but much earlier, almost immediately after the

Party's re-election in March 1966. The usual honeymoon period which governments often enjoy in the first few months after a general election victory was denied to the re-elected Labour Government, which faced serious economic problems from the outset. Indeed, some of these were indirectly exacerbated by its 1966 election victory, because Labour's re-election with a comfortable ninety-seven-seat Parliamentary majority caused consternation among senior industrialists and financiers that the Government might now feel sufficiently strengthened and emboldened to pursue a programme of radical economic and social reform and wealth redistribution, and *inter alia* significantly increase public expenditure.

Thereafter, the Labour Government struggled to win the confidence of the business community, as Ministers struggled to tackle a plethora of economic and industrial problems. Indeed, even though the Government responded by pursuing the traditional policies of deflation, entailing curbs on public expenditure and wage restraint via incomes policies, coupled with increased prescription charges in the NHS and postponing the planned raising of the school leaving age (from 15 years of age to 16), it continued to face scepticism from senior industrialists and investors about the Party's economic competence and probity. As noted in a mid-1960s editorial in *The Economist*, titled 'Labour men, Tory measures', 'when orthodox financial policies are pursued by a left-wing government, they do not attract the same return in financial confidence as exactly the same policies pursued by the Tories' (*The Economist*, 1965: 416). Yet whilst the Labour Government's deflationary policies failed to foster confidence among the business community, they did seemingly alienate some of Labour's working class and trade union supporters.

The second reason why it is over-simplistic to attribute Labour's 1970 electoral defeat to *In Place of Strife* is that, as noted above, during May and early June 1970 Labour enjoyed comfortable leads over the Conservatives in opinion polls, and performed well in local government elections. This strongly suggested that the Party's relatively recent problems over industrial relations had not prompted a significant desertion of former supporters, otherwise Labour would have trailed the Conservatives in the polls consistently throughout the campaign. As it was, Labour's support dissipated right at the very end of the campaign, during the last couple of days.

This last point strongly implies that the late collapse of Labour's support was largely prompted by unfavourable economic data published a couple of days before the election, which then prompted last-minute doubts about the Party's credibility and competence *vis-à-vis* its future stewardship of the British economy. For example, official statistics published on the Monday before the (Thursday) election revealed that Britain's trade/balance of payments deficit had increased in May, while polling day itself was accompanied by the publication of figures showing an increase in unemployment. Such data probably persuaded some voters that the apparent economic recovery which had occurred during the previous twelve months or so was rather more ephemeral or fragile than had been assumed. According to Shirley Williams, for example, '[t]he single most important factor reversing the public's favourable view of the government was … the publication three days before election day of trade figures' which fuelled concerns that 'the government was not out of the woods as far as the economy was concerned' (Williams, 2009: 208).

Of course, if one particular set of economic data had such a major and damaging impact on Labour's electoral support in the last forty-eight hours or so of the campaign, then its apparent recovery in the opinion polls must have been fragile anyway. In fact, Williams herself notes that '[o]ne month's trade figures would not have so radically altered the course of the election had there not been a deep-seated unease about the administration's economic and industrial management' (Williams, 2009: 208–9). Or as Ponting averred, 'taken in isolation at a critical time', such figures seemed to vindicate Conservative claims that 'the economy was still weak and fragile' (Ponting, 1990: 388).

Moreover, an in-depth study of the 1970 general election suggested that there were already early indications that the British electorate, which had hitherto been notable for its high degree of party loyalty via class and partisan alignment, was starting to become more volatile, and thus somewhat less inclined to vote consistently for the same party at every general election. In this respect, dealignment had three consequences for general elections and voting behaviour, namely a greater willingness by voters to switch their support to another party, a higher propensity to abstain from voting and, as a consequence of the latter, a decline in electoral turnout.

Certainly, some of the data for the 1970 general election suggested that, instead of Labour suffering millions of the Party's erstwhile supporters switching to the Conservatives, a much more significant factor in its defeat was abstention by many disgruntled Labour supporters. As one eminent political scientist suggested at the time, '[t]he absolute fall in the Labour vote, by more than three-quarters of a million, is best interpreted as a positive decision by Labour voters to abstain' (Rose, 1970: 31; see also Panitch, 1976: 221).

That Labour was strongly affected by abstentions among its former supporters was acknowledged by some of the Party's MPs. Ian Mikardo, for example, reported that in his Poplar [East London] constituency:

> [w]hat I heard on the doorsteps was not that a lot of people who had voted Labour in 1966 were going to vote Tory or Liberal in 1970, but that a lot of people who had voted Labour in 1966 were, in 1970, not going to vote at all.

After the election, Mikardo somehow succeeded in locating 116 of these abstainers, and asked them what had prompted their decision not to vote. The standard response was that 'they couldn't see much, if any, difference between what the Labour Government had done in the last four years, and what a Conservative Government would have done' (Mikardo, 1988: 181, 182).

The impact of late abstentions on Labour's electoral support was also observed by the Foreign Secretary, Michael Stewart, in his Fulham constituency. He recalled that '[i]t was not till 6.00 pm on polling day ... that I saw what was happening; that is when one can see whether Labour voters are coming out in sufficient numbers. They were not' (Stewart, 1980: 254). Likewise, in his Coventry East seat, Richard Crossman recognised that, by the evening of polling day, 'it was obvious that something was going very badly wrong. The poll [turnout] was only just over 50, 52, 55 per cent, even in our safest, biggest wards, and by 9 o'clock, it was only 60 per cent'. Upon reflection, Crossman concluded that, although some erstwhile Labour voters might have switched to the Conservative Party, most of the electoral swing to the Conservatives 'was the result of Labour abstentions' (Crossman, 1977: 949, diary entry for 19 June 1970).

What compounded the deleterious impact of abstentions on Labour's electoral performance in June 1970 was that the Conservative Party had benefited from an increase in turnout (compared to 1966) among its supporters. In several seats, the increase in the number of Conservative votes was much greater than the decline in Labour's vote, thereby reaffirming Crossman's contention that Labour suffered primarily from abstentions, rather than former supporters switching to the Conservative Party *en masse*. For example, in the Merseyside constituency of Bebington, Labour polled just ten votes fewer than in 1966, whereas the Conservatives won an additional 3,000+ votes in 1970. Meanwhile, in Bedfordshire South, the Labour Party vote fell by 1,442 in 1970 (compared to 1966), while the Conservative vote increased by 7,776.

Furthermore, in a few constituencies Labour actually won more votes than in 1966, but still lost because the Conservatives won an even larger increase. This was certainly the case in the Derbyshire constituency of High Peak, where the 1970 election saw Labour attract an extra 1000+ votes compared to 1966, whereas the Conservatives vote increased by 3,000+. In such constituencies, the Conservatives seemed to have benefited from a significant increase in turnout among their own supporters compared to 1966.

One other voting variable which seems to have damaged Labour's performance in the 1970 election, while correspondingly benefiting the Conservatives, was the role of the Liberal Party and its candidates. In particular, there were some constituencies where the Liberals did not field a candidate in 1970, having previously done so in 1966. In many such constituencies, much of the Liberals' former support was transferred to the Conservatives in 1970, rather than to Labour. For example, having won 6,382 votes in Stretford in 1966, the Liberal Party did not field a candidate in 1970, whereupon the Conservatives won an additional 7,255 votes, while Labour's support fell by just 125 votes.

Conversely, there were some constituencies which the Liberals had *not* contested in 1966, but did contest in 1970, and in some of these, that Party's tally of votes was remarkably similar to the Labour Party's loss of votes compared to 1966. Indeed, in thirteen of the seats which the Conservatives won from Labour in 1970, the Liberal Party fielded a candidate having *not* done so in 1966. For example, in Brighton Kemptown, Labour's vote fell by 3,831 in 1970, while the Liberal candidate won 3,833 votes – just two more than Labour's loss. This enabled the Conservatives to win the seat by a margin of 3,103 votes, even though their candidate only won 103 votes more than in 1966. A similar scenario ensued in Stockport North, where Labour's 1970 vote was 4,330 lower than in 1966, whereas the Liberals won 4,022 votes. Again, the Liberals' intervention benefited the Conservatives, who won the seat from Labour by a margin of just 871 votes, having attracted only 130 votes more than in 1966.

This suggests that, alongside abstentions by some former Labour supporters who were disappointed with the record of the 1966–70 Labour Government, at least some of those who had voted for the Party in 1966 switched to the Liberals (rather than to the Conservatives) four years later. This, in turn, would have split the non-Conservative vote in some constituencies, and – owing to the operation of Britain's simple plurality (first-past-the-post) electoral system – this enabled the Conservative candidate to win the seat, irrespective of whether they had significantly increased the number of people voting for them.

Consequently, rather than treating *In Place of Strife* as if it was the key variable in explaining Labour's defeat in the 1970 election, the White Paper should be comprehended in the context of Labour's overall record in office, and the sundry economic problems the Government faced, coupled with its consequent policy responses (for a fuller account of why Labour lost the 1970 general election, see Dorey, 2013a).

Furthermore, it could be argued that the battle over *In Place of Strife* was, or subsequently became, symptomatic and symbolic of more significant and substantive dilemmas which face(d) Labour governments, and which periodically fuelled tensions between the Labour Party and the trade unions – the political and industrial wings of the organised labour movement in Britain. The economic and industrial problems affecting Britain in the 1960s, and the 1964–70 Labour Government's policy responses, brought, these dilemmas and tensions to the fore, but then, in turn, had fatal consequences for Labour's electoral support and performance.

The 'national interest' and electoralism vs sectional interests

One of the most obvious and general sources of tension between the Labour Party and the trade unions, which was particularly pronounced during the latter half of the 1960s, concerns the different perspectives and pressures faced by Labour Governments, which brought them into conflict with the trade unions. In fact, there are two broad aspects to this conflict of interests. The first is that, whereas the trade unions have just one socio-economic interest – albeit one which has been inextricably linked to the Party financially and organisationally – Labour has had to appeal to a much wider range of interests and sections of society in order to be electable and evince governmental competence, which has meant addressing two other crucial 'constituencies'.

The first of these is big business, financiers and industrialists, all of whom have feared the Party's professed Socialist principles and hostility to capitalism (such fears strongly imply that they took Labour's egalitarian rhetoric far too seriously or literally), and/or harboured grave doubts about Labour's economic competence, in terms of its ability to provide the economic conditions or circumstances in which capital accumulation, profitability and shareholder value could continually be increased. This has historically placed the Labour Party in an almost impossible situation, for the Party has simultaneously sought to pledge or deliver material and tangible improvements to workers and trade unions, while promising capital and 'the City' that it will pursue business-friendly policies which boost profitability and shareholder value. The latter will often entail convincing the business community that a Labour government will secure the compliance of the trade unions in *not* pursuing 'excessive' wage increases which would result in higher labour costs, and thus erode profit margins. In other words, the Labour Party has repeatedly been obliged to reassure big business and 'the City' that it will 'contain' or restrain the trade unions and hold down wages, while the Conservatives have never felt compelled to reassure the trade unions that a Conservative government will keep big business or employers 'under control' by curbing huge profits, or curtailing enormous salaries and bonuses in company boardrooms or 'the City'.

The second way in which the Labour Party has had to appeal far beyond the trade unions and their members in order to be elected (or merely viewed as electable – a credible government-in-waiting) is by rendering itself attractive to ordinary or middle-of-the-road voters, many of whom are not trade unionists, or working class. Indeed, particularly in recent decades, as the traditional working class has declined and trade union membership has plummeted, the Labour Party has been obliged to broaden its electoral appeal by seeking to attract support both from the growing middle class, and the increasing number of non-trade unionists; in effect, becoming a genuinely catch-all party, as exemplified by the post-1994 phenomenon of New Labour.

Certainly, much of the impetus for *In Place of Strife* and the ensuing Industrial Relations Bill was the perceived need to pacify the concerns of both the business and financial communities, and the wider electorate, about the industrial disruption and consequent economic damage attributed to unconstitutional and unofficial strikes. Yet seeking to assuage such concerns inevitably brought the Labour Government into conflict with the trade unions. However, the unions' hostility to *In Place of Strife* was exacerbated by the fact that this recourse to industrial relations legislation not only defied the main recommendations of the Donovan Report, but also followed several years of Ministerial efforts to curb wage increases, and *inter alia* inflation, via increasingly stringent incomes policies.

Of course, pay restraint had also owed much to the Labour Government's need to assuage the serious concerns of business elites and capital about Labour's stewardship of the British economy, but it also highlighted a further tension between a Labour Government's response to economic exigencies, namely incomes policies to restrain pay increases, and a fundamental principle of Britain's trade unions, namely the commitment to free collective bargaining to increase earnings.

Incomes policies vs free collective bargaining

Britain's trade unions have long been strongly committed to 'free collective bargaining', in which wage determination is, or should be, 'free' from political interference or State control. Even when Britain has had a Labour government, the trade unions have generally remained committed – at least in principle – to free collective bargaining, insisting that wages could only ever be planned and controlled by the State when capitalism had been superseded by Socialism, and the rest of the economy itself planned and placed under 'democratic' control. Until such time, in the words of Frank Cousins when addressing the TUC's 1956 conference (while he was leader of the TGWU, Britain's largest trade union at the time), 'in a period of freedom for all, we are part of the all'. Indeed, in 1966, Cousins resigned as a Cabinet Minister when the Labour Government adopted an incomes policy as an integral component of its economic and industrial strategy.

Trade unions also resented the manner in which incomes policies – even when adopted by Labour governments – reflected the premise that it was workers' wage increases which were the underlying cause of domestic inflation, rather than price increases intended to boost profits and shareholders' dividends (although companies often retorted that their price rises were often caused by the need to cover the higher labour costs accruing from wage increases). Certainly, the unions could argue that curbs were rarely imposed on high pay or bonuses in Britain's boardrooms or 'the City'; it was only workers' wages – not bosses' salaries – that were condemned as being excessive, economically damaging, greedy, inflationary and liable to increase unemployment through 'pricing people out of work'.

Although many trade union leaders initially acquiesced in the recourse of incomes policies, they did so for two main reasons: a) it was a Labour government adopting such a policy, rather than the Conservatives, so it was expected to be 'fairer' or more equitable; b) incomes polices were assumed to be a short-term emergency measure to tackle a particular economic crisis, after which there would be a return to free collective bargaining. However, as Labour governments sought to extend or renew each incomes policy on an annual basis, so trade union support diminished, thereby fuelling tensions between the political and industrial wings of organised labour, particularly as a new generation of more left-wing trade union leaders emerged in the 1960s, most notably Jack Jones and Hugh Scanlon: 'militant free collective bargainers' (Ackers, 2018: 272). As noted earlier, some critics suggested that the attempt by the 1966–70 Labour Government to hold down workers' wages via incomes policies – while also cutting public expenditure and the social wage – was a key reason (but certainly not the only one) for the Party's defeat in the 1970 general election.

Alongside the disjuncture between governmental incomes policies and the trade unions' commitment to free collective bargaining, the 1964–70 Labour Government's recourse to formal pay restraint encountered or exacerbated another practical problem, namely that of 'wage drift', for as we noted in chapter 1, as pay increasingly became formally determined centrally at national level, and often between union leaders and government Ministers, there was a counter-trend whereby local-level, more informal, wage bargaining increased, and this often yielded wage increases which were higher than those officially agreed nationally. This, in turn, served to enhance the authority, loyalty and respect enjoyed, in the workplace, by local-level union officials and shop stewards, for these were visibly pursuing the material interests of their members, whereas the national union leadership seemed to have become out of touch, and appeared to be colluding with Ministers to hold down workers' wages via incomes policies.

Of course, it was this gulf which underpinned the 'two systems' (formal and informal) of industrial relations and collective bargaining, as noted by the Donovan Report, and which largely prompted Barbara Castle's proposed reform of industrial relations via *In Place of Strife*, although Ministers and officials harboured divergent views about whether this was intended to make incomes policies more viable and effective, or render them unnecessary, on the grounds that reform would yield more stable, orderly and 'responsible' collective bargaining.

Yet pay determination, be it free collective bargaining or incomes policy, encountered another problem derived from the structure of British trade unionism, namely the fact that Britain's unions have been organised primarily on occupational grounds and, in this regard, become an inadvertent or unintentional source of (working) class fragmentation, rather than the basis of workers' solidarity (Ackers, 2018: 272–73; see also Anderson, 1967). Although there has always been a left romanticism about the *organised* working class as a vehicle for consciousness-raising and Socialist transformation, this long-term vision has repeatedly conflicted with the essentially sectional and short-term interests of trade unions, which seek to improve the material conditions and wages of their members (based on occupation or industrial sector) within capitalism. Many trade unions have pledged their commitment to Socialism, but this has often been a rhetorical or vague future goal, and in the meantime they have, in effect, competed against each other to secure the best deal for their members, with little genuine regard for other workers and trade unionists.

In this particular regard, trade unions are themselves a paradoxical product of capitalism, simultaneously providing their members with some protection against the worst forms of exploitation and immiseration – or lobbying for such protection – but nonetheless internalising the functional logic of capitalist competition when seeking the 'best deal' for their members. Just as a company is not concerned with the material well-being or welfare of other companies against which it is competing, so Britain's trade unions have rarely evinced much concern for the fate of other unions and their members, even when denouncing the inequities and injustices of capitalism. This further exacerbated the problems encountered by Labour Governments in the 1960s and 1970s in persuading the trade unions collectively to adopt both more responsible industrial behaviour and a longer-term perspective in response to Britain's economic problems and governmental policies to tackle them.

The longer-term consequences: from the 1969 White Paper to the 'winter of discontent'

Having lost the 1970 general election, the Labour Party and the trade unions naturally sought to foster a *rapprochement*, to put the bitterness engendered by *In Place of Strife* behind them and thenceforth ensure that the political and industrial 'wings' of organised labour could work more harmoniously together next time there was a Labour government. Indeed, it was recognised that Labour's future electoral prospects would be greatly enhanced by being able to convince voters that it was the only party which could establish, and then sustain, a more constructive and fraternal long-term relationship with the trade unions. Yet in the context of these observations, this new *rapprochement* was almost inevitably doomed to fail, although it was initially facilitated by joint Labour-trade union hostility to the Conservative 'enemy', before fracturing when the next Labour government again fatally foundered, and thereupon proved unable to 'deliver', in the face of severe economic difficulties in the latter half of the decade.

The Conservatives' 1971 Industrial Relations Act

Initially, a closer relationship and relative unity between the Labour Party and the trade unions was facilitated by their combined opposition to the newly elected Heath Government's Industrial Relations Bill, which also sought to impose a series of statutory curbs and regulations on the trade unions, but which were rather more extensive than those proposed by *In Place of Strife*. However, the Conservatives' Industrial Relations Bill unwittingly enshrined sundry inconsistencies, some of which were highlighted by Conservative MPs during the legislation's Parliamentary debates and (committee stage) scrutiny.

One of these concerned the provisions for weakening the 'closed shop', a system of compulsory trade union membership under which obtaining or retaining a job was dependent on being, or immediately becoming, a member of a trade union; often a specific, designated, union. In attempting to weaken the closed shop, Conservative Ministers were immediately confronted with a problem which had perennially faced their Party in denouncing such compulsion, namely the tension between promoting individual liberty and maintaining industrial order (Dorey, 2009a). On one hand, many Conservatives instinctively or ideologically condemned the closed shop for constituting a form of industrial conscription and trade union tyranny, because some workers were required to join a union against their wishes; indeed, they might have conscientious objections to belonging to a trade union. Yet failure to be(come) a union member could result in loss of employment, or failure to be appointed in the first place, even though they might be ideally qualified and/or perform extremely well at the job interview.

On the other hand, some Conservative MPs (particularly those originating from industrial or managerial backgrounds) recognised that maximum trade union membership could facilitate greater industrial order, because if all workers in a company or industry belonged to a specific trade union there would be far fewer demarcation and/or inter-union disputes. Moreover, management would benefit by only needing to negotiate with one set of trade union leaders or officials during pay bargaining, or discussions over other terms and conditions of employment. Conversely, for the Conservatives to encourage non-union membership, or permit workers to join any trade union they wished (in the guise of freedom of choice), the result was likely to be the fragmentation of trade unionism. Not only would this seriously undermine the Government's over-riding objective of imbuing industrial relations with greater order and stability, it would also make the role of management and employers much more onerous.

Some Conservative MPs also pointed out that maximising union membership would ensure that 'moderates' were trade unionists, and therefore more able to counter the influence of the left, whereas if union membership was solely a matter of individual choice then many 'moderates' would feel less inclination or motivation to join, and thereby inadvertently enable the (more active and organised) left to dominate the unions (Dorey, 2009a: 227–8). In the face of such arguments, the Industrial Relations Bill's provisions to outlaw the closed shop were amended, so that maximum union membership was to be encouraged, but with statutory safeguards for workers who harboured strong moral objections to being, or becoming, trade union members.

The official trade union response to the Industrial Relations Bill was one of 'passive non-co-operation', although this did not preclude extra-Parliamentary action in the form of demonstrations, marches and rallies seeking to 'kill the Bill' whilst it was still wending its way through Parliament. Once the Bill had become law, most trade unions simply refused *en masse* to register with the new Registrar of Trade Unions and Employers Associations, as they were required to do if they were to retain their legal immunities.

However, it was the judiciary – not normally known for its comradely sympathy towards the trade unions – which grievously undermined the Industrial Relations Act, quite unwittingly. In one instance, dock-workers who were members of the TGWU refused to handle the containers of Heaton's, a firm on Merseyside, because it was employing non-dock labour at its terminals. The TGWU defied an instruction by the National Industrial Relations Court (NIRC) to order the dockers to stop this refusal to deal with Heaton's containers, whereupon it was fined £5,000 for contempt of court,[3] this subsequently being increased to £50,000 when the 'boycott' continued.[4]

When the TGWU then took the case to the Appeal Court, claiming that it could not be held responsible for the actions of individual members who acted without the union's authorisation and who rejected the union's request to desist, its appeal was upheld. This favourable judicial decision was subsequently overturned by the 'Law Lords' (then Britain's highest judicial body and court of final appeal), but by this stage some of the inconsistencies in the Industrial Relations Act, in this case, the tension between the freedom of individual trade union members and the authority of their leaders, had become fully apparent. As with the closed shop, the twin Conservative tenets of liberty and order could not always be easily reconciled.

What ultimately proved fatal to the Industrial Relations Act was another bitter industrial dispute involving dock-workers, which resulted in five shop stewards being sent to prison after defying an order by the NIRC to stop picketing a firm employing non-dock labour. Their imprisonment provoked a national dock strike, accompanied by sympathy or solidarity action from other workers and trade unions. However, the Law Lords' verdict in the earlier Heaton's case, in which it had judged that the trade unions, not individual members, were ultimately legally responsible for industrial action, effectively absolved the 'Pentonville Five' dockers from legal liability, thereby ensuring their immediate acquittal and release from prison in August 1972.

The manner in which these judicial decisions highlighted inherent flaws and inconsistencies in the Industrial Relations Act, coupled with the willingness of trade unions to mobilise in support of fellow trade unionists who were prosecuted (and sometimes imprisoned) for defying the Act, effectively destroyed the credibility and effectiveness of the legislation. Although the Conservative Prime Minister, Edward Heath, refused to repeal the Act, it was tacitly acknowledged that it would no longer be invoked and instead, a new partnership with the trade unions sought instead as the primary means of improving industrial relations (on the failure of the Act, see Campbell, 1993: chapter 24; Moran, 1977: chapters 8 and 9; Taylor, 1993: 186–202; Taylor, 1996: 169–76; Whitehead, 1985: chapter 4; Williamson, 2015: 174–7).

Had the Conservative Government's 1971 Industrial Relations Act proved successful, it would almost certainly have proved problematic for Labour, because a pledge by the latter to repeal the Act would inevitably have been portrayed, by the Conservatives (and their many allies in the press) as both a recipe for returning to industrial chaos and trade union militancy, and evidence that Labour placed the interests of its trade union 'pay-masters' above those of the nation itself. However, the *de facto* defeat of the Industrial Relations Act, within a year of being placed on the statute book, meant that Labour's subsequent pledge to repeal it was much less contentious than it would otherwise have been.

The Labour-trade union 'social contract'

Meanwhile, the pursuit of a *rapprochement* between the Labour Party and the trade unions yielded the 1972 'social contract', which decreed that if the trade unions exercised *voluntary* wage restraint, and took into account the overall state of the economy when submitting pay claims, the next Labour government would enact a tranche of policies to improve the social wage, such as increasing old-age pensions and introducing subsidies for transport fares, rents and some food items. The 'social contract' also entailed a commitment by the Labour Party to repeal the Industrial Relations Act, strengthen employment protection and workers' rights, and introduce industrial democracy (Coates, 1980: 82–3; Taylor, 1978; Taylor, 1993: chapter 7; Trades Union Congress, 1973a; Trades Union Congress, 1973b; Whitehead, 1985: chapter 6).

The Labour Party's leadership clearly hoped that improvements in the social wage would deter the trade unions from pursuing significant increases in 'real' wages, and thereby simultaneously facilitate sustained economic growth and full employment without fuelling inflation. Indeed, the success or failure of the 'social contract' would depend upon this, as was made clear in Labour's October 1974 election manifesto, which declared that:

> [a]t the heart of this manifesto and our programme to save the nation lies the Social Contract between the Labour Government and the trade unions … The Social Contract is no mere paper agreement approved by politicians and trade unions. It is not concerned solely or even primarily with wages. It covers the whole range of national policies. It is the agreed basis upon which the Labour Party and the trade unions define their common purpose … the firm and detailed commitments which will be fulfilled in the field of social policy, in the fairer sharing of the nation's wealth, in the determination to restore and sustain full employment. The unions in response confirm how they will seek to exercise the newly restored right of free collective bargaining. Naturally the trade unions see their clearest loyalty to their own members. But the Social Contract is their free acknowledgment that they have other loyalties – to the members of other unions too, to pensioners, to the lower-paid, to invalids, and to the community as a whole. (Labour Party, 1974: 5)

However, when Labour was returned to Office in 1974 – initially as a minority government after an inconclusive February election and Heath's failure to secure Liberal Party support for a coalition government (Dorey, 2008–09), and then with a wafer-thin Parliamentary majority in October 1974 – the new Cabinet was immediately beset by serious economic problems. The most notable of these was a rate of inflation which peaked at 25 per cent in 1975, largely due to the knock-on effects of a 400 per cent increase in international crude oil prices during 1973, which filtered through the economy and impacted on prices during the next eighteen months or so. Although Heath's Conservative Government had been in office at the time of this increase, the enormous surge in inflation coincided with Labour's first full year in government, and thus significantly contributed to the subsequent doubts about the Party's economic competence and credibility.

Just as in 2008, when the global financial crash occurred, followed by a decade of austerity policies in Britain entailing major cuts to public expenditure and welfare, and pay freezes for millions of workers, Labour were given the blame for a major economic crisis which originated overseas but was then attributed to Labour's own fiscal policies and 'excessive' spending. In short, both during the late 1970s and late 2000s, Labour governments incurred the opprobrium for problems emanating from the periodic crises and inherent contradictions of capitalism, 'market' neo-liberalism and globalisation, yet in both instances the Conservatives readily persuaded much of the electorate that these were crises of Socialism or social democracy.

The circumstances facing Labour when it entered office in 1974, and many of the new Government's subsequent policy responses, bore several similarities to those which had pertained following Labour's 1966 election victory. History did indeed repeat itself a decade later, albeit as further tragedy, not farce. Having promised the trade unions higher public expenditure and improvements in the social wage in return for voluntary pay restraint – 'responsible' collective bargaining – the post-1974 Labour Government, just like its predecessor a decade earlier, immediately embarked upon a series of increasingly stringent incomes policies to curb pay increases (in order to both curb inflation and win the confidence of industrialists, investors and financiers), coupled with cuts in public expenditure (which were deepened under the conditions imposed by the International Monetary Fund when it granted the Government an emergency loan in 1976) and the social wage (see Dorey, 2001: chapter 6, for an examination of the 1974–9 Labour Government's incomes policies and the trade unions' response).

For the first two years, the TUC again grudgingly accepted the Labour Government's recourse to formal incomes policies, partly through cognizance of the seriousness of the economic situation, and partly because the trade unions were convinced that these were temporary measures ahead of a return to free (but responsible) collective bargaining once the crises had abated. Yet economic recovery proved much more elusive than had been envisaged, so that by late 1976 Ministers were faced with a serious dilemma; the economic circumstances which would make the trade unions hostile to continued pay restraint – high inflation (which thus eroded workers' living standards), rising unemployment, cuts in public expenditure and the social wage – also made incomes policy more necessary, at least from the Government's perspective. Indeed, as in the latter half of the 1960s, some Ministers who had initially viewed incomes policies as a temporary, short-term, response to dire economic circumstances, subsequently saw them as a permanent tool of economic management and counter-inflation strategy (Callaghan, 1987: 521).

Towards the 'winter of discontent' and subsequent electoral defeat

Thus it was that when the Labour Government sought to impose a fourth successive year of pay restraint in 1978–9, with wage increases to be limited to 5 per cent (while the inflation rate was 8 per cent), many trade unions effectively rebelled. In some cases, it was employers who proved willing to exceed the Government's 5 per cent pay limit, either to avert strike action over pay claims or to improve their recruitment of workers to fill key vacancies by offering higher wages, regardless of the levels or limits decreed by Ministers. For example, in November 1978 a nine-week strike by Ford car workers was called off when the union accepted the management's offer of a 17 per cent pay rise. At about the same time, road haulage drivers accepted a 21 per cent pay increase after striking for three weeks, while a threatened strike by petrol tanker drivers, in pursuit of a 25 per cent pay rise, was only averted when the employers offered a 20 per cent increase, which was accepted. Each time a trade union or category of workers secured a pay rise much higher than the 5 per cent decreed by the Government, other trade unions and workers felt emboldened or compelled to follow suit, while claiming 'comparability'.

Consequently, early 1979 heralded several strikes in support of 'large' pay claims, the most serious of which involved low-paid workers, often employed in the public sector. By their very nature, these strikes caused widespread disruption and inconvenience, and greatly exacerbated public hostility towards 'selfish' trade unions, because many of those most seriously affected by these stoppages were not capitalist employers or 'greedy bosses' but ordinary citizens, and sometimes people who were particularly vulnerable, such as those who had recently experienced the death of a spouse or close family member, but who had to delay the funeral owing to a strike by local council grave-diggers, triggering press headlines claiming that 'They won't even let us bury our dead'.

Other public sector strikes which caused widespread disruption and inconvenience during early 1979 included one by school caretakers, which led to schools being closed, and some parents thus having to take time off work to look after their children (particularly in the absence of a child-minder, which they might have been unable to afford). Another major strike involved refuse collectors (or 'dustmen', as they were widely known), which meant that household and commercial waste was not collected for several weeks: in an era long before recycling and separate containers for different types of waste, bin-bags and dustbins containing rotting food posed a considerable health risk, as well as attracting rats. This strike also provided pro-Conservative newspapers with ample opportunities to publish damning pictures of bags of festering, stinking rubbish piled high in Britain's streets.

This spate of strikes became known as 'the winter of discontent', and placed the Labour Government in a no-win situation. If it stood firm and refused to yield to 'excessive' pay claims, it was liable to be condemned by the public and the press for being complacent, incompetent or out-of-touch, and for allowing the widespread disruption of public services to continue unchallenged. Yet if it sought to end the strikes by acceding to the pay claims, it would doubtless have been accused of being weak, and surrendering to trade union militancy. In attempting to extricate itself from this quandary, the Cabinet hurriedly established a Commission on Pay Comparability, chaired by Professor Hugh Clegg, which it was envisaged would provide the Government with a pretext for awarding pay rises above 5 per cent.

In the meantime, Ministers also desperately sought to reach a new *concordat* with the TUC, which 'at least give us a piece of paper on which to fight an election' (Barnett, 1982: 176). What transpired was a 'joint statement' committing Labour and the trade unions to reduce inflation to 5 per cent within three years, with an annual 'economic assessment' being conducted to gauge what level of pay increases was affordable, and commensurate with this inflation target (Donoughue, 1987: 177–8). Under pressure from Ministers, the TUC also issued guidance to affiliated unions concerning the conduct of future strikes, most notably urging greater responsibility when engaging in such activities as picketing or pursuing 'secondary' industrial action; for example, the targeting of other firms which were not directly involved in a dispute, but which were supplying materials to the firm which was at the heart or source of the strike.

These responses were too little, too late. Many trade unionists had become deeply disillusioned with incomes policies, and *inter alia* the Labour Government, not merely because of their *a priori* commitment to free collective bargaining, but because of the impact on wages. In fact, by early 1979 workers' opposition to pay restraint emanated from two distinct sources. On one hand, low-paid workers understandably viewed repeated wage restraint as a major reason for their poverty wages and material hardships, even though Labour's incomes policies had sometimes permitted somewhat higher increases for the lowest-paid. On the other hand, skilled workers, on higher wages, increasingly resented the erosion of 'differentials' which accrued from incomes policies that were slightly more generous to those on the lowest wages. In effect, Britain's 'labour aristocracy' baulked at incomes policies which were perceived to be too egalitarian, and 'levelled down' higher-paid workers. Consequently, in the May 1979 general election, the largest swing to the Conservatives (of

11 per cent) was among skilled workers (the C2s as they have often been referred to subsequently), who were evidently attracted by the Conservatives' pledge of a return to free collective bargaining, coupled with a professed commitment to restoring pay differentials linked to skills (Kellner, 2015: 229).

More generally, the 'winter of discontent' had appalled and alienated many voters, and caused considerable resentment of the trade unions, which in turn damaged Labour's credibility and popularity. Having previously been widely viewed as organisations which fought for fairness, justice and the underdog, many people now viewed the trade unions as selfish tyrants and swaggering bullies who were devoid of decency and compassion, rather than the 'wicked capitalists' or 'greedy bosses' routinely denounced by the left. This public revulsion manifested itself in the strong leads enjoyed by the Conservatives in opinion polls during early 1979: an Ipsos MORI/*Daily Express* poll in early February, for example, reported a 55 per cent–36 per cent lead over Labour, while 51 per cent of respondents considered strikes/trade unions to be the most important issue facing Britain (in contrast, only 1 per cent cited education, and 2 per cent cited the NHS). The poll also revealed that 89 per cent of respondents believed both that trade unions should be required to ballot their members prior to a strike, and that 'secondary picketing' should be banned.

Senior Labour Ministers were virtually resigned to electoral defeat in the imminent general election. The previous August, James Callaghan had contemplated calling an autumn 1978 general election, which is what many of his Ministerial colleagues and advisers were advocating. However, the ultra-cautious Callaghan decided that the opinion polls were too close, with Labour and the Conservatives virtually neck-and-neck; it was too risky.[5] He therefore resolved to defer the election until 1979, hoping that the economic situation would steadily improve during the winter months, in tandem with Labour's poll ratings, sufficient to secure electoral victory in a spring election (Dorey, 2016a).[6]

In so doing, Callaghan also assumed that, whilst the trade unions were unhappy at the 5 per cent pay limit, they would refrain from widespread defiance and industrial action during the winter of 1978–9, lest they jeopardise Labour's prospects of re-election in the Spring.[7] This, of course, proved to be a deeply erroneous assumption, one which a Cabinet colleague attributed to 'a tragic over-estimation of his own influence with the trade union leaders, and of their influence over their members' (Williams, 2009: 248). The clear implication was that Callaghan would be able to call in a favour from the trade unions in return for having opposed *In Place of Strife* a decade earlier. It proved to be a fatal miscalculation, for as Callaghan himself subsequently noted, '[t]he serious and widespread industrial dislocation caused by the strikes of January 1979 … sent the government's fortunes cascading downhill' (Callaghan, 1987: 540). His Chancellor, Denis

Healey, was rather blunter, asserting that '[t]he cowardice and irresponsibility of some union leaders ... at this time, guaranteed her [Margaret Thatcher's] election' (Healey, 1990: 462; see also Donoughue, 1987: 180, 187; Donoughue, 2008: 498–9).

However, as in 1970, some on Labour's left insisted that electoral defeat was primarily the fault of those Ministers who had refused to heed or understand the frustration of ordinary trade unionists in the context of repeated wage restraint and public expenditure cuts. Eric Heffer, for example, argued that 'the government was responsible for its own unpopularity, and certainly laid the basis for its defeat' by alienating its own working-class supporters. Indeed, Heffer singled out Healey for particular criticism, by denouncing the ex-Chancellor's 'colossal arrogance' in blaming workers and trade unions, rather than Healey's own economic policies. Heffer claimed that Healey had 'little real understanding of ordinary working people', and tartly suggested that '[p]erhaps if he had listened to rank-and-file workers, rather than those in the City ... things might have gone better' (Heffer, 1991: 167).

Meanwhile, on the day *before* the 1979 general election, Tony Benn (who had moved decisively to the left since the late 1960s, when he had supported *In Place of Strife*) complained that 'we've had a right-wing leader, a right-wing policy, a right-wing Cabinet, a right-wing manifesto and a right-wing campaign' (Benn, 1990: 493, diary entry for 2 May 1979). Benn also reported a conversation he had had, a few days after the election, with one of Labour's former whips, Joe Ashton, during which the latter asserted that 'incomes policy had been the cause of Labour's trouble' (Benn, 1990: 499, diary entry for 8 May 1979).

Regardless of who was to blame, the 'winter of discontent' effectively guaranteed the Conservative Party's victory in the May 1979 election – whereupon Labour was consigned to impotent Opposition for the next eighteen years (on the 'discursive' and 'ideological' representations of the 'winter of discontent' by the Thatcherite right of the Conservative Party, see the discourse analysis of Hay, 1996; Hay 2010). Electoral victory also persuaded the Conservatives that there was now a strong appetite for trade union reform among a British public which was exasperated with strikes and the associated economic damage and social disruption – as were many trade union members.

As a biographer of Thatcher notes: 'Not only was Callaghan's credibility destroyed, but public anger at the unions' indiscipline silenced the objections of her Tory critics, and gave Mrs Thatcher's incoming Government the mandate to tackle the abuses of trade union power which she had lacked the previous autumn' (Campbell, 2000: 414–15). Or, as one of her senior Cabinet colleagues averred: 'It needed further hard experience, culminating in the Winter of Discontent ... before the British people were ready to give continuous backing to a Government for trade union reform' (Whitelaw, 1989: 75–6).

Furthermore, by this time the Conservative Party had spent its period in Opposition honing a new approach to industrial relations and trade union reform, one which aimed to achieve many of the objectives originally pursued by the Heath Government, but avoiding the 'big bang' approach symbolised by the all-encompassing 1971 Industrial Relations Act; it was widely acknowledged inside the Thatcher-led Conservative Party that the 1971 legislation had attempted too much, too soon, and had been overly legalistic. Thus did the 1974–9 Conservative Opposition devise a more strategic, longer-term, step-by-step, industrial relations policy to curb the trade unions irrevocably (Dorey, 2009b; Dorey, 2014; Dorey, 2016b), with breaches of the law cast as civil, not criminal, offences (thus avoiding trade unionists being sent to prison and becoming martyrs), a discourse of 'democratisation' deployed to render the reforms more popular to ordinary union members, and careful planning in advance of major industrial 'battles', which would be provoked only when the Government had amassed sufficient resources to ensure its victory: the 1984–5 miners' strike being the most obvious example (Dorey, 2013b).

For the Conservatives, the success of this legislative approach was greatly assisted and reinforced by wider economic and structural changes which occurred or accelerated during the 1980s and beyond, most notably de-industrialisation, globalisation, privatisation and the general shift towards a post-Fordist economy. All these trends had a deleterious impact on trade union membership, and further weakened the unions, in tandem with the Thatcher Government's legislation. Furthermore, as the unions became weaker, fewer workers deemed them worth joining, which obviously meant that the decline in their membership and diminution of their strength continued unabated.

There was no attempt or desire to reverse these trends during the thirteen years of New Labour government which began in 1997. On the contrary, aligning itself with big business, pursuing supply-side economics and promoting 'labour market flexibility' were key characteristics of New Labour. In stark contrast, the trade unions were to be kept at arm's length, and in a clearly subordinate position. There was to be no return to 'beer and sandwiches' at 10, Downing Street, nor late nights sipping brandy with trade union leaders while brokering deals.

Notes

1   NA CAB 128/45, CC (70), 23rd Conclusions, 7 May 1970.
2   NA CAB 128/45, CC (70), 23rd Conclusions, 7 May 1970.

3 About £73,500 in 2018.
4 About £735,000 in 2018.
5 Callaghan Papers, Box 113, Hand-written note, 23 August 1978.
6 NA PREM 16/1621, Kenneth Stowe [Callaghan's PPS], 'Note for the Record', 6 September 1978.
7 NA PREM 16/1667, Prime Minister's Notes, undated but *circa* September 1978.

Bibliography

Books, articles and chapters

Abrams, Mark (1970) 'The Opinion Polls and the 1970 British General Election', *Public Opinion Quarterly* 34.3, 317–24.

Ackers, Peter (2011) 'Finding the Future in the Past? The Social Philosophy of Oxford Industrial Relations Pluralism' in Keith Townsend and Adrian Wilkinson (eds) *Research Handbook on the Future of Work and Employment Relations*, Cheltenham: Edward Elgar, 45–66.

Ackers, Peter (2014) 'Game Changer: Hugh Clegg's Role in Drafting the 1968 Donovan Report and Redefining the British Industrial Relations Policy-Problem', *Historical Studies in Industrial Relations* 35, 63–88.

Ackers, Peter (2018) 'Saving Social Democracy? Hugh Clegg and the Post-War Programme to Reform British Workplace Industrial Relations: Too Little, Too Late?' in Stefan Berger and Marcel Boldorf (eds) *Social Movements and the Change of Economic Elites in Europe after 1945*, Basingstoke: Palgrave Macmillan, 257–77.

Alford, Bernard (1996) *Britain in the World Economy since 1880*, London: Pearson.

Anderson, Perry (1967) 'The Limits and Possibilities of Trade Union Action' in Robin Blackburn and Alexander Cockburn (eds) *The Incompatibles: Trade Union Militancy and the Consensus*, Harmondsworth: Penguin, 263–80.

Barnes, Denis and Reid, Eileen (1980) *Governments and Trade Unions: The British Experience 1964–79*, London: Heinemann/Policy Studies Institute.

Barnett, Joel (1982) *Inside the Treasury*, London: André Deutsch.

BBC (2011) 'How Britain converted to decimal currency', 5 February (www.bbc.co.uk/news/business-12346083).

Benn, Tony (1988) *Office Without Power: Diaries 1968–1972*, London: Hutchinson.

Benn, Tony (1990) *Conflicts of Interest: Diaries 1977–80*, London: Hutchinson.

Brittan, Samuel (1969) *Steering the Economy*, London: Secker and Warburg.

Bugler, Jeremy (1968) 'The New Oxford Group', *New Society*, 15 February, 221–2.

Butler, David and Pinto-Duschinsky, Michael (1971) *The British General Election of 1970*, London: Macmillan.

Butt, Ronald (1969) *The Power of Parliament*, second edition, London: Constable.

Callaghan, James (1987) *Time and Chance*, London: Collins.

Campbell, John (1993) *Edward Heath: A Biography*, London: Jonathan Cape.
Campbell, John (2000) *Margaret Thatcher, Volume One: The Grocer's Daughter*, London: Jonathan Cape.
Campbell, John (2014) *Roy Jenkins: A Well-Rounded Life*, London: Jonathan Cape.
Castle, Barbara (1990) *The Castle Diaries 1964–70*, London: Weidenfeld and Nicolson.
Castle, Barbara (1993) *Fighting all the Way*, London: Pan Books.
Clegg, Hugh (1970) *The System of Industrial Relations in Great Britain*, Oxford: Blackwell.
Clegg, Hugh (1983) 'Otto Kahn-Freund and British Industrial Relations' in Lord Wedderburn, Roy Lewis and Jon Clark (eds) *Labour Law and Industrial Relations: Building on Kahn-Freund*, Oxford: Clarendon Press, 14–28.
Clements, Richard (1969) 'The trade unions, the government, and what happened at Downing Street', *Tribune*, 16 May.
Clements, Richard (1970) 'The General Election result: why it happened – and what we are going to do', *Tribune*, 26 June.
Coates, David (1980) *Labour in Power? A Study of the Labour Government, 1974–1979*, London: Longman.
Coates, David (1984) *The Context of British Politics*, London: Hutchinson.
Cohen, Michael, March, James and Olsen, Johan (1972) 'A Garbage Can Model of Organizational Choice', *Administrative Science Quarterly*, 17.1, 1–25.
Conservative Political Centre (1968) *Fair Deal at Work*, London: Conservative Political Centre.
Cousins, John (1969) 'The dangers which face the unions', *Tribune*, 3 January.
Crosland, Susan (1982) *Tony Crosland*, London: Jonathan Cape.
Crossman, Richard (1963) 'Introduction' to Walter Bagehot, *The English Constitution*, London: Fontana. First published in 1867.
Crossman, Richard (1970) 'Labour after defeat', *New Statesman*, 10 July.
Crossman, Richard (1972) *Inside View: Three Lectures on Prime Ministerial Government*, London: Jonathan Cape.
Crossman, Richard (1977) *Diaries of a Cabinet Minister, Volume 3: Secretary of State for Social Services, 1968–1970*, London: Hamish Hamilton/Jonathan Cape.
Dalyell, Tam (1998) 'Obituary: Lord Mellish', *The Independent*, 10 May (www.independent.co.uk/news/obituaries/obituary-lord-mellish-1159549.html).
Davenport, Nicholas (1974) *Memoirs of a City Radical*, London: Weidenfeld and Nicolson.
Davies, Paul and Freedland, Mark (1999) *Labour Legislation and Public Policy: A Contemporary History*, Oxford: Clarendon Press.
Dintenfass, Michael (1992) *The Decline of Industrial Britain: 1870–1980*, London: Routledge.
Donoughue, Bernard (1987) *Prime Minister: Conduct of Policy under Harold Wilson and James Callaghan, 1974–79*, London: Jonathan Cape.
Donoughue, Bernard (2008) *Downing Street Diary, Volume Two: James Callaghan in No. 10*, London: Jonathan Cape.
Dorey, Peter (2001) *Wage Politics in Britain: The Rise and Fall of Incomes Policies since 1945*, Brighton: Sussex Academic Press.
Dorey, Peter (2006) 'From a "Policy for Incomes" to an Incomes Policy' in Peter Dorey (ed.) *The Labour Governments 1964–70*, London: Routledge, 73–91.

Dorey, Peter (2008–09) 'Asking Too Much and Offering Too Little? The Conservative–Liberal Coalition Talks of 1–4 March 1974', *Journal of Liberal History* 61, 28–37.
Dorey, Peter (2009a) 'Individual Liberty versus Industrial Order: Conservatives and the Trade Union Closed Shop, 1946–90', *Contemporary British History* 23.2, 221–244.
Dorey, Peter (2009b) 'Conciliation or Confrontation with the Trade Unions? The Conservative Party's "Authority of Government Group", 1975–1978' *Historical Studies in Industrial Relations* 27/28, 135–51.
Dorey, Peter (2013a) 'The Fall of the Wilson Government, 1970' in Timothy Heppell and Kevin Theakston (eds) *How Labour Governments Fall: From Ramsay Macdonald to Gordon Brown*, Basingstoke: Palgrave Macmillan, 83–112.
Dorey, Peter (2013b) '"It Was Just Like Arming to Face the Threat of Hitler in the Late 1930s." The Ridley Report and the Conservative Party's Preparations for the 1984–85 Miners' Strike', *Historical Studies in Industrial Relations* 34, 173–214.
Dorey, Peter (2014) 'The Stepping Stones Programme: The Conservative Party's Struggle to Develop a Trade-Union Policy, 1975–79', *Historical Studies in Industrial Relations* 35, 89–116.
Dorey, Peter (2016a) '"Should I Stay or Should I Go?": James Callaghan's Decision not to Call an Autumn 1978 General Election', *British Politics* 11.1, 95–118.
Dorey, Peter (2016b) 'Weakening the Trade Unions, One Step at a Time: The Thatcher Governments' Strategy for the Reform of Trade-Union Law, 1979–1984', *Historical Studies in Industrial Relations* 37, 169–200.
Dorfman, Gerald A. (1979) *Government versus Trade Unionism in British Politics since 1968*, Basingstoke: Macmillan.
Eatwell, Roger and Wright, Anthony (1978) 'Labour and the Lessons of 1931', *History* 63.207, 38–53.
Economist, The (1965) 'Editorial: Labour men, Tory measures', 31 July.
Edmonds, John (1968) 'The Worker' in Brian Lapping and Giles Radice (eds) *More Power to the People: Young Fabian Essays on Democracy in Britain*, London: Longmans, 34–56.
Elbaum, Bernard and Lazonick, William (eds) (1986) *The Decline of the British Economy*, Oxford: Oxford University Press.
Feather, Victor (1963) *The Essence of Trade Unionism*, London: The Bodley Head.
Feather, Victor (1968) 'The Royal Commission's Analysis: A Trade Union Appraisal', *British Journal of Industrial Relations* 6.3, 339–45.
Flanders, Allan (1964) *The Fawley Productivity Agreements: A Case Study of Management and Collective Bargaining*, London: Faber.
Flanders, Allan (1974) 'The Tradition of Voluntarism', *British Journal of Industrial Relations* 12.3, 352–70.
Flanders, Allan (1975) *Management and Unions*, London: Faber.
Foot, Michael (1969a) 'The maddest scene in modern history', *Tribune*, 18 April.
Foot, Michael (1969b) 'It is fatal in politics, as in other fields, to desert friends in order to appease enemies', *Tribune*, 25 April.
Foot, Michael (1970) 'What's wanted: a big shift leftwards', *Tribune*, 3 July.
Fox, Alan (1974) *Beyond Contract: Work, Power and Trust Relations*, London: Faber.
Fox, Alan (1985) *History and Heritage: Social Origins of the British Industrial Relations System*, London: Allen and Unwin.

Gamble, Andrew (1981) *Britain in Decline: Economic Policy, Political Strategy and the British State*, London: Macmillan.
Goodman, Geoffrey (1984) *The Awkward Warrior: Frank Cousins, His Life and Times*, second edition, Nottingham: Spokesman Books.
Gormley, Joe (1982) *Battered Cherub*, London: Hamish Hamilton.
Griffith, James (1991) *The Politics of the Judiciary*, fourth edition, London: Fontana.
Haines, Joe (1977) *The Politics of Power*, London: Jonathan Cape.
Haines, Joe (2003) *Glimmers of Twilight: Harold Wilson in Decline*, London: Politico's.
Hall, Robert (1961) 'Britain's economic problems', *The Economist*, 16 September.
Hansard (1911) *House of Commons Debates*, 5th series, 30 May.
Hansard (1966) *House of Commons Debates*, 5th series, 20 June.
Hansard (1968) *House of Commons Debates*, 5th series, 16 July.
Hansard (1969a) *House of Commons Debates*, 5th series, 3 March.
Hansard (1969b) *House of Commons Debates*, 5th series, 16 April.
Hattersley, Roy (1970) 'Could Labour have won?', *New Statesman*, 31 July.
Hay, Colin (1996) 'Narrating Crisis: The Discursive Construction of the "Winter of Discontent"', *Sociology* 30.2, 253–77.
Hay, Colin (2010) 'Chronicles of a Death Foretold: the Winter of Discontent and Construction of the Crisis of British Keynesianism', *Parliamentary Affairs* 63.3, 446–70.
Healey, Denis (1990) *The Time of My Life*, Harmondsworth: Penguin Books.
Heffer, Eric (1970) 'Attack the Tories, fight for Socialism', *Tribune*, 3 July.
Heffer, Eric (1973) *The Class Struggle in Parliament: A Socialist View of Industrial Relations*, London: Victor Gollancz.
Heffer, Eric (1991) *Never a Yes Man: The Life and Politics of an Adopted Liverpudlian*, London: Verso.
Hinden, Rita (1970) 'Not without comfort', *Socialist Commentary*, 18 July.
Houghton, Douglas (1969) 'The Labour Backbencher', *The Political Quarterly* 40.4, 454–63.
Hyman, Richard (1972) *Strikes*, London: Fontana.
Hyman, Richard (2003) 'The Historical Evolution of British Industrial Relations' in Paul Edwards (ed.) *Industrial Relations: Theory and Practice*, second edition, Oxford: Blackwell, 37–57.
Ince, Sir Godfrey (1960) *The Ministry of Labour and National Service*, London: George Allen and Unwin.
Jenkins, Peter (1970) *The Battle of Downing Street*, London: Charles Knight.
Jenkins, Roy (1991) *A Life at the Centre*, London: Macmillan.
Jones, George W. (1965) 'The Prime Minister's Power', *Parliamentary Affairs* 18 (Spring), 167–85.
Jones, Jack (1969) 'Why I still think Barbara Castle is wrong', *Tribune*, 14 February.
Jones, Jack (1986) *Union Man: An Autobiography*, London: Collins.
Kahn-Freund, Otto (1959) 'Labour Law' in Morris Ginsberg (ed.) *Law and Opinion in England in the 20th Century*, London: Stevens, 215–63.
Kahn-Freund, Otto (1972) *Labour and the Law*, London: Stevens.
Kavanagh, Dennis and Morris, Peter (1989) *Consensus Politics: From Attlee to Thatcher*, Oxford: Blackwell.

Kellner, Peter (2015) 'James Callaghan' in Charles Clarke and Toby S. James (eds) *British Labour Leaders*, London: Biteback, 217–30.

Kingdon, John W. (1984) *Agendas, Alternatives, and Public Policies*, Boston: Little, Brown.

Kirby, Maurice W. (1981) *The Decline of British Economic Power Since 1870*, London: HarperCollins.

Labour Party, The (1964) *Let's Go with Labour for the New Britain: The Labour Party's Manifesto for the 1964 General Election*, London: The Labour Party.

Labour Party, The (1974) *Labour Party Manifesto October 1974*, London: The Labour Party.

Lewis, Roy (1976) 'The Historical Development of Labour Law', *British Journal of Industrial Relations* 14.1, 1–17.

Lewis, Roy (1983) 'Collective Labour Law' in George Sayers Bain (ed.) *British Industrial Relations*, Oxford: Blackwell, 361–92.

Lindblom, Charles (1965) *The Intelligence of Democracy: Decision Making through Mutual Adjustment*, New York: The Free Press.

Lovell, John and Roberts, B. C. (1968) *A Short History of the TUC*, London: Macmillan.

Macmillan, Harold (1972) *Pointing the Way, 1959–1961*, London: Macmillan.

Marsh, Richard (1978) *Off the Rails: An Autobiography*, London: Weidenfeld and Nicolson.

Martineau, Lisa (2011) *Politics and Power: Barbara Castle*, London: André Deutsch.

McCarthy, W. E. J. (1992) 'The Rise and Fall of Collective *Laissez-faire*' in W. E. J. McCarthy (ed.) *Legal Intervention in Industrial Relations*, Oxford: Blackwell, 1–78.

Michels, Robert (1911/1962) *Political Parties: A Sociological Study of the Oligarchical Tendencies of Modern Democracy*, New York: Collier Books.

Middlemas, Keith (1991) *Power, Competition and the State, Volume 3: The End of the Post-War Era, Britain since 1974*, London: Macmillan.

Mikardo, Ian (1988) *Backbencher*, London: Weidenfeld and Nicolson.

Miliband, Ralph (1973) *The State in Capitalist Society*, London: Quartet.

Ministry of Labour (1957) *Industrial Relations Handbook*, revised edition, London: HMSO.

Ministry of Labour (1965) *Written Evidence of the Ministry of Labour to the Royal Commission on Trade Unions and Employers' Associations*, London: HMSO.

Moran, Michael (1977) *The Politics of Industrial Relations: The Origins, Life and Death of the 1971 Industrial Relations Act*, London: Macmillan.

Morgan, Kenneth, O. (1997) *Callaghan: A Life*, Oxford: Oxford University Press.

Norton, Philip (1975) *Dissension in the House of Commons: Intra-Party Dissent in the House of Commons' Division Lobbies, 1945–1974*, London: Macmillan.

Organisation for European Economic Co-operation (1961) *The Problem of Rising Prices*, Paris: OEEC.

Owen, David (1992) *Time to Declare*, Harmondsworth: Penguin.

Panitch, Leo (1976) *Social Democracy and Industrial Militancy: The Labour Party, the Trade Unions and Incomes Policy 1945–1974*, Cambridge: Cambridge University Press.

Perkins, Anne (2003) *Red Queen: The Authorized Biography of Barbara Castle*, Basingstoke: Macmillan.

Pimlott, Ben (1993) *Harold Wilson*, London: HarperCollins.
Ponting, Clive (1990) *Breach of Promise: Labour in Power 1964–1970*, Harmondsworth: Penguin.
Robbins, Keith (1983) *The Eclipse of a Great Power: Modern Britain 1870–1975*, London: Longman.
Rogin, Michael (1962) 'Voluntarism: The Political Functions of an Anti-Political Doctrine', *Industrial and Labour Relations Review* 15.4, 521–35.
Rose, Richard (1970) 'Voting Trends Surveyed' in *The Times Guide to the House of Commons 1970*, London: Times Newspaper Limited, 31–2.
Royal Commission on Trade Unions and Employers' Associations, 1965–8 (1968) *Report*, Cmnd 3623, London: HMSO.
Sandbrook, Dominic (2006) *White Heat: A History of Britain in the Swinging Sixties*, London: Little, Brown.
Shanks, Michael (1961) *The Stagnant Society*, Harmondsworth: Penguin.
Shore, Peter (1993) *Leading the Left*, London: Weidenfeld and Nicolson.
Silver, Eric (1973) *Victor Feather, TUC: A Biography*, London: Victor Gollancz.
Sinclair, Geoffrey (1969) 'What all good political reporters must learn about the Left and incomes policy', *Tribune*, 17 January.
Smith, Geoffrey and Polsby, Nelson W. (1981) *British Government and Its Discontents*, New York: Basic Books.
Smith, Paul (2011) 'Order in British Industrial Relations: From Donovan to Neoliberalism', *Historical Studies in Industrial Relations* 31/32, 115–154.
Stewart, Michael (1980) *Life and Labour: An Autobiography*, Sidgwick and Jackson.
Supple, Barry (1994) 'Fear of Failing: Economic History and the Decline of Britain', *Economic History Review*, 47, 441–58.
Syrett, Keith (1998) '"Immunity", "Privilege", and "Right": British Trade Unions and the Language of Labour Law Reform', *Journal of Law and Society* 25:3, 388–406.
Taylor, Robert (1978) *Labour and the Social Contract*, Fabian Tract 458, London: The Fabian Society.
Taylor, Robert (1993) *The Trade Union Question in British Politics: Government and the Unions since 1945*, Oxford: Blackwell.
Taylor, Robert (1996) 'The Heath Government and Industrial Relations: Myth and Reality' in Stuart Ball and Anthony Seldon (eds) *The Heath Government 1970–74*, London: Longman, 161–90.
Taylor, Robert (2004) 'The Rise and Fall of the Social Contract' in Anthony Seldon and Kevin Hickson (eds) *New Labour, Old Labour; The Wilson and Callaghan Governments, 1974–79*, London: Routledge, 70–104.
Terry, Michael (1983) 'Shop Steward Development and Management Strategies' in George Sayers Bain (ed.) *Industrial Relations in Britain*, Oxford: Oxford University Press, 67–71.
Trades Union Congress (1966) *Trade Unionism: The Evidence of the TUC to the Royal Commission on Trade Unions and Employers' Associations*, London: TUC.
Trades Union Congress (1968a) *Report of the 100th Annual Trades Union Congress*. London: TUC.
Trades Union Congress (1968b) *Action on Donovan: Interim Statement by the TUC General Council in Response to the Royal Commission on Trade Unions and Employers' Associations*, London: TUC.

Trades Union Congress (1969a) *Report of the 101st Annual Trades Union Congress*, London: TUC.
Trades Union Congress (1969b) *Industrial Relations – Programme for Action: Report of a Special Trades Union Congress held at Fairfield Hall, Croydon, 5 June 1969*.
Trades Union Congress (1973a) *Economic Policy and Collective Bargaining in 1973*, London: TUC.
Trades Union Congress (1973b) 'Collective Bargaining, Prices and Social Priorities' in TUC, *Report* 1973, Annex B, London: TUC, 377–83.
Trades Union Congress (1999) 'Interview with James Callaghan', TUC Millennium Film Project, 31 March (www.unionhistory.info/equalpay/display.php?irn=10 62&mediaindex=3).
Tribune (1969a) Editorial, 'The government needs "a cooling off" period', 3 January.
Tribune (1969b) Editorial, 'Recipe for disaster', 10 January.
Tribune (1969c) Editorial, 'Wilson versus the unions', 21 April.
Tribune Group of Labour MPs (1969) 'The Cabinet, the Labour Party and the trade union legislation', *Tribune*, 11 April.
Turner, David (1969a) 'Will the TUC Special Congress oppose the whole White Paper?', *Tribune*, 2 May.
Turner, David (1969b) 'What the TUC plan means for the unions', *Tribune*, 23 May.
Tyler, Richard (2006) 'Victims of our History? Barbara Castle and *In Place of Strife*', *Contemporary British History* 20.3, 461–76.
Undy, Roger (2015) 'An Overview of Bill McCarthy's Academic and Political Engagement with Industrial Relations', *Industrial Relations Journal* 46.1, 1–6.
Urwin, Harry (1969) 'The trade unions must go into the attack', *Tribune*, 9 May.
Wedderburn, K. W. (1971) *The Worker and the Law*, second edition, Harmondsworth: Pelican Books.
Wedderburn, Lord (1989) 'Freedom of Association and Philosophies of Labour Law', *Industrial Law Journal* 18:1, 1–38.
Westergaard, John and Resler, Henrietta (1976) *Class in a Capitalist Society*, London: Pelican.
Whitehead, Philip (1985) *The Writing on the Wall*, London: Michael Joseph.
Whitelaw, William (1989) *The Whitelaw Memoirs*, London: Aurum.
Wigham, Eric (1961) *What's Wrong with the Unions?*, Harmondsworth: Penguin.
Wigham, Eric (1968) 'The arduous path to consensus', *The Times*, 14 June.
Williams, Marcia (1972) *Inside Number 10*, London: Weidenfeld and Nicolson.
Williams, Shirley (2009) *Climbing the Bookshelves*, London: Virago.
Williamson, Adrian (2015) *Conservative Economic Policy-Making and the Birth of Thatcherism, 1964–1979*, Basingstoke: Palgrave Macmillan.
Wilson, Harold (1971) *The Labour Government 1964–70*, London: Weidenfeld and Nicolson.

Index

Note: Page numbers in *italic* refer to tables. 'n' after a page number indicates the number of a note on the page.

Ackers, Peter 36, 37, 39, 134, 200, 201

balance of payments 10–11
Barnes, Denis 47, 52, 55
Benn, Tony 74, 76, 81, 85, 103, 104, 183, 210
Bevan, Aneurin 68
Blackburn constituency Labour Party 117
Bridlington Agreement 180, 181, 187n.35
Burgh, John 52, 59, 65
business community
  concern over strikes 90
  Labour Party need to appeal to 198

Cabinet, Labour 73–109
  annoyance at TUC being briefed first on White Paper 74–5
  Callaghan's role in opposing *In Place of Strife* 84–90
  Castle presents *In Place of Strife* to 74–82
  ebbing away of support for industrial relations legislation 73–4, 98–103, 106–7
  irked by Wilson's rejection of TUC counter-proposals 106

and junior Ministers concerns at intransigence over TUC counter-proposals 100–1
  response to 'solemn and binding' agreement 182–3, 185–6
  varying degrees of support for Industrial Relations Bill 75–9, 92–4, 105–6
  views on timing of industrial relations legislation 82–4
Callaghan, James
  breach of collective responsibility 86–7
  critical of colleagues' lack of trade union experience 85, 89
  defers general election to 1979 209
  on Feather's views of Wilson and Castle 97
  –Houghton axis in opposition to Industrial Relations Bill 119–20
  miscalculates trade unions 209
  at NEC meetings 86, 87
  objections to draft of *The Battle for Downing Street* 89–90
  opposition to Industrial Relations Bill 93, 119–20, 152
  opposition to *In Place of Strife* 78, 84–90, 103

Index 221

relations with Castle 84, 85, 86, 105
removal from Inner Cabinet 88
suspected of leadership ambitions 85–6
trade union background 85, 88–9
Wilson's refusal to sack 86–8
Carr, Robert 49
Castle, Barbara
 anger over replacing of Silkin as Chief Whip 95, 97–8
 annoyed at Wilson's rejection of Croydon proposals 173–4
 attendance at 1st June Chequers meeting 96, 170–1, 172
 on Callaghan and Houghton working in unison 102, 119
 confidential code names between Wilson and 170–1
 criticised for her 'academic' approach to industrial relations 119–20, 129, 148, 154, 159
 DEP influence over 5, 55–7, 123–4, 146
 Donovan Report, views on 49
 views on 43, 46, 47–8, 51–2, 69–70
 failure to foresee depth of opposition to *In Place of Strife* 69, 76, 112, 130
 handling of industrial relations legislation criticised 183–4
 presenting *In Place of Strife* to Cabinet 74, 76, 77–8, 79–80, 81
 relationship with Wilson 97–8
 relations with Callaghan 84, 85, 86, 105
 secret TUC meetings to discuss White Paper 68–9, 74–5, 141–3
 sexism towards 153–4
 at Sunningdale Conference 64, 65, 70
 support for 'solemn and binding' agreement 180–1, 183
 threatens to resign 104–5
 at Trade Union Group of MPs meeting 126
 TUC leaders' perceptions of Wilson and 96–7, 172
 view on timing of industrial relations legislation 83
 –Wilson axis driving industrial relations legislation 95–8
 and Wilson left increasingly isolated 74, 102, 106, 178–9, 182
CBI (Confederation of British Industry) 48–9, 50–1, 55, 140, 141
Chequers meeting (1 June 1969) 96, 170–3
Churchill, Winston 138
CIR (Commission for Industrial Relations) 61–2, 76, 92, 125, 127, 136, 140
the 'City' 76, 90, 121, 125, 147, 192, 198, 200, 210
Clegg, Hugh 26, 36, 37, 39, 44, 58, 208
'closed shop' 20, 46, 134, 201–3, 204
code-names 170–1
Cohen, Michael 56
collective agreements
 legally binding 38–9, 41, 44, 54, 63, 66, 127, 141
 Ministry of Labour submission to Donovan Commission 33
 registering 37, 40, 41–2
 voluntarist approach to 34
collective bargaining
 'Alternative Approach' to 59
 ambiguity in desire for reform of 54–5
 Donovan Report recommendations 24, 27, 36, 38, 39, 40, 43
 incomes policies and free 53, 54–5, 144, 199–201
 state intervention 34, 49, 60–1, 92, 93, 121
 TUC response to Donovan Report recommendations 139, 140
 voluntarism and commitment to free 2, 139, 146

collective *laissez-faire see* voluntarism
collective responsibility, Callaghan's breach of 86–7
Commission for Industrial Relations (CIR) 61–2, 76, 92, 125, 127, 136, 140
'conciliation pause' 63, 66
　measure in draft Industrial Relations Bill 92
　Ministerial concerns over 77–8, 79–81, 99
　Ministerial support for 169
　PLP opposition to 112, 128
　possible deferment of 109
　responsibility for invoking 67, 92
　TUC opposition to 92, 142, 143, 148–9
Confederation of British Industry (CBI) 48–9, 50–1, 140
Conservative Party
　1970 general election victory 196, 197
　1979 general election victory 208–9
　decides not to support interim Industrial Relations Bill 118
　Fair Deal at Work 46, 49, 91, 118, 192
　Macmillan's government 14
　Thatcher's government 210–11
　see also Industrial Relations Act (1971)
cooling-off period 32, 42, 46, 63, 127
　Donovan Report rejection of 55, 141
　see also 'conciliation pause'
Cousins, Frank 74, 145, 157, 199
Crosland, Anthony Tony 76, 93, 99, 184
Crossman, Richard 81, 87, 88, 91, 93, 96, 99, 100, 102, 105, 150, 169, 170, 183
　criticism of Wilson and Castle 183–4
　on general election defeat in 1970 196
　on rise of Prime Ministerial government 184–5
　suggests way out of impasse 101–2
　on timing of legislation 83–4, 150
　on TUC manoeuvres at Croydon Conference 178
　on Wilson's threats to resign 182
Croydon Conference, TUC 106, 116, 117, 118, 128, 130, 152–3, 154–8, 164, 170
　government response to 173–82

Davenport, Nicholas 154
Davies, Paul 12, 40, 44
DEA (Department of Economic Affairs) 54, 146
deflationary policies 144, 194
demarcation disputes, trade union 13, 51, 70, 166, 202
Department of Economic Affairs (DEA) 5, 54, 146
Department of Employment and Productivity (DEP) 54–7, 62, 83, 141, 149–50
　influence over Castle 5, 55–7, 123–4, 146
　keen to move beyond voluntarist approach 59, 70
dockers' strikes
　Heaton's dispute 203–4
　national strike 204
Donovan Commission 24–33
　establishing 25–7
　evidence to 28–32
　　Ministry of Labour written 32–3
　　TUC written 28, 30–2
　membership 25–6
　remit 26–7
　'survey' questions 27–8
　TUC views on 27
　work of 27–8
Donovan, Lord Terence 25, 37, 41
'Donovan Plus' 51, 65, 70
Donovan Report 24–5, 33–43, 43–4
　Addendum 41
　collective bargaining recommendations 24, 27, 36, 38, 39, 40, 43

'deregistering' of trade unions 42
disappointing for Wilson and
    Castle 43, 46, 48, 69–70
on formal and informal systems of
    industrial relations 34–5
legally binding collective
    agreements rejected 38–9, 41,
    54
main proposals 37–8
Orme on 126
'Oxford School' influential role in
    36–7, 38
Parliamentary debate on 49
qualified defence of voluntarism
    34, 39–40, 43, 44
registration of collective
    agreements 37, 40, 41–2
Shonfield's note of reservation
    42–3
statutory curbs on unofficial
    strikes rejected 39
strike ballots rejected 38, 39
supplementary notes 41–2
TUC reaction to 139–45
unwillingness to recommend
    legislation 35–6, 41
Doughty, George 158

economic decline, relative 10–11,
    21–2
economic growth rate 10
The Economist 194
Edmonds, John 135
electoral appeal, broadening Labour
    198–9
Ennals, David 100
export markets 10

Fair Deal at Work 46, 49, 91, 118,
    192
Feather, Vic 27, 69, 113, 135, 151,
    155, 172, 174
    address to TUC Special
        Conference 156
    cosy relationship with Wilson
        98
    key role in negotiations 163–4,
        180
    views on Castle and Wilson 96–7

fines, individual trade union member
    60
    attachment-of-earnings orders for
        non-payment of 143
    Clive Jenkins on 157
    concerns over custodial sentences
        for non-payment of 77–8,
        80–1, 142–3
    Mikardo on 123
    Orme on 127
    Pannell on 128
    Wilson looks for guarantees from
        TUC on 168
fines, trade union 60, 169
Flanders, Allan 18, 28, 36, 134–5,
    137
Foot, Michael 120, 124, 129
Ford, Ben 111
Ford strike 207
Fraser, John 57, 65, 112
Freedland, Mark 12, 40, 44

'garbage can model' of policy process
    56
general election 1970
    abstention by Labour voters
        195–6
    comparing results for 1966 and
        191, *191*
    decision on timing of 189–90,
        192–3
    economic data published just
        prior to 194–5
    increase in Conservative vote 196
    Liberal Party and role in Labour
        defeat 196–7
    partisan dealigmnent 195
    In Place of Strife as a reason for
        Labour defeat 189, 191–3
    reasons beyond *In Place of Strife*
        for Labour defeat 8–9, 193–7
general election 1979 209–10
    skilled workers' swing to
        Conservatives 208–9
Girling Brakes factory 51–2, 70
Gormley, Joe 86, 135, 146, 148
    warns Wilson on election timing
        192–3
Gunter, Ray 25, 26, 48

224 Index

Haines, Joe 154, 188, 189, 190, 192
Hart, Judith 80, 81
Hattersley, Roy 57, 64
Healey, Denis 88, 93–4, 99, 164, 169
   on Callaghan 86
   Heffer criticises 210
   on losing 1979 general election 209–10
Heaton's dispute 203–4
Heffer, Eric 113, 122, 123–4, 126, 129, 193
   on 1979 election defeat 210
Helsby, Sir Laurence 53
Houghton, Douglas 102, 106, 110, 178
   –Callaghan axis in opposition to Industrial Relations Bill 119–20
   warns Wilson on PLP attitude to 'penal clauses' 117–18

incomes policies 11, 14–16, 18, 31, 34, 35, 53–4, 67, 125
   Donovan Report on 34, 35
   free collective bargaining and 53, 54–5, 144, 199–201
   industrial relations an alternative to 93–4
   'labour aristocracy' baulks at overly egalitarian 208–9
   post-1974 Labour government 206–7
   reinforcing antipathy to *In Place of Strife* 122
   straining relations with trade unions 143–4
   Sunningdale Conference discussion of 61–2
   trade unions rebel against 207–8
industrial disputes
   attributed to capitalism and employers 121–4
   incidence and impact 13–14
   media reporting on 90–1
   Rule 11, *Programme for Action* 165–6
      negotiations on redrafting and strengthening 174–7, 179–80, 181

   Sunningdale Conference on how to tackle 62–3
   TUC hostility to government intervention in 157–8
   see also strikes; unconstitutional/'wildcat' strikes; unofficial strikes
Industrial Relations Act (1971) 202–4, 211
   failure of 204
   judicial decisions highlighting flaws in 203–4
   Labour pledge to repeal 205
   trade unions' response to 203–4
   see also 'closed shop'
Industrial Relations Bill, short 90–5
   announcement in House of Commons 93
   Cabinet's varying degrees of support for 75–9, 92–4, 105–6
   Callaghan and Houghton in opposition to 119–20
   draft measures 92
   PLP opposition to 110–11, 112–13, 113–15, 130–1
   left-wing 124–5
   Trade Union Group 128–30
   PLP support for 111–12
   pressure from Labour Whips on 115–16
   timing 82–4, 91, 99, 150, 151, 156, 163
   TUC counter-proposals to obviate *see* Trade Union Congress (TUC) *Programme for Action*
   TUC reaction to 150–3, 156
   warnings of impending defeat on 114, 117–19
   Wilson addresses PLP on 104, 113, 114
   Wilson threatens to resign over 104
industrial relations legislation, Labour
   Cabinet support ebbs away 73–4, 98–103, 106–7
   Castle convinced of need for 47–8
   and changing culture at Ministry of Labour 53–7, 146

Index   225

drafting of White Paper 52–3, 65–8, 70–1
initial consultations with TUC and CBI 48–9, 50–1, 140
meetings from April to June 1969 162–3
option of one or two Bills 49–51
Orme's discussion paper prior to 126–8
political considerations prompting 46–7
threats of resignation over 103–5
two-stage approach adopted 91
Wilson–Castle axis driving 95–8
Wilson's options, May 1969 169–70
see also Industrial Relations Bill, short; *In Place of Strife*
inflation 11, 199–200, 205–6
'joint statement' on 208
In Place of Strife
battle over, symbolic of wider economic and industrial problems 197–8
blamed in part for 1970 Labour election defeat 125, 189, 191–3
Cabinet response to 74–82
Callaghan's opposition to 78, 84–90
Castle's secret meetings with TUC to discuss 68–9, 74–5, 141–3
dispensing with Green Paper prior to 52
drafting of 52–3, 65–8, 70–1
lengthy consultation period agreed prior to legislation 98–9, 149–50
main proposals 66–7
Orme's discussion paper prior to publication of 126–8
to pacify concerns of business and electorate 199
PLP opposition to 110–11, 112–13, 130–1
left-wing 120–4
Trade Union Group 125–30

PLP support for 111–12
title 67–8
transcending of orthodox left/right divisions 79
TUC given advance notification of draft 68–9, 74–5
TUC hostile response to 133, 145–50
voting on 110, 127–8
inter-union disputes 33, 62, 70, 78–9, 90, 92, 129, 149, 155, 162, 167, 169
'An Alternative Approach' 59
Girling Brakes factory 51–2
Programme for Action Rule 12 166

Jenkins, Clive 157
Jenkins, Peter 99
The Battle of Downing Street 4, 88–9
Jenkins, Roy 84, 88, 165, 169
on 1970 election defeat 193
announces short Industrial Relations Bill 92, 93
changing views on industrial relations legislation 75–6, 99
criticism of Wilson and Castle 184
on timing of industrial relations legislation 91, 99, 150
Jones, G.W. 185
Jones, Jack 95, 96, 143, 146, 148, 164, 170, 172, 174, 180, 200
judiciary
decisions highlighting flaws in Industrial Relations Act 203–4
Rookes v Barnard decision 20–1
trade unions' scepticism towards 134, 137–9
TUC evidence to Donovan Commission on 31–2

Kingdon, John 56

Lestor, Joan 100–1, 115
Liberal Party 196–7, 205

226 Index

MacDonald, Ramsay 132n.26
Macmillan, Harold 14
March, James 56
Marsh, Richard 78–9, 93, 105
Mellish, Bob 95, 97, 106, 115, 118–19, 131, 169, 178
middle class vote 199
Mikardo, Ian 122–3, 129, 195–6
Ministry of Labour
   changing culture at 53–7, 146
   merger with DEA 54
   written evidence to Donovan Commission 32–3
modernisation policies 5, 21, 47, 79–80, 164

National Executive Committee (NEC) 86, 87, 108n.24
national interests vs sectional interests 198–9
nationalised industries 11
National Opinion Poll 90
National Union of Seamen 113, 144
New Labour 199, 211

Olsen, John 56
Organisation for European Economic Co-operation (latterly OECD) 16
Orme, Stan, discussion paper on trade union reform 126–8
Owen, David 100, 179
'Oxford School' of industrial relations 24, 36–7, 38, 44

Pannell, Charles 128
Parliamentary Labour Party (PLP) 110–32
   Callaghan–Houghton axis 119–20
   Chair and Chief Whip warn Wilson of impending defeat 117–19
   discipline 94–5
   Orme's discussion paper 126–8
   response to pressure from Labour Whips 115–16
   strengthening of opposition to industrial relations legislation 91, 110–11, 112–13, 113–15, 128–30, 130–1
   left-wing 120–5
   Trade Union Group 125–6
   support for industrial relations legislation 111–12
   support for TUC *Programme for Action* 116–17, 125, 129, 131
   Wilson addresses, on Industrial Relations Bill 104, 113, 114
   Wilson appoints a new Chief Whip 94–5, 97–8
'pay pause' 14
Peart, Fred 50, 76, 82–3, 169
'penal clauses'
   Cabinet opposition to 73, 77, 78, 80–1, 103
   Callaghan's objections to 84, 85, 86
   Castle's CLP implores her to abandon 117
   Feather's address to TUC Special Conference 156
   Houghton warns Wilson on PLP opposition to 117–18
   PLP opposition to 7, 100, 110–11, 112, 123, 125, 126, 128, 136
   proposals in *In Place of Strife* 66–7
   responsibility for invoking 67
   and timing of introduction of Industrial Relations Bill 82, 83–4, 91
   TUC concerns over 2, 142–3, 147, 148, 151, 156, 168
   TUC threatens to withdraw counter-proposals over 158, 167–8, 173
   Wilson's conditions for reconsideration of 104, 113–14, 149, 151–2, 158, 168, 169–70, 175
   Wilson threatens to resign over 104
policy-making models
   'garbage can model' 56
   'policy streams' approach 56–7

Prime Ministerial government, rise of 184–6
private sector oligopolies 11, 22
Programme for Action see Trade Union Congress (TUC) *Programme for Action*
public opinion on trade unions 90, 209, 210–11

Rookes v Barnard 20–1
Rose, Paul 115–16
Royal Commission on Trade Unions and Employers' Associations *see* Donovan Commission
Rule 11, *Programme for Action* 165–6
  negotiations on redrafting and strengthening 172, 174–7, 179–80, 181

sanctions *see* fines, individual trade union member; fines, trade union
Scanlon, Hugh 96, 98, 164, 170, 172, 200
Scrutton, Lord Justice Thomas 138
sectional interests vs national interests 198–9
sexism 153–4
Shanks, Michael 16
Shonfield, Andrew 26, 33–4, 42–3
shop stewards 12–13, 14, 15, 22, 32, 34, 35, 53, 63, 200, 204
Shore, Peter 58, 63, 64, 65, 76, 79, 85, 102–3, 106, 184, 190
Silkin, John 94–5, 97, 115
social contract (1972) 204–7
'solemn and binding' agreement 3, 8, 180–2, 185
  Cabinet response to 182–3, 185–6
  Crossman suggests a way out of impasse 101–2
  immediate aftermath 183–5
  saves Wilson and Castle from complete humiliation 3, 179, 185
Stagg, Norman 157
Stewart, Michael 178, 191–2, 196

strike ballots 66, 92
  Mikardo's objection to 123
  Ministry of Labour submission to Donovan Commission on 32
  rejected by Donovan Commission 38, 39
  responsibility for invoking 63–4, 67
strikes 22, 90
  attributed to capitalism and employers 31, 121–4, 147
  dockers 203–4
  Ford 207
  Ministry of Labour submission to Donovan Commission on 32–3
  National Union of Seamen 144
  refuse collectors 207–8
  school caretakers 207
  TUC evidence to Donovan Commission 31
  TUC guidance on future 208
  in 'winter of discontent' 207–8
  see also unconstitutional/'wildcat' strikes; unofficial strikes
structure of British industry, changing 11–13, 22
Sunningdale Conference 57–65, 70
  'An Alternative Approach' 59–61
  Castle on consensus reached at 64, 65
  Castle's draft policy proposals 65
  legal enforcement of collective agreements 63
  objectives of State intervention 61–2
  tackling industrial disputes 62–3
  themes and papers for discussion 58

Tangley, Lord Edward 26, 41, 42
Taylor, Robert 4, 16, 22, 56, 204, 205
Thomas, George 81, 183
timing of industrial relations legislation 82–4, 91, 99, 150, 151, 156, 163
Trade Disputes Act (1906) 18, 19, 20, 40, 42

Trade Disputes Act (1965) 24, 25
Trade Union (Amalgamations, etc.)
    Act (1964) 12
Trade Union Congress (TUC)
  Action on Donovan 141
  concerns over Conservative
    extensions to legislation
    147–8
  hostile response to *In Place of
    Strife* 145–50, 159
  initial consultations on industrial
    relations legislation 48–9,
    50–1, 140
  issues guidance on future strikes
    208
  'joint statement' on inflation 208
  lack of authority over affiliated
    trade unions 18–20
  leaders' perceptions of Wilson and
    Castle 96–7, 172
  meetings with Castle to discuss
    White Paper 68–9, 74–5,
    141–3
  nominations to Donovan
    Commission 26
  reaction to Donovan report 139–45
  reaction to short Industrial
    Relations Bill 150–3, 156
  response to *Rookes v Barnard*
    judicial decision 20–1
  sexism towards Castle 154
  social contract with Labour Party
    204–7
  suspect Wilson of withholding
    timing information 151, 163
  'voluntarist myth' 134
  written evidence to Donovan
    Commission 28, 30–2
Trade Union Congress (TUC)
    Programme for Action 164–70
  1st June Chequers meeting 170–3
  18th June meeting 178–82
  Croydon Conference 116, 152–3,
    154–8
    government's response to
    173–82
  junior Ministers' concerns at
    Wilson's intransigence over
    100–1
  negotiations on 166–70
  Paragraph 42 165, 174–5
  PLP support for 116–17, 125, 129,
    131
  Rule 11 165–6
    negotiations on redrafting and
    strengthening 174–7, 179–80,
    181
  Rule 12 166
  Rule 13 166
  'solemn and binding undertaking'
    on 180–2, 185
  TUC threatens withdrawal of 158,
    167–8, 173
  Wilson and Castle under pressure
    to reach an agreement based
    on 116, 125, 129, 178–9
  Wilson claims willing to consider
    counter-proposals 113–14,
    149, 151–2
  Wilson's dismissal of 96, 98, 101,
    116–17, 158, 160, 173–4
trade unions 16–20, 20–1
  Callaghan miscalculates 209
  commitment to voluntarism 30,
    133–9, 156, 158–9, 168
  competition between 200
  conduct of TUC affiliated 166
  demarcation disputes 13, 51, 70,
    166, 202
  'deregistering' of 42
  disputes between TUC affiliated
    166
  government concerns over 11–13,
    22
  gulf between national leaders and
    local workplace 12, 13, 15, 17,
    22
  incomes policies straining
    relations with Labour
    government 143–4
  membership 12
  numbers 12
  paradox of 'too powerful'/'not
    powerful enough' 17, 18–20,
    22
  public opinion of 90, 209, 210–11
  rapprochement with Labour Party
    200–1, 204–7

response to Industrial Relations
Act 203–4
Rookes v Barnard judicial decision
20–1
shop stewards 12–13, 15
TUC lack of authority over 18–20
weakening of 210–11
'winter of discontent' 207–10
trade union sponsored MPs
opposition to *In Place of
Strife* 125–6
Transport and General Workers'
Union dockers strike 203–4
Trend, Burke 50
Tribune 123, 124
Tribune Group opposition to *In
Place of Strife* 120–5
TUC *see* Trade Union Congress
(TUC); Trade Union
Congress (TUC) *Programme
for Action*

unconstitutional/'wildcat' strikes 1,
14, 19, 22, 35, 140, 149
disagreement over priorities in
resolving 167–8, 168–9,
172–3, 177–8
Donovan Commission findings 35,
36, 38, 39, 40, 41
negotiations on Rule 11 and
resolution of 174–7, 179–80,
181
Orme on 127
Sunningdale 'Alternative
Approach' and discussion on
59–60, 63–4
TUC 'solemn and binding
undertaking' 3, 8, 180–2,
185
Wilson rejects TUC counter-
proposals 96, 98, 158, 160,
173–4
unemployment 55, 195, 200, 206
unofficial strikes 3, 13, 14, 16, 18, 19,
22, 44, 49, 57, 64, 77, 78, 84,
111, 112, 113, 117, 123, 131,
140, 146, 165, 170, 177, 199
Conservative Opposition
proposals for tackling 46

Donovan Commission findings 35,
36, 38, 39, 40, 41
Girling Brakes factory 51–2,
70
Ministry of Labour submission to
Donovan Commission on
32–3
Orme on 127
power vacuum underpinning 19,
22, 35
TUC 'solemn and binding
undertaking' 3, 8, 180–2,
185

voluntarism 9–10
Action on Donovan on 141
Callaghan's support for 84
DEP keen to move beyond 59,
70
Donovan Report qualified defence
of 34, 39–40, 43, 44
an empiricist tradition 135–6
of individual unions vis-a-vis TUC
18, 157–8
Ministry of Labour shift in
perspective on 32–3, 53–4
of 'Oxford School' 36–7, 38
In Place of Strife a break with
tradition of 2, 145–6
principle of 134–5
scepticism towards judiciary and
137–9
Sunningdale consideration of
moving beyond 59, 60, 61,
64–5, 70
suspicion of motives of would-be
reformers 136–7
trade unions' commitment to 30,
133–9, 156, 158–9, 168

'wage drift' 15, 18, 34, 35, 54, 61,
200
wage restraints 14–16
see also incomes policies
Wedderburn, K.W. 19, 28, 138
White Paper on industrial relations
reform *see In Place of Strife*
Wigham, Eric 16–17, 26, 43
Williams, Marcia 94

Williams, Shirley 116, 117, 195
Wilson, Harold
  accepts 'solemn and binding' agreement 180–1, 182, 183
  addresses PLP on Industrial Relations Bill 104, 113, 114
  appoints a new Chief Whip 94–5, 97–8
  –Castle axis driving industrial relations legislation 95–8
  and Castle left isolated 74, 102, 106, 178–9, 182
  on Castle presenting White Paper to TUC prior to Cabinet 75
  conditions for reconsideration of 'penal clauses' 104, 113–14, 149, 151–2, 158, 168, 169–70, 175
  confidential code names between Castle and 170–1
  criticised for 'academic' approach to industrial relations 119–20, 129, 148, 159
  decides on date for 1970 general election 190, 192–3
  declines to sack Callaghan 86–8
  disingenuous over timing of legislation 151, 163
  dismisses TUC counter-proposals 96, 98, 101, 116–17, 158, 160, 173–4
  Donovan Commission and 24, 26, 43, 46, 48, 69–70
  handling of industrial relations legislation criticised 183–4
  on National Union of Seamen strike 144
  praise for *Programme for Action* 166–7
  record of 1st June Chequers dinner 172
  relationship with Castle 97–8
  reminds Cabinet of collective responsibility requirement 87
  suggests he addresses Croydon Conference 155
  threatens to resign 103–4, 182
  on trade union attempts to dictate proceedings 179
  TUC leaders' perceptions of Castle and 96–7, 172
  urges Castle to consider industrial relations reform 47
  willing to consider TUC counter-proposals 113–14, 149, 151–2
'winter of discontent' 207–10
Woodcock, George 26, 27, 39, 68–9, 136, 163

EU authorised representative for GPSR:
Easy Access System Europe, Mustamäe tee 50,
10621 Tallinn, Estonia
gpsr.requests@easproject.com

www.ingramcontent.com/pod-product-compliance
Lightning Source LLC
Chambersburg PA
CBHW082105250426
43673CB00067B/1833